Sexuality and
Social Work

Transforming Social Work Practice – titles in the series

Applied Psychology for Social Work	ISBN: 978 1 84445 071 8
Collaborative Social Work Practice	ISBN: 978 1 84445 014 5
Communication and Interpersonal Skills in Social Work	ISBN: 978 1 84445 019 0
Courtroom Skills for Social Workers	ISBN: 978 1 84445 123 4
Effective Practice Learning in Social Work	ISBN: 978 1 84445 015 2
Groupwork Practice in Social Work	ISBN: 978 1 84445 086 2
Loss and Social Work	ISBN: 978 1 84445 088 6
Management and Organisations in Social Work	ISBN: 978 1 84445 044 2
New Directions in Social Work	ISBN: 978 1 84445 079 4
Practical Computer Skills for Social Work	ISBN: 978 1 84445 031 2
Reflective Practice in Social Work	ISBN: 978 1 84445 082 4
Service User and Carer Participation in Social Work	ISBN: 978 1 84445 074 9
Social Work and Human Development (second edition)	ISBN: 978 1 84445 112 8
Social Work and Mental Health (second edition)	ISBN: 978 1 84445 068 8
Social Work in Education and Children's Services	ISBN: 978 1 84445 045 9
Social Work Practice: Assessment, Planning, Intervention and Review (second edition)	ISBN: 978 1 84445 113 5
Social Work with Children and Families	ISBN: 978 1 84445 018 3
Social Work with Children, Young People and their Families in Scotland	ISBN: 978 1 84445 031 2
Social Work with Drug and Substance Misusers	ISBN: 978 1 84445 058 9
Social Work with Looked After Children	ISBN: 978 1 84445 103 6
Social Work with Older People	ISBN: 978 1 84445 017 6
Social Work with People with Learning Difficulties	ISBN: 978 1 84445 042 8
Sociology and Social Work	ISBN: 978 1 84445 087 9
Thriving and Surviving in Social Work	ISBN: 978 1 84445 080 0
Using the Law in Social Work (third edition)	ISBN: 978 1 84445 114 2
Values and Ethics in Social Work	ISBN: 978 1 84445 067 1
What is Social Work? Context and Perspectives (second edition)	ISBN: 978 1 84445 055 1
Youth Justice and Social Work	ISBN: 978 1 84445 066 4

To order, please contact our distributor: BEBC Distribution, Albion Close, Parkstone, Poole, BH12 3LL. Telephone: 0845 230 9000, email: **learningmatters@bebc.co.uk**. You can also find more information on each of these titles and our other learning resources at **www.learningmatters.co.uk**.

Sexuality and Social Work

JULIE BYWATER
RHIANNON JONES

Series Editors: Jonathan Parker and Greta Bradley

LearningMatters

First published in 2007 by Learning Matters Ltd.

© 2007 Julie Bywater and Rhiannon Jones

British Library Cataloguing in Publication Data
A CIP record for this book is available from the British Library.

ISBN: 978 1 84445 085 5

Cover and text design by Code 5 Design Associates
Project management by Deer Park Productions
Typeset by Pantek Arts Ltd, Maidstone, Kent

Learning Matters Ltd
33 Southernhay East
Exeter EX1 1NX
Tel: 01392 215560
info@learningmatters.co.uk
www.learningmatters.co.uk

Contents

Introduction   vii

1   Sexuality, terminology and theoretical perspectives
of sexuality   1

2   (Hetero)sexuality and diversity   16

3   Sexuality, young people and social work   35

4   Sexuality, older people and social work   56

5   Sexuality, disabled people and social work   74

6   Sexuality, HIV and social work   92

7   Sexuality, sexual violence and social work   111

8   Sexuality, best practice and social work   127

Conclusion   133

References   135

Glossary   152

Index   154

Acknowledgements

Julie would like to thank all the social work students at the University of Leeds, particularly the graduates of 2007, for their inspiration and encouragement. Rhiannon would like to thank social work colleagues at Manchester Metropolitan University for their support. Thanks to the Learning Matters editorial team for their enthusiasm and constructive feedback. Finally we would like to dedicate this book to each other and for ourselves.

Introduction

This book is written primarily to support student social workers on the new degree programme in their academic work as well as practice placements. Whilst it is aimed at students in their first or second year/level of study, it will also be useful for final-year students depending on how individual programmes are designed. The book may also appeal to experienced social workers as well as students and practitioners in other health and social care fields.

Sexuality remains a neglected and largely taboo area within social work practice yet it can be a difficult and demanding aspect of social work. Social workers may be more accustomed to thinking about the importance of issues such as gender and ethnicity than considering sexuality. Yet sexuality is a very significant part of our lives in terms of relationships, identities, beliefs and a sense of who we are. This book will introduce readers to the topic of sexuality, by considering the diversity of sexualities and exploring issues and their implications for social work assessment and intervention with a range of service users.

Requirements for social work education

Social workers are faced with many issues relating to sexuality of diverse populations and together with the development of the new social work degree and the national occupational standards it is important that issues of sexuality are addressed. Issues of diversity and anti-oppressive practice are central to good social work practice and the GSCC requirements support this stating that 'social work education is to ensure that the principles of valuing diversity and equalities awareness are integral to the teaching and learning of students' (www.gscc.org.uk accessed 6/1/06). This book aims to enable students to identify situations where issues of sexuality need to be considered and addressed when working to the National Occupational Standards set up for social workers. Social workers are expected to:

- prepare for and work with people to assess their needs and circumstances;
- plan, carry out, review and evaluate social work practice;
- support individuals to represent their needs, views and circumstances;
- manage risk;
- manage and be accountable, with supervision and support, for their own social work practice;
- demonstrate professional competence in social work practice.

The academic subject benchmark statement identifies four core areas in which students need to acquire knowledge, understanding and skills. These are:

- social work services and service users;

- values and ethics;

- social work theory;

- the nature of social work practice.

A theme that runs through the core areas is one of being able to critically analyse the processes within a diverse society that lead to sources of disadvantage and result in marginalisation, social exclusion and isolation. Students are expected to analyse and take account of the impact of inequality and discrimination. Throughout this book we encourage students to analyse issues of sexuality that explore these types of processes and in particular the intersection between social divisions and sexuality.

Book structure

This book will introduce the topic of sexuality by considering the diversity of sexualities using a predominantly social constructionist approach and explore the implications for social work assessment and intervention with a range of service users.

Chapter 1 introduces students to the terminology and two contrasting perspectives, that of naturalist and social constructionist, in relation to sexuality. Students will be encouraged to explore definitions, assumptions and constructs which will be used throughout the book.

Chapter 2 introduces students to a range of different sexualities while also looking at issues of power, oppression, heterosexuality and 'normality'. This chapter will consider the impact of social divisions such as gender, ethnicity and class on people's experiences of sexuality.

Chapter 3 considers a range of issues of sexuality that are relevant to young people, such as the development of a sexual identity and sexual orientation, consensual sex and sexual health needs. The chapter will encourage students to consider issues of power and oppression and the way that society's view of young people can impact negatively upon their experiences of sex and sexuality.

Chapter 4 considers the issues of sex and sexuality in relation to older people. Students will be encouraged to consider the impact of ageism on older people's sexuality and specific issues such as sexual health needs, residential care and sexual abuse will be considered. The needs of older lesbians and gay men will be discussed, as will the needs of older heterosexual people and the way that older people's sexual needs are generally ignored.

Chapter 5 considers the issues of sex and sexuality in relation to disabled people and in particular examines the influence of the medical and social models of disability. A range of impairments are discussed such as physical disabilities, learning difficulties and mental health issues and their impact on the issues of sexuality.

Chapter 6 considers the issues of sexuality in relation to HIV. Students are introduced to the basic facts of HIV whilst also considering the impact of social and cultural aspects on the experiences of people living with HIV. Social work practice is discussed in terms of the social worker's dual role, that of working with people living with HIV and HIV prevention.

Chapter 7 considers sexual violence and details the relevant legal and policy frameworks when working with adults and young people. Issues of social work practice will be explored in relation to rape.

Chapter 8 succinctly discusses sexual rights and offers guidelines for social work best practice when working with a range of different service users in relation to issues of sexuality.

Throughout the chapters we will be encouraging students to use a social constructionist approach to the issues of sexuality and the application of theoretical discussions to social work practice.

Learning features

This book contains activities to enable students to participate in their own learning as they progress through the different chapters. Many of the activities include case studies where students are asked to imagine that they are the worker involved in the given situation. We provide commentary which will guide the student towards considering the range of issues and identifying best social work practice. We hope that these activities will encourage reflection on possible courses of action as well as giving students ways of working that they can utilise on placement and in practice. Each chapter provides references to further learning material and web links.

Chapter 1

Sexuality, terminology and theoretical perspectives of sexuality

A C H I E V I N G   A   S O C I A L   W O R K   D E G R E E

This chapter will help you to meet the following National Occupational Standards.
Key Role 1: Prepare for and work with individuals, families, carers, groups, and communities to assess their needs and circumstances.
- Prepare for social work contact and involvement.
Key Role 6: Demonstrate professional competence in social work practice.
- Research, analyse, evaluate and use current knowledge of best social work practice.

It will also introduce you to the following academic standards set out in the social work subject benchmark statement.
3.1.1 Social work service and service users.
- The social processes that lead to marginalisation, isolation and exclusion and their impact on the demand for social work services.
3.2.2 Problem solving skills.
- Analyse and take account of the impact of inequality and discrimination.

Terminology and meanings

Before reading any of the following chapters it is important that we share a common understanding of the terms and their meanings. One of the reasons why it is important to clarify and understand the meaning of terms is that words around issues of sex, sexuality and sexual orientation can often be perceived by others as offensive or oppressive or to mean different things to different people. The following activity will provide you with an opportunity to check out your initial thoughts and understandings.

ACTIVITY *1.1*

Use of language/terminology
What do you think are the meanings of the following terms?

Sex	*Heterosexual*	*Homophobia*
Sexuality	*Bisexual*	*Heterosexism*
Sexual orientation	*Homosexual*	*Sexism*
Gender	*Gay*	
	Lesbian	

Who and what do you think has influenced your understanding of these terms?

Comment

You may have been very clear about the meaning of some of the terms and others you may have been more uncertain about. Our understanding of certain words is obviously influenced by many aspects of our lives such as family, friends, education, work, politics, media, culture and belief systems. It would be helpful for you at this stage to refer to the Glossary for the words and meanings that are going to be used throughout this book.

The remainder of the chapter will include a discussion around these terms and give us an opportunity to explore their interrelationship.

Sex, sexuality and sexual orientation – the meanings

It is useful at this stage to consider in more detail the terms sex, sexuality and sexual orientation.

Sex

In the English language 'sex' has several meanings. It can be used to categorise biological or anatomical differences between male and female, and it can also be used to describe a physical act between people, that of 'having sex'. For the purpose of this book we have generally used the word 'sex' to mean the anatomical differences between male and female and have used the terms 'sexual practice', 'sexual activity' or 'having a sexual relationship' to refer to 'having sex'. There are a few obvious exceptions when we have used the word 'sex' to mean sexual practice, for example in Chapter 6 when we discuss 'safer sex'. How then do the terms 'sex' and 'gender' differ? One view is that sex is about the biological and anatomical differences whereas gender refers to the psychological, social and cultural differences between male and female (Giddens, 2006). It is useful at this point to reflect back to the nature versus nurture debate concerning human growth and development (Crawford and Walker, 2003) and consider to what extent the differences between men and women are determined by their sex (i.e. biological) or by their gender (i.e. psychological, social and cultural). Are aspects of masculinity and femininity constructed and influenced by biology or society's structures? Current feminist theorists would dispute this division by stating that society influences all the differences between women and men and using the terms 'sex' for biological differences and 'gender' for social and cultural differences is unhelpful. Scott and Jackson (2006) argue that the term 'gender' should be used to cover all aspects of what it means to be a woman or a man in terms of biological, psychological, social and cultural differences and that the term 'sex' should be used for sexual and erotic activity. These are debates that we will return to in later chapters.

Sexuality

Sexuality is a difficult term to define as it depends on what theoretical perspective of sexuality you hold. An example is that if you believe that issues relating to sex, sexuality and sexual orientation are determined by biology and natural processes then your definition will be simple, concrete and immovable. Your definition will state that *sexuality is that which is concerned with the reproduction of the species* (Jackson, 1999, p.5). However, we would argue that sexuality is complex, fluid and involves many facets of human behaviour and being, which in turn is influenced by the historical, social, cultural and political context that we live in. Sexuality includes beliefs, acts, behaviours, desires, relationships and identities (Jackson, 1999; Weeks, 2003).

Sexuality explained

Bremner and Hillin (1994) argue that sexuality is made up of sex and sexual practices, sexual orientation, sensuality, social relationships and political dimensions. These aspects all add up to how we define ourselves as sexual beings. Sexuality involves our relationships with ourselves, those around us and the society in which we live, whether we identify as gay, heterosexual, lesbian, bisexual or celibate. Below are the different aspects of sexuality and what each aspect may include.

Sex/sexual practice	Sexual orientation	Sensuality	Social relationships	Political dimensions
With oneself	Heterosexual	Massage	Marriage	Feminism
	Lesbian	Music	Civil partnership	Gay men
With partner(s) of	Gay	Touch	Living together	Lesbians
same or other gender	Bisexual	Intimacy	Partnerships	Bisexuals
		Fantasy	Families	Black people
Celibacy		Food	Monogamy	Disabled people
		Smells	Non-monogamy	Older adults
		Exercise	Friendships	Women
		Emotions (love, anger, desire, delight, pleasure)		Transgender people Transsexual people

The lists above are not exhaustive and you may be able to think of other aspects that are missing. It is important to note that the sexual identities of the people within the political dimensions column are important in relation to anti-discriminatory social work practice. Some of their issues and struggles in relation to inequality, power and oppression within society will be explored in later chapters.

Sexual orientation

Sexual orientation is a term used to describe the direction of a person's sexual attractions and desires. Common terms for describing people's sexual orientation are heterosexual, bisexual, homosexual, lesbian or gay. These are terms that you have considered earlier when undertaking Activity 1.1. Sexual identity and sexual preference are also terms which are used to mean sexual orientation. All these different terms reflect the debate about whether sexual attraction and desire is fluid and incorporates an element of choice or whether it is an immovable entity which is fixed early in life.

ACTIVITY 1.2

Looking at Bremner and Hillin's (1994) dimensions of sexuality, consider your own sexuality. What do you think has influenced the development of your sexuality? What messages did you receive about your sexuality and about sexuality generally in your childhood, young adulthood and later adulthood? Write down your thoughts so that you can refer back to them throughout the rest of the chapter when we are considering the aspects of the nature versus nurture debate.

Comment

You will have identified many influences regarding the development of your sexuality. You may find that the influences are similar to the ones you identified in the first activity in relation to your understanding of different concepts. How much of your sexuality has been influenced by nurture and how much by nature? You may find that one aspect particularly dominates as an influence. Has your sexuality changed significantly during the course of your life? If so, what were the influences for the changes? You may feel that your sexuality is fluid and changeable, or you may feel that it has been a constant in your identity.

RESEARCH SUMMARY

The nature versus nurture debate in relation to sexuality

Nature

The debate about whether there is a gene responsible for determining male homosexuality began in 1993 following a report in the journal Science *by Dean Hamer, PhD in which he claimed to have identified a segment of the X chromosome (at marker Xq28) considered to be influential in determining sexual orientation. The report was based upon a study of 40 pairs of gay brothers and observed the same marker in 33 of the pairs. This led to claims that sexual orientation is hereditary and not a choice. However, in 1999 a team from the University of Western Ontario reported results of their study involving 52 pairs of gay brothers in the journal* Science *which disputed the presence of the Xq28 'gay gene' or any other gene influencing sexual orientation. In the most recent research in 2005 undertaken by Brian Mustanski, PhD at the University of Illinois, Chicago, a wider study of genetic information was undertaken on all of the chromosomes, not just the X*

RESEARCH SUMMARY *continued*

chromosome. This study of 456 men from 146 families with two or more gay brothers, found the same pattern among the gay men on three chromosomes which were shared by 60 per cent of the gay men in the study. This study strengthens the earlier claims that sexual orientation is innate (WebMD, 2005).

Nurture

Accepted types of sexual practices and orientation vary between different cultures, highlighting that most sexual responses are learned rather than occurring 'naturally'. For example, in some societies/cultures it is believed that frequent sexual intercourse leads to physical illness and debilitation. Some cultures actively encourage or tolerate homosexuality, others are condemning and discouraging. There are also diverse cultural norms in relation to what is considered to be sexually attractive. For example, in most countries there is more focus upon the physical looks of women rather than of men, and traits of what is defined as beautiful in women differ greatly. In the UK and mass media globally today, for example, the traits most identified as beautiful and sexually attractive in women are those of a slim, 'hour-glass' shaped body, whilst other societies may identify more with the colour of eyes, shape of face, lips and nose. Ford and Beach (1951), Davenport (1965), Plummer (1975), Shephard (1987), Plummer (1995) and Trumbach (2003) are a sample of references spanning 50 years for further reading about the way sexuality is constructed by aspects other than nature.

Sexuality – diversity and power

As sexuality involves everyone, diversity and difference become its main appeal. For example, Lorber (1994) distinguished ten different sexual orientations/identities: heterosexual male/female; lesbian; gay man; bisexual male/female; transvestite female/male and transsexual female/male. In addition, there is a diversity of sexual practices and sexual tastes. For example, a man or woman can have a sexual relationship with a man or a woman or both, and sexual practices can take place on a one-to-one basis or with more people participating. We can perform sexual practices with ourselves (masturbation) or with no one (celibacy). People may also choose to have sexual relationships involving erotic materials and/or sexual devices. However, although these ranges of differences are recognised they are not all equal in terms of acceptability, perceived normality or power. Jackson and Scott (2006) for example, argue that what is regarded as sexuality and sex depends on the society in which it exists and whether it is regarded as acceptable or deviant is largely a matter of power relations.

At this point we would like to introduce you briefly to Michael Foucault's ideas on power, which he claimed operated on all levels of social interaction, in all social institutions and by all people. The crucial aspect of power is the role of discourse, which Foucault referred to as the way people talk and think about a particular topic where they are united by common assumptions (Giddens, 2006). Discourse can be defined as the *written, spoken or enacted practices organised so as to supply a coherent claim to a position or perspective* (Fox, 1993, p.161). Foucault claimed that power worked through discourses to shape particular and popular attitudes towards certain things such as sexuality (Giddens, 2006). It is important to recognise that although power is everywhere, not all discourses have equal power. Some discourses have more power than others, for example, medical discourses. These powerful discourses, also referred to as knowledge, can restrict alternative ways of thinking and speaking. For Foucault power and knowledge are closely linked and reinforce one another and in relation to sexuality, construct what is and what is not acceptable. These ideas will be returned to later in the chapter.

In modern Western societies there is a hierarchical system of sexual value (Rubin, 1993). The most valued *at the top of the erotic pyramid* (Rubin, 1993, p.14) are married heterosexual people who have or are having children. The least valued at the bottom of the pyramid are transsexuals, transvestites and sex workers. This hierarchy tends to reflect the power relations within society, that is, the people at the top of the pyramid have the most power whilst the people at the bottom of the pyramid have the least power. Obviously a hierarchical system such as this would be different in different societies. It is important to note however, that as well as gender and sexual orientation determining people's place in the hierarchy the other important social divisions that are also linked to power or lack of it are ethnicity and age (Calasanti and Slevin, 2001; Stephen, 2002). This interrelationship between sexuality and other social divisions such as gender, ethnicity, age, disability and class will be explored in later chapters.

Sexuality through the ages

Familiarising ourselves with a history of sexuality actually involves looking through history at the changing ideas about sexuality. It is a useful exercise for three reasons. Firstly, it can help us to work out the origins of our own beliefs, why we hold them, and to what extent they influence our social work practice. Secondly, through enabling us as individuals and professionals to look at our own beliefs about sexuality it may help us respect the different beliefs of others. This reflexivity is so central to professionalism, as without it, we may be more concerned to 'protect' our sense of what is right than to safeguard the integrity of our service users (Wilton, 2000). Thirdly, it gives us a sense that sexuality, and in particular our ideas and preoccupations with it, change and that these changes are influenced by different structures in society (Weeks, 2003). In a sense, this challenges the perspective that there is 'one true sexuality' that is natural and biologically determined. This 'naturalist approach' will be explored later in the chapter when we look at two contrasting perspectives in relation to sexuality. In this section we intend only to consider a few examples of some particular aspects of sexuality that have changed through the ages. For more comprehensive accounts of the history of sexuality please see the references in 'Further reading' at the end of the chapter.

There is a popular assumption that ancient Greeks were tolerant of homosexuality. Philosophers such as Plato and Aristotle, leaders such as Alexander the Great, and writers such as Sappho, were all Greek and all were openly lovers of members of their own sex. If we examine their society a bit closer it is apparent that they did not have the concept of 'homosexuality' and 'heterosexuality', i.e. sexual orientation, as we do today. They regarded sexual orientation as more a matter of taste or preference as opposed to being integral to someone's identity. However, sexuality was firmly linked to power and status. The only people eligible to vote and run the country were adult male citizens who were free (i.e. not slaves). These men were free to choose anyone for their sexual partner regardless of gender. The important 'division' was in the sexual act itself. The free Greek adult male citizen, as a reflection of his power and status, would be expected to be the 'active' partner in relation to any sexual acts, that is, to penetrate his sexual partner with his penis. If a person was penetrated it was a sign of low status and power, and in effect shameful (Wilton, 2000). During some of the periods in the history of the ancient Greeks and Romans, the love of men for boys was idealised as the highest form of sexual love and men who preferred to have sex with women were seen to be undermining their virility, not enhancing it (Giddens, 2006).

Moving on in time to the eighteenth and early nineteenth centuries, in Britain many middle-class women had relationships with each other which included declarations of love, passionate nights spent in bed together, and long-term relationships without attracting the least adverse comment. Historians have tried to ignore this or explain it away so that it could not challenge their heterosexual account of history (Jeffries, 1985). Running parallel to this also during the eighteenth century in Britain women were sexually active, whilst men were viewed as being sexually passive (Lewis, 1984). However, early in the nineteenth century in Victorian Britain there was a significant shift in the way female sexuality was constructed. The ideal woman came to be portrayed as being passive, pure and innocent and someone who would only ever participate in sexual practices with her husband as an act of marital duty. Many Victorian men who were 'devoted' to and respectful of their wives, subsequently and regularly visited 'prostitutes' or 'kept mistresses'. By contrast however, wives who had lovers were regarded as scandalous and shunned by society. These different standards for men and women were regarded as acceptable and still act as a moral basis for certain attitudes today (Giddens, 2006). Again we see the connection between sexuality and power. What emerged from Victorian times was the notion of the 'good' and 'bad' woman, and the ideal of the 'good' woman was a way of socially controlling female sexuality. A good example of the social control of women is the Poor Law Amendment Act 1834 which contained a Bastardy Clause. Within this clause unmarried mothers were regarded as undeserving of any welfare and were made totally responsible for their child(ren) with no support from the father. This reinforced the message that poverty and immorality were negative aspects of female sexuality, for which there were consequences and condemnation. It can be recognised from these few examples how the way sexuality is perceived has changed and what is and what is not acceptable is very much influenced by social structures.

Religion and sexuality

Before we move on to look at different perspectives of sexuality it is useful to spend some time considering the influence of religion. Giddens (2006) states that Christianity has been the main influence on sexuality in Western culture and that the dominant view of the Christian Church was that the only acceptable sexual behaviour was the one needed for reproduction. This Christian view was particularly thought out and supported by St Thomas Aquinas in the thirteenth century. He placed an emphasis on a 'natural' sexuality where semen was intended by 'nature' for reproduction and any other use of it was 'contrary to nature' and therefore against God's will. This resulted in all other sexual acts being condemned as 'unnatural' and a sin. Masturbation, oral sex, anal sex, homosexual relationships and heterosexual intercourse that failed to produce children were all seen to be 'unnatural' and evil. This perspective made rape more acceptable than sodomy (which as Foucault (1978) points out was a word collectively used to mean masturbation, oral sex, anal sex and same-sex sexual relationships) because rape could result in pregnancy. Although this perspective has been challenged and rejected by many contemporary theologians it still has the power to influence our thinking and emotions about human sexuality (Reiss and Reiss, 2003). The powerful notion of 'natural' versus 'unnatural' sexual practices and relationships is still around today and demonstrates how religion continues to play an important part in shaping cultural attitudes towards sexuality. An example of this is the Catholic Church's resistance to sanction safer sexual practices in relation to condoms in many of the African countries in response to the HIV crisis (Bradshaw, 2003).

RESEARCH SUMMARY

Same-sex marriages

It is often cited that the Bible condemns homosexuality, linking this to the notion that the only acceptable sexual relationship is between a man and a woman within the structure of a marriage. It depends more on how the biblical texts are interpreted as opposed to what the texts literally state that influences Christian moulding of acceptable sexuality. There is surprising evidence of Christian same-sex 'marriage ceremonies' taking place in the Middle Ages which tends to strongly suggest that medieval Christians cannot have believed that this biblical condemnation existed. There are periods in the last 2,000 years when people have reacted against or ignored the Christian Church's teachings on sexuality.

Source: Wilton (2000) and Giddens (2006)

What are the views of other religions and faiths on sexuality? It is a difficult question to answer within a short discussion, so a few examples will be highlighted. In order to be able to present a comparative structure within this section of the chapter, we will use the example of same-sex relationships. Although same-sex relationships are not supported by the Hindu and Sikh religions today, the homoerotic carvings in ancient Indian temples may indicate evidence of past acceptance (Channel 4, 2006). The view on same-sex relationships amongst Muslims is extremely diverse, ranging from condemnation (and possible execution) through to the Muslim Canadian Congress welcoming legislation redefining marriage to include same-sex partners. The root of this diversity of opinion is reflected in the different Islamic schools of thought, such as the Maliki and Shaefi denominations, and comes from the different interpretations of the Qur'an. In fact, a number of Islamic scholars point out that the Qur'anic verse, 'we created you as partners', need not be limited to male–female couples and have upheld that this diversity of interpretation of the Qur'an lies at the heart of traditional Islamic practice. People can therefore align themselves to whichever interpretation they feel represents them most (Channel 4, 2006). It is important however, to refer here to Sharia, which is an Islamic religious code for living and governs the lives of people in ways which are not governed by the secular law. Although whether Sharia is adhered to is a matter of personal conscience for many Muslims, many Islamic countries have incorporated elements of Sharia into their state laws, hence Sharia law. For our present discussion it is worth noting that within Sharia law there is a specific set of offences known as the Hadd offences which cover so-called 'sexual offences' (Steiner, 2002). Homosexual behaviour is seen as a 'sexual offence' and therefore lesbians and gay men are executed in countries which carry out this law to the letter (Wilton, 2000; Petrelis, 2005).

The main theme that unites the Hindu, Sikh, Muslim and Christian religions is that their attitudes towards same-sex relationships are not consistent. Some denominations accept the diversity of human sexuality, others use religious teachings to justify human rights abuses against lesbians, gay men and others who transgress sexual protocols. Wilton (2000) distinguishes between religion and fundamentalism, stating that it is clearly possible to hold religious beliefs and remain tolerant of sexual diversity. Many lesbians, gay men and bisexuals are active members of their own religious cultures and strive to integrate their sexuality and their faith.

RESEARCH SUMMARY

What is religious fundamentalism?

Religious fundamentalism was a term originally applied to conservative, Bible-centred Protestant Christians (many of whom now prefer to call themselves 'evangelicals'), but can now apply to the range of religions including classical Christians, Jews, Muslims, Hindu and Sikhs. Fundamentalists of these religions interpret their scriptures and holy books literally and favour a strict adherence to certain traditional doctrines and practices. Fundamentalists usually demand that their doctrines and practices are legally enforced. It can lead to extreme prejudice and violence; for example, the Crusades, the Inquisition, and witch-burning were due to fundamentalist ideals. It is important to remember that fundamentalists make up only one part of any religion's followers, who usually fall along a wide spectrum of different interpretations, values and beliefs, as we have noted in the preceding discussion.

This was compiled by a range of definitions accessed from www.google.co.uk/search? hl=en&q=define%3AFundamentalism&btnG=Search&meta= (accessed 27/05/06).

Theoretical perspectives of sexuality

There are two broad perspectives to consider when we are defining and explaining sexuality. The first perspective can be referred to as a 'naturalist approach' to sexuality and at its simplest maintains that sexuality is biologically determined with minimal influence from the structures of society. It is important to note that the proponents of this approach believe that traits are fixed and there is no variation. The second perspective directly challenges this view and can be loosely referred to as a 'social constructionist' approach to sexuality which at its simplest seeks to explore how sexuality is constructed and influenced by societal structures. However, the proponents of this perspective suggest that sexuality could also be seen as giving us a potential for choice, change and diversity. Again we are reminded of the 'nature versus nurture' debate that was referred to at the beginning of this chapter and you may find it helpful to refer back to your notes from Activity 1.2 as you are reading about the different approaches. Although we recognise that within the two main perspectives there are varying points of view, we would like to present the main themes of the contrasting views under the two main headings of 'naturalist' and 'social constructionist' approaches.

The naturalist approach

The naturalist approach (which includes as its proponents sexologists such as Havelock Ellis 1859–1939 and psychoanalysts such as Sigmund Freud 1856–1939) uses the biological anatomical differences between male and female to claim that there is a biological basis to sexuality. The traditional gender traits, for example, activity and passivity for men and women respectively, are believed to develop 'naturally' from this biological basis. When considering sexuality the starting point is the male heterosexual sex 'drive' which is viewed as a natural urge that is 'uncontrollable' and needs to be satisfied. Some would argue that men are 'naturally' more sexually active than women, in order to impregnate as many women as possible to ensure the continuation of the blood-line (Giddens, 2006). *All sexuality is derived from or developed in relation to a male heterosexual drive…[where] men are active sexual agents with 'natural' sexual urges that cannot be ignored; women are passive recipients of men's sexual desires* (Stephen, 2002, p.30). Following on from this is the view that heterosexuality is the normal expression and identity of sexuality. This view is backed up by the prolific amount of studies that are undertaken on the causes of sexualities other than heterosexuality, which is presumed as having no cause as it is viewed as natural (Johnson, 2004). This approach is extremely influential and echoes some of the fundamentalist ideas within religion that we touched on in the previous section of this chapter. It could be argued that this perspective, through its similarities has in turn replaced the religious presumptions about sexuality.

CRITICAL THINKING

If something is natural why does it need to be encouraged?

Within the context of a general alarm about female sexuality in the nineteenth and twentieth centuries, which we have referred to earlier, the norm of heterosexuality was forcibly established by deploying enormous efforts to control female sexuality in monogamous, heterosexual marriage, which became institutionalised through the enforcement of chastity belts, property laws and welfare restrictions (Wilton, 2000). An example is the Vagrancy Act 1898 which criminalised homosexual 'soliciting' addressing a growing concern to map out and contain the legitimate boundaries of accepted sexuality. Heterosexuality became the linchpin of maintaining patriarchal structures still evidenced to date, which is currently defined as 'hetero-patriarchy' (Jackson and Scott, 2006).

Before turning to the 'social constructionist' approach we would like you to engage with the following activity which we have called 'How is sexuality viewed by society?' The activity consists of five sections and is similar to a jigsaw. Each of the four sections is a part of the jigsaw and highlights part of the picture. The fifth section involves you putting the four sections together to make the whole picture. We have provided some commentary at the end of each part.

How is sexuality viewed by society?

We would like you to consider the images, photographs and printed texts of how sexuality is viewed by our society. To do this you could look through journals, magazines, newspapers, adverts, leaflets, the web and television. However you choose to do this we would like you then to analyse the material you have chosen under the four section headings below of 'representation', 'silence/absence', 'proliferation', and 'address'.

1.3a Representation

How does your material:

- *represent men's sexuality?*
- *represent women's sexuality?*
- *represent people's sexual relationships?*
- *represent people of different sexual orientations?*
- *represent the emotional states of people?*
- *represent people's physical traits?*

Comment

Representation is about how an issue, in this case sexuality, is conveyed through images, photographs and written text. When analysing your material you will want to consider whether certain ways of representing sexuality dominate. For example, how often are slim white able-bodied men and women dressed in fashionable clothing, with smiling and happy faces portrayed? Are men and women presented together assuming heterosexuality? Is any other sexual orientation represented? How are other sexual orientations represented? These are some critical questions that you can be asking of your material. You may think of others in relation to this section on representation.

1.3b Silence/absence/invisibility

When considering your material:

- *which groups of people are not represented?*
- *which groups of people are missing?*
- *which groups of people have very little representation?*

Comment

Silence, absence or invisibility are self-explanatory. In relation to this section the critical question is who is not represented or who is missing. If certain groups of people are invisible or underrepresented, what does this say about their sexuality? Are some groups of people, due to their invisibility, assumed to be asexual or is

ACTIVITY 1.3 *continued*

their sexuality seen as 'abnormal' and so should not be portrayed? Sometimes certain groups of people may have some aspects of their sexuality represented and in relation to other aspects there is a silence.

1.3c – Proliferation

When considering your material:

- *which groups are presented more often and in what way are they presented?*

- *what types of images are presented most frequently?*

- *what effect do you think the frequently presented images have?*

- *what kinds of norms are being represented?*

Comment

When analysing your material in relation to proliferation you are considering in relation to sexuality what and who have an enormous amount of representation. Who and what do you see and read a lot about in relation to sexuality? In certain situations people who are underrepresented may only have one particular aspect of their sexuality portrayed and this particular aspect is portrayed excessively. This links into the previous section in relation to certain aspects of a person's sexuality being invisible.

1.3d Address

When considering your material:

- *what assumptions are being made about the readers?*

- *is it being targeted at particular groups of people – if so, who? and why?*

- *what messages does it give to people who do not feel it is for them?*

Comment

This section called 'address' is about who the material is intended for, in other words who is being targeted. This is a complex but important area because you will find that if some material is being targeted at a particular group then assumptions will be made about the way that particular 'readership' views sexuality. An example of this is when health journals address the sexual needs of older people then the issues are presented in a very medicalised way. This does two things: (1) it assumes that the readership is only interested in a medical viewpoint of the sexuality of older people; and (2) it builds a medical model of older people's sexuality.

> **ACTIVITY 1.3** *continued*
>
> ### 1.3e Building a viewpoint of sexuality
>
> *After completing your analysis of your material try to draw some conclusions for yourself about how sexuality is viewed within society by putting together your comments from the four areas of 'representation', 'silence/absence', 'proliferation' and 'address'.*
>
> ## Comment
>
> To conclude the exercise you are putting together the four aspects to help you to complete a picture of how a range of materials (images and texts) build a viewpoint(s) of sexuality. You could argue at this point that these images have helped to 'construct' a way of seeing and considering sexuality and by analysing these areas you have engaged with an activity that 'deconstructs' sexuality.
>
> *Source: Adapted from T Wilton (2000) Sexualities in health and social care: A textbook. Buckingham: Open University. Reproduced by kind permission of the Open University Press.*

We will be returning to some aspects of this exercise towards the end of this chapter, but at this point we would like to briefly summarise the approach that we have referred to as 'social constructionist'. Again we would like to reiterate that there are varying viewpoints and positions within this approach but we hope to do it justice by presenting to you its main themes.

The social constructionist approach

A social constructionist approach (includes as its proponents philosophers such as Michael Foucault (1926–1984) and sociologists such as Jeffrey Weeks (1945–), to considering sexuality is in direct contrast to the naturalist approach that we summarised earlier in the chapter. This perspective is based on the premise that although there are biological anatomical differences between men and women, the rest of a person's sexuality is influenced by society's structures. It is interesting to note that although sexuality is frequently portrayed as the most natural aspect of life, social constructionists would claim that it is a part of life that is most susceptible to being moulded, constructed and organised by social, political, cultural and historical forces (Weeks, 2003). If we follow this line of argument other important themes follow when considering sexuality. Foucault (1978) argues that sexuality is made up of erotic concepts of desires, identities and relationships and what is deemed as erotic varies across cultures, history and social contexts. This makes sexuality difficult to analyse as it is not a fixed entity but something that is fluid and changing. What is erotic, and therefore sexual, depends on what is defined as such, by whom, and in what specific social contexts (Jackson, 1999). Sexuality is a socially constructed set of meanings and behaviours that have to be learnt and practised. Traditional gender traits are learnt through, for example, 'gender-appropriate' toys such as dolls for girls and guns for boys, which directly link to 'gender-appropriate' work such as mother and soldier respectively. Sexual behaviour for men and women is different and again is learnt and supported by a range of societal structures, such as language. Language controls and moulds sexual behaviour, for example it is acceptable for men to have many sexual partners before they 'settle down' and they are referred to as 'sowing their wild oats' or 'stud'. There is no comparable positive term for women who for the same behaviour risk being called 'slag', 'whore' and 'nymphomaniac'. Sexual orientation is viewed by social constructionists as a choice and not a fixed identity that people are born with. Research studies over the last half a century (Kinsey et al., 1948; Humphreys, 1970; Wilton, 2004) support the fact that many people change their sexual orientation during the course of their lives. Obviously social constructionists would argue that the 'choice' element in sexual orientation is heavily weighted towards heterosexuality and that it is reinforced by powerful social regulations and institutions (Foucault, 1978; Butler, 1990).

Social construction and analysing discourse

So how do we explore the way that issues and concepts such as sexuality are constructed and supported by society and its structures? We introduced you earlier to the concept of discourse as a system of ideas or knowledge that is used to control and regulate alternative ways of thinking. The important aspect in any discourse that is said to be influential is the fact that it needs to be coherent and have some authority. Therefore taking a piece of discourse and analysing it is a method of exploring how concepts such as sexuality are constructed. Analysing sexuality in this way allows us to challenge how it is defined and explained and to highlight which person's sexuality it includes and excludes, that is, who it discriminates against. In effect, through analysing discourse we can deconstruct the concept of sexuality and hence allow the potential for choice, change and diversity (Stephen, 2002).

When you were undertaking Activity 1.3 you were analysing the discourses around sexuality and how they are constructed, by examining a range of different discourses through the materials you decided to use. Although discourses represent sets of generally accepted and widespread opinions and ideas about the way things are and the way things should be, it is important to understand that they do not just reflect what the current reality is as we experience it, but they also act to promote, contribute and police what we experience as reality. They promote certain values and perspectives and marginalise others even to the point of some becoming invisible in relation to what is natural, inevitable, desirable and appropriate in human behaviour (Foucault, 1981; Phillips, 2000). A good example of this is the way disabled people in our society are often regarded as non-sexual adults. Sexual activity is very much associated with youth and physical attractiveness, and when it is not, it is often seen as 'unseemly'. If sexuality and disability are discussed, it is very much in terms of capacity, technique and fertility, in particular, male capacity and technique and female fertility, with no reference to sexual feelings. This approach ignores other aspects of sexuality, such as touching, caressing, affection and emotions (McCarthy, 1999). If we accept that sexual expression is a natural and important part of human life, then perceptions that deny sexuality for disabled people deny a basic human right of expression. These are themes that we explore further in Chapter 5 when we discuss issues of sexuality and disabled people.

The social construction of sexuality and the analysing of discourses around sexuality are themes that will be revisited in later chapters throughout the book. The work that you have undertaken for Activity 1.3 will be invaluable when we look in more detail at sexuality in relation to different groups of people.

C H A P T E R   S U M M A R Y

This chapter has introduced you to some of the key issues in relation to sexuality. As well as being able to demonstrate your understanding of the terminology, you should also feel confident to be able to identify contrasting perspectives and analyse some of the assumptions in relation to sexuality. A key learning point from the chapter is the link between sexuality, power and oppression. You should be able to demonstrate your understanding of the relationship between sexuality and discrimination and be starting to think of the impact this has on anti-discriminatory social work practice.

FURTHER READING

Beasley, C (2005) *Gender and sexuality – critical theories, critical thinkers*. London: Sage Publications.

A comprehensive book that offers a critical overview of the key theorists and debates in the area of sexuality and gender.

Weeks, J (2003) *Sexuality*. 2nd edition. London and New York: Routledge.

Good comprehensive introduction to the social and cultural understanding of sexuality. It covers the central issues needed for a full understanding of sexual life.

Wilton, T (2000) *Sexualities in health and social care – a textbook*. Buckingham and Philadelphia: Open University Press.

Good introduction to human sexuality within the context of health and social care practice.

Chapter 2

(Hetero)sexuality and diversity

Sexuality and diversity – an introduction

Sexuality is made up of a range of diverse aspects in terms of relationships, sexual orientations, sexual practices and sexual preferences. This diversity is the central backbone to sexuality which makes it an interesting and challenging area to engage with as social workers. The two theoretical perspectives, naturalist and social constructionist, that you were introduced to in the first chapter, both recognise the diverse aspects of sexuality, but the similarity stops here. The naturalist approach views any deviation from a monogamous heterosexual relationship as unnatural and unacceptable. The social constructionist approach views all the different aspects of sexuality as acceptable, valid and equal. As we have seen in Chapter 1, this approach also offers a way of exploring how diverse sexualities are constructed as 'unacceptable', by analysing discourses and their interrelationship with power and oppression. The focus of this chapter is the exploration of sexuality and its diversities.

Heterosexuality, homophobia and heterosexism

Heterosexuality

Any discussion about sexuality and diversity has to start with some discussion about hetero-sexuality. So what is heterosexuality? You will have familiarised yourself with the definition whilst undertaking Activity 1.1. To recap, heterosexuality refers to a sexual orientation where people are exclusively or almost exclusively sexually and/or romantically attracted to people of the opposite sex or with opposite gender identity. We would argue however, that this definition only contributes to a small part of the meaning of heterosexuality within Western societies. So what does it mean to be a heterosexual person in our society?

> *Being a heterosexual person is being a 'normal' person. 'Other' people have 'sexuality' but heterosexual people are 'just people'.*

> (Best, 2005, p.213)

This statement reiterates some of the discussion we introduced to you in the first chapter, notably that heterosexuality is viewed as the 'natural' and 'normal' form of human sexual-ity. We highlighted how this was supported by religion, biological determinism (i.e. naturalist approach) and the emphasis on reproduction. It is important to understand at this stage that by 'constructing' heterosexuality as 'normal', people who are not heterosex-ual are referred to as 'abnormal' or seen as 'other' people. This can be referred to as 'othering', which is a way of defining and securing a positive identity through the stigmati-sation of 'other' people's identity. This can lead to a 'us' and 'them' situation and in order for 'us' to feel positive, then 'them' are belittled and seen as inferior. This process can take place with a range of differences such as ethnicity, gender, class, age and disability.

Heterosexuality is an institution and an identity. It is constructed and enforced within Western societies through powerful social processes such as the law, the state, social con-ventions, and marriage is its central institution (Jackson, 1999). Foucault used the notion of dominant discourses as a way of enforcing particular behaviour, and identified powerful structures and institutions within society, such as hospitals, prisons and schools, which supported these dominant discourses (Giddens, 2006). Although men and women may not have to 'come out' as heterosexual, many of their identities such as wife/husband, fiancée, girlfriend/boyfriend, daughter/son or mother/father are derived from their hetero-sexual relationships. Heterosexuality structures men and women's social, work, domestic and sexual lives, and has many opposing aspects.

> *It is both sexual and asexual, publicly institutionalised yet often experienced as private and intimate, maintained through everyday practices yet so taken for granted that it appears unremarkable.*

> (Jackson, 2006, p.44)

ACTIVITY 2.1

The term 'compulsory heterosexuality' was first introduced by Adrienne Rich (1980) to emphasise that heterosexuality is imposed on us rather than freely chosen. Do you think that heterosexuality is enforced and/or encouraged in modern Western societies? Write down your answer and support it with examples from your life experiences, your reading/ research and knowledge.

Comment

You may have come up with examples to support the view that heterosexuality is encouraged in our society, such as the way that opposite-sex relationships are predominantly featured to promote commodities, for example 'his/her' mugs and towels, or enforced through violence against lesbians, gay men, bisexuals and transgender people. You may also have argued against heterosexuality being enforced because of recent major changes in the UK in legislation supporting the rights of lesbians, gay men, bisexuals and transgender people. A good example is the Civil Partnership Act 2004 which gives same-sex couples who enter into a civil partnership the same treatment as opposite-sex couples who enter into a civil marriage, in relation to a wide range of legal matters. We would argue that although there has been a massive positive shift in policy in favour of lesbians, gay men, bisexuals and transgender people, heterosexuality is still the dominant discourse and this manifests itself through homophobia and heterosexism.

RESEARCH SUMMARY

Hate crime against lesbian, gay, bisexual and transgender (LGBT) communities

The extent of homophobic incidents is very high, though under-reporting means the actual level of anti-gay hate crime is unclear. Statistics suggest that in East London 48 per cent of LGBT people had experienced hate crime, but only 44 per cent of these reported the incident to the police. Two studies by GALOP (1998, 2001), a London-based independent voluntary sector organisation which lobbies for changes and improvements in police services and practices relating to LGBT people, found that black LGBT people were 10 per cent more likely to experience physical abuse than white LGBT people, reflecting a combination of racism and homophobia.

Source: Victim Support (2006) Crime and prejudice: the support needs of victims of hate crime: a research report

---

Homophobia and heterosexism

Both of these terms were introduced in the first chapter and need to be explored here in more depth so that we can understand the power and dominance of heterosexuality. Homophobia refers to the intolerance, fear and hatred that some heterosexual people have of lesbians, gay men and bisexuals. It is, however, an inadequate term as the word 'phobia' tends to imply possible mental health issues, a degree of irrational and unconscious behaviour and implies the phobia is only located within the individual concerned (King, 2003). It therefore gives the impression that anti-gay attitudes are only a problem for the minority of heterosexual people and ignores the fact that much anti-gay prejudice is perpetrated quite consciously through society's cultural and structural institutions and values. You may come across the term 'internalised homophobia' which is used to describe a self-loathing that lesbians, gay men and bisexuals may develop as a response to homophobia. Again this term tends to individualise the problem by focusing on the lesbian, gay or bisexual person and prevents us from exploring the cause of the anti-gay prejudice. Homophobia is only a part, albeit an extremely destructive part, of heterosexism. For this reason we prefer to use the word 'heterosexism' as opposed to 'homophobia', as we feel it best describes all the levels of prejudice and oppression experienced by lesbians, gay men and bisexuals.

The term heterosexism refers to a set of assumptions and practices which promote heterosexuality as the only normal, acceptable and viable way to live our lives. Heterosexuality is used as a standard against which other sexual orientations are judged, policed and rendered inferior (Scott and Jackson, 2006). A powerful part of heterosexism is the assumption that everyone is heterosexual unless someone indicates to the contrary. This assumption of heterosexuality supports the view that it is natural and therefore does not have to assert its existence. The superiority and assumption of heterosexuality is perpetuated through personal, cultural and structural levels of society (Thompson, 2006), such as laws, media, education, religions, public services, cultural values, language, stereotypes and prejudices. This institutionalised heterosexuality serves to marginalise lesbians, gay men and bisexuals and gives rise to discrimination and oppression (Scott and Jackson, 2006). The discrimination and oppression of people who do not identify as heterosexual can take many forms. An explicit example is a person not being able to take up certain religious posts because of their sexual orientation. However, if you reflect back on Activity 1.3 where you were 'deconstructing' sexuality, you will remember the power of 'silence/absence/invisibility' in constructing a view of sexuality. Heterosexism uses the implicit form of silence as a way of constructing lesbians, gay men and bisexuals as invisible. This is done through, for example, lack of representation and presence within the media, or through exclusive language such as 'what contraception do you use?'. Challenging heterosexism, particularly heterosexual privilege and dominance, is a tricky business because of the complexities of the power relations between heterosexual people and lesbians, gay men and bisexuals. Many heterosexual people deny, ignore or are not conscious of the privileges they have from being heterosexual. This makes the power that a privileged position holds, such as that of heterosexual people, very difficult to challenge and to change.

ACTIVITY 2.2

We would like you to imagine that you are heterosexual. What do you think are some of the privileges or advantages that you have over someone who may be lesbian, gay or bisexual?

Comment

You may have come up with a range of different privileges and advantages. Fish (2006) highlights many privileges that heterosexual people can enjoy and we list some of the main ones so that you can compare them with the list that you have come up with.

19

- Heterosexual people do not need to consider whether or not to tell someone that they meet for the first time about the fact that they are heterosexual.

- Children of heterosexual people will not be taunted or bullied because of their parents' sexual orientation.

- Heterosexual teenagers will not have their sexual orientation dismissed as something that they will probably grow out of.

- The media can show two heterosexual people kissing or holding each other without it being considered as either remarkable or risqué.

- Heterosexual students can be sure that their course material will represent their sexual orientation and represent it positively.

For further privileges refer to Fish (2006, pp.12–13).

From the above list we can see that heterosexual privilege operates on different levels of society, therefore heterosexism is neither completely determined by social structures, nor is it just about people's individual behaviour. Individual beliefs, values and actions are inter-related with society's norms and expectations, which in turn are underpinned and influenced by social structures. The different levels support and constrain one another.

Heterosexuality and social divisions

Social divisions

Society is made up of social divisions, the main ones being gender, ethnicity, class, disability, age and sexual orientation. They are categories or groups which are socially constructed and will differ depending on the type of society. In Western societies everybody belongs to every social division, and within each there is an internal division(s). For example, the social division of gender has a division between men and women. The relationships between these internal divisions or groups are unequal in terms of privilege and power, and usually one group is seen as superior and the other group(s) seen as inferior. This results in social inequalities and oppressions, such as sexism, racism, classism, disablism, ageism and heterosexism (Payne, 2006).

ACTIVITY 2.3

Consider each of the main social divisions, that is, gender, class, race, disability, sexual orientation and age, in relation to yourself. In which social divisions do you think you have privileges and power and in which do you feel less powerful?

Comment

As we all belong to all of the social divisions, the membership of one can give us privileges and power whereas the membership of another will give us no privileges and make us feel powerless. For example, a black man will have power in terms of gender but none or limited power in terms of ethnicity. The social divisions often connect and overlap, reinforcing powerlessness so that the person in question experiences multiple oppressions, for example a disabled lesbian. Another example is a middle-class heterosexual woman, who will have power in terms of her sexual orientation and class but none, or limited, power in terms of her gender. It is this multiple membership of the social divisions which complicates the issue of power and inequality.

For the purpose of this chapter we shall be considering the interrelationship of gender, ethnicity and class with heterosexuality. The social divisions of disability and age will be considered in later chapters. Although we will be considering each separately it is necessary to bear in mind that people will experience their heterosexuality, gender, ethnicity and class simultaneously.

Heterosexuality and gender

It is impossible to have a discussion about heterosexuality without discussing gender (Jackson, 2006). Heterosexuality by its definition is gendered and being heterosexual does not have the same experience or consequences for men as for women. Gender is a social division where men have more power than women, and are able to control women through political, economic, social and physical power (Abbott, 2006). The oppression of women by men is referred to as sexism, which is based on the belief that men are superior to women, and used as a justification of women's inequality. This inequality is present within heterosexual relationships which are, it is argued, based on male dominance and female subordination (Scott and Jackson, 2006). Over the last 40 years feminist theorists have made a particular contribution to the analysis of power relationships between men and women. It is important for you to have an overview of the main themes of the debate which we have put in the following research summary. We do recognise that we risk oversimplifying what is a complex and diverse debate, but hope you will be encouraged to do further reading within this area so that you are able to appreciate the nuances.

RESEARCH SUMMARY

Power relationships between men and women – patriarchy versus discourse?

When analysing the power relationships between men and women within modern Western societies feminist theorists have offered a range of perspectives. Their major difference is how they view power in terms of where it is located and how it is manifested. The two major concepts to emerge from the recent debates are patriarchy and discourse.

- *Patriarchy*

The ideology of patriarchy, which involves male superiority, domination and power over women, is manifested in different ways. Some theorists regard male domination as being manifested through the system of social, political and economic structures and practices which in turn support men's oppression of women. Examples of these structures and practices would be paid work (women's economic inequality in terms of wages, pensions and benefits), the family (women's 'role' being the {re}production, management and ultimate responsibility for the family), and sexuality (women's lack of control over their own

---

bodies, for example, reproduction and abortion). However, other theorists regard male domination as being manifested through men and women's day-to-day relationships, in particular, men's use of aggression and sexual power in rape, domestic violence and sexual harassment. Through the differences of interpretation there is an agreement about the existence of the patriarchy as a system of male domination.

• **Discourse**

Postmodernist feminists analyse power relationships between men and women by considering discourses that men and women use in their day-to-day lives about each other. It is through these discourses that male power is constructed and supported. For example, the discourses such as 'stud' and 'real man' for men and 'tart' and 'slapper' for women construct and control both men and women's sexual behaviour as masculine and feminine respectively. Power in terms of discourse is seen to be everywhere and involving all people at all levels of society, as opposed to being located in one system such as patriarchy.

Source: Abbott (2006)

When evaluating these perspectives it is important to recognise that both men and women are affected by the predominance of the male-dominated cultures that exist in most Western societies. However, gender power is complex and is embodied in structural, cultural, personal and historical aspects of society. Despite this we must not assume that it is a natural and intractable aspect of society. Women and men do resist and challenge pressure to conform to the 'way they should' relate to each other.

So how do heterosexual women and men experience their sexuality? The claim that women and men are biologically and therefore 'naturally' different extends to differences in their sexuality, in terms of sexual identity, desires and inclinations. These differences are reinforced through being presented as the basis for attraction, desire and compatibility, hence the saying *women and men are 'made for each other'* (Jackson, 2006, p.53).

Women

For a heterosexual woman, her sexuality is being defined and redefined during her life in relation to what is seen as feminine. It could be argued that for heterosexual women their gender is the main determining influence of how they experience their sexuality within a heterosexual context. For example, women's femininity or womanliness is confirmed by her sexual attractiveness to men (Holland et al., 1998). In the first chapter female sexuality was briefly introduced in relation to passivity and control. We would like now to explore these two concepts in more detail and their effects on women.

Historically female sexuality within a heterosexual concept has always been constructed as passive to 'complement' the active male sexuality. This passivity has encouraged the view that women do not have a sexuality in their own right. For example, the age of consent for young men was not considered a legal issue until the Sexual Offences Act 1993. The age of consent legislation up until that date had focused only on young women and girls, supporting the view that it was men that initiated sexual activities and women consented (or not) to them (Waites, 2005). Also in direct contrast to gay men, lesbianism has never been criminalised, nor have lesbians had an age of consent until the implementation of the Sexual Offences Bill 2003. The dominant discourse regarding lesbians has always been focused on the lack of a penis and cries of 'what do they do in bed?'. Closely related to this issue of passivity are the ideas that women are there to please and prioritise men's sexual needs as well as often being *identified and evaluated in terms of their sexual availability to men* (Jackson, 2006, p.54). Again legislation has supported these ideas, with the example of rape within marriage only becoming a criminal offence in 1991 (Waites, 2005), implying that sexual intercourse (with or without consent) is a married man's right. These discourses have however been challenged as women have found their clitorises, questioned the view that being sexual is solely about the penile penetration of the vagina, and asserted their rights to sexual pleasure (Scott and Jackson, 2006).

RESEARCH SUMMARY

The National Survey of Sexual Attitudes and Lifestyles in 1991 (Wellings et al., 1994) found that penile penetration of the vagina was the most common sexual activity for heterosexual people. There is an all-pervasive discourse that suggests that heterosexual sexual intercourse is the best and only true expression of sexuality (Gott, 2005). Bill Clinton's denial of sexual relations with Monica Lewinsky because sexual intercourse had not taken place supports this dominant discourse (Best, 2005). Research (Hawkes, 1996, cited in Gott, 2005) analysing female sexuality in women's magazines found that heterosexual sexual intercourse was regarded as the height of sexual experience. It was found that young women were encouraged:

> ...to 'please their man' through finding the most satisfying sexual position for intercourse – 'More' magazine helpfully illustrates a new 'position' every fortnight for such educational purposes.

Source: Gott (2005, p.17)

Women receive contradictory messages about their sexuality and negotiating the discourse around being 'sexually available for men' can create confusion, anxiety and danger for many women. Women who are being sexually active can often be judged as immoral and women who choose not to be sexually active can be accused of being 'frigid', 'a tease', and may also be labelled as 'lesbian'. The moral discourse surrounding women's sexual history is often played out in courtrooms in relation to rape or sexual assault. Convictions for rape are at an all-time low, with reported rapes being at an all-time high (Office for Criminal Justice Reform, 2006). With the majority of perpetrators being known to the survivors and the increase in 'date' rape, we do need to question the role played by the construction of male sexuality as being predatory and female sexuality as being available for men. Pornography plays an influential part in the social construction of the relationship between female and male sexuality. Pornography depicts women enjoying being overpowered, humiliated and degraded (usually by men) which encourages violence against women (Saul, 2003). Control, or lack of it, has historically been a significant aspect of women's experiences of their sexuality from the threat and fear of sexual violence to lack of control over their own bodies in relation to reproductive rights. Reproductive rights for all women include the right to be pregnant, free from the threat and reality of compulsory sterilisation and compulsory abortion, as well as the right of access to effective contraception and termination facilities (Weeks, 2003).

ACTIVITY 2.4

Case study – challenging heterosexism and sexism

You are on placement in a residential unit for young people and have been asked to run a series of four group sessions lasting an hour and half each, on the topic of sexuality, with four young women aged 14 years old who live in the unit. As part of your planning, we would like you to think about your value base and how you are going to practise in an anti-discriminatory way. Write down a list of things that you would need to be aware of and do that would help you to create and promote a positive, inclusive and empowering atmosphere for the group.

Comment

We have come up with a list of the main points we think are important. This list is not exhaustive and you may have highlighted a few more.

- The sessions need to be person-centred with a focus on feelings, emotions and self-esteem. It is good to develop an open style and in relation to the language of sexuality check for common understandings.

- Sexuality needs to be explored in its fullest sense, which will enable the group to view being sexual as more than just penetrative heterosexual sexual intercourse.

- Sexual relationships should be explored in terms of their complexities and diversities. It is important to create an atmosphere that does not assume heterosexuality.

- Sexual rights and responsibilities should be discussed highlighting the young women's right to say 'no' to sexual activity at any time in their sexual relationships.

- Sexual pleasure and how women achieve this is an important area to discuss as this tends to be neglected in relation to young women.

Through your anti-discriminatory value base you are attempting to challenge the assumption that these young women only need to know about the biological aspects of heterosexual sexual intercourse and its link to reproduction.

Men

Although we provide a fuller discussion about the development of masculinity and its effect on male sexuality in the next chapter focusing on young people, we wanted to draw your attention to a couple of points. Holland et al. (1998) argue that heterosexuality is not just about the oppression of women by men but the conditioning and promotion of masculinity. Therefore male (hetero)sexuality is also regulated and constrained by the hierarchical division within gender, but not quite as much as for women. For a heterosexual man, being sexually active confirms his masculinity but unlike women, men can have their gender confirmed in other areas of their lives such as through their physical and mental skills and abilities. However, despite this gay men may find that their masculinity is in doubt because of their sexual orientation. Heterosexual men experience themselves as the 'norm' and women as 'different', as 'them', as 'other' (Jackson, 2006). There are powerful pressures on men to conform in terms of their sexuality and any nonconformity results in personal and social consequences.

Recent analysis of relationships between heterosexual women and men has led to new understandings and awareness in some areas of life; for example, sexual harassment at work is now illegal. However, globalisation and capitalist chic lifestyle that package heterosexual sexual activity as fun and glamorous can help to obscure the inequalities and oppression. It is claimed that *women are made to feel a permanent insecurity of becoming ugly* (Best, 2005, p.263). Like the most effective social divisions, gender is assumed to be fundamentally based on biological differences which produce all the stereotypes and social constructs that we have been discussing in relation to heterosexuality. There have obviously been some changes over the years, but we would argue that it is the amount and type of difference that are changing as opposed to challenging that there is a fundamental and natural difference at all (Jackson, 2006).

Heterosexuality and ethnicity

We are using the following definitions for the terms 'ethnicity' and 'race'.

> *Ethnicity* [refers to the] *differences between individuals and groups in skin colour, language, religion, culture, national origin/nationality, or sometimes geographic region. Ethnicity subsumes both nationalism and race. Current notions of race are centred exclusively on visible (usually skin colour) distinctions among populations.*

> (Nagel, 2003, p.6)

The impact of ethnicity on heterosexuality is significant, but complex, therefore we cannot hope to cover all the different aspects. We hope however to raise your awareness of some important points, illustrating these with examples. There has been little public discussion on the connections between race and sexuality, and much of the theoretical discussion has tended to be dominated by reference to the sexuality of white/European people (Richardson, 2000).

An important starting point in relation to any discussion about black people and sexuality is the impact of slavery, apartheid and colonisation. The system of slavery which was not abolished until mid-nineteenth century was about white people, and in particular white men, owning black women and men. Therefore black women's experience of gender and heterosexuality was through the system of slavery, as opposed to the experience of white women which was through the system of marriage. White women had specific rights as they were not only regarded sexually, but also as potential wives, mothers and human. This need for racially pure offspring gave white women a position over black women (Haraway, 2007). Black women on the other hand were seen in racial, sexual and inhuman terms, and white men often assumed sexual rights over black women slaves who were regarded as their property (hooks, 1992). Rape was used routinely by white men within the slavery system to shame and suppress black people. On the other hand, if a black man was suspected of being sexually intimate with a white woman, he would be accused of being a rapist and killed. This happened in the USA until the mid-twentieth century. The term 'rape' was constructed along race lines as opposed to the issue of consent:

> *Many black men were lynched and publicly castrated in the USA last century as a way of 'protecting white womanhood'. In other words, white men had social and economic rights which enabled them to engage in coercive non-consensual sex with non-white partners, at a time when black men were being denied the right to choose a consensual sexual partner 'across race lines'.*

(Richardson, 2000, p.113)

Apartheid, or the system of racial segregation, gave rise to anti-miscegenation laws (laws against inter-racial marriage) in many countries, for example in South Africa until 1985 and in the USA until 1967. These policies were instigated because white people wanted to maintain the 'purity' of the race.

The systems of slavery and apartheid constructed a dominant and racist view of black sexuality that is prevalent today. Black people are often portrayed as oversexed, promiscuous, immoral and dangerous, with black women often being perceived as sexually available. Black female sexuality is often associated with deviancy, for example prostitution, and then perceived as a risk or a threat to white heterosexual men. These perceptions are directly related to how black women were viewed within the slavery system (hooks, 1992). Western pornography portrays black women as masseuses, geishas and being in possession of erotic secrets. The process of globalisation has resulted in an expanding global sex trade which involves in particular marginalised and economically disadvantaged women from black and minority ethnic communities (Best, 2005).

Heterosexuality and class

Social class can be defined in many ways and broadly refers to the socioeconomic differences between groups of people in society. Within the social class structure in the UK there are three divisions, generally referred to as working class, middle class and upper class. As with the other social divisions the relationship between the classes is one of inequality resulting in people from the middle and upper classes having more power and privileges than working-class people. In order to examine the impact class may have on heterosexuality we are going to highlight some examples.

Although the development of a middle-class sexual morality in the nineteenth century in the UK was in response to the perceived immorality of both upper- and working-class people, it was the sexuality of working-class people that was regulated through social policy. The sexuality of working-class men and women was portrayed as animal-like, uncontrollable and linked to disease (Hawkes, 1996). People from the upper and middle classes were having fewer children and poverty was seen as being caused by working-class people having too many children. The Poor Law 1834 regulated the heterosexual sexual practices of working-class people by segregating men and women living in the work-houses and demanded that working-class people show a marriage certificate in order to apply for poor relief and military allowances (Carabine, 2004).

> *Both charitable and state support for the poor was becoming tightly mapped onto the model of a family consisting of a breadwinner husband and his dependent wife and children, suggesting that social policies were increasingly becoming linked to the promotion and regulation of certain kinds of sexual practices and relationships.*

(Carabine, 2004, p.65)

This model of the heterosexual family became synonymous with respectability for many working-class people. Concerns about parenthood, sexuality and class can be seen to exist today, in particular over the issue of young working-class women and unplanned pregnancies. This issue will be discussed further in Chapter 3.

It could be argued that sexuality is a middle-class concept because of the way it defined and united the middle classes in the nineteenth century (Weeks, 2003). We would argue that the stereotypical views held by society of working-class people have resulted in their views on the issues of sexuality being marginalised. For example, working class masculinity has been associated with *stark homophobia, misogyny and domestic patriarchy* (Connell, 2003, p.55) and traditional socialist politics has promoted a view of working class as masculine and heterosexual (Richardson, 2000). As a result the views of lesbians, gay men, bisexuals and heterosexual women from working-class communities have been marginalised. Challenges to the oppressive aspects of sexual relationships and heteronormativity have tended to come from political movements dominated by the middle-classes, for example feminism (Carabine, 2004). There is an assumption that issues of sexuality are a luxury for working-class people and that there is rigidity, particularly around working-class masculinity, that acts as a barrier to any change in terms of heterosexual relationships. However, the masculinity of working-class men is no more rigid than the masculinity of middle- and upper-class men (Connell, 2003).

Sexuality and diversity

Any discussion so far of the lives and experiences of lesbians, gay men and bisexual people has been in relation to the oppressive impact of heterosexuality in the form of heterosexism. This shared experience of oppression can give the impression that people from these communities are a homogenous group. The aim of this section is to present examples that highlight the diversity.

Lesbians, gay men and bisexuals

Whilst undertaking Activity 1.1 you will have reflected on the meaning of the terms 'lesbian', 'gay' and 'bisexual'. In this book we use the terms 'lesbian' for women, 'gay' for men, and 'bisexual' for men and women. It is vital to recognise that self-definition is an important part of the process of identity development and acceptance and people may use other words to describe their sexual orientation, such as 'homosexual', 'gay woman', or even reclaiming pejorative terms such as 'dyke' and 'queer'. There is also an important distinction between behaviour and identity. For example, some people may have or be having same-sex experiences and relationships but not identify as lesbian, gay or bisexual. For other people, being lesbian or gay is very much part of their identity, going beyond sexual behaviour to include beliefs, values, support networks, language and institutions that make up different lesbian and gay subcultures (Weeks, 2003).

Bisexuality

Major research into sexuality has situated bisexuality on a scale in between heterosexuality and homosexuality (Kinsey Institute, 1999). This has fuelled many misconceptions. For example, bisexuality is often regarded as a transitional phase usually to becoming lesbian/gay, or it is viewed as unstable in the sense that the bisexual person can switch from heterosexuality to homosexuality and vice versa. Although bisexuals experience heterosexism they have often been viewed by lesbians and gay men as retaining the privileges, power and acceptability of heterosexuality. Bisexuality is often regarded as a comment on someone's sexual behaviour as opposed to being a reference to their sexual identity. This can be attributed to the fact that we tend to view sexual identity as fixed, either as heterosexual or homosexual, as opposed to fluid. This fluidity (which is referred to again in the section 'Queer theory') leads people to argue that:

> bisexuality has the potential to end sexual categories because it poses a unique challenge to the institution of heterosexuality.

> (Fish, 2006, p.75)

Ethnicity and class

ACTIVITY **2.5**

Lesbians, gay men and bisexuals from working-class and black and minority ethnic communities are not particularly visible and struggle to find a voice. Why do you think this is?

Comment

As we have seen from our previous discussions, historically the sexuality of people from working-class and black and minority ethnic communities has been regulated through social policy and slavery. This has involved a process of heterosexualisation (Richardson, 2000) which has left a strong 'assumption of heterosexuality' that is present today. Another contribution to the invisibility of lesbians, gays and bisexuals from these communities has been the fact that discourse, political action around issues of sexuality and sexual politics in general have tended to be dominated by white middle-class people. This has not only excluded working-class and black experiences but has also served to give the impression that sexuality is an issue that only concerns white middle-class people.

In an attempt to go some way to addressing this invisibility we would like to highlight the following points.

Class

Working-class lesbians, gay men and bisexuals have featured strongly in the history of the gay rights movement and were in the forefront of the 1969 Stonewall rebellion which saw lesbian, gay, bisexual and transgender people fighting back against police raids (Fish, 2006). The Stonewall Riots were the catalyst that launched the Gay Liberation Movement. (See Donnellan, 2005, for a history of significant events of lesbian/gay struggles and victories in the twentieth century in 'Further reading').

RESEARCH SUMMARY

Social class is the least explored aspect in terms of research relating to sexual identity. McDermott (2006) has undertaken a study on the influence of social class for lesbians in how they manage their sexual identity in the workplace. The study found that middle-class lesbians are more likely than working-class lesbians to be in positions of power and authority, more likely to be employed in liberal and safer work settings and therefore more likely to be able to be open about their sexual orientation, which benefited their psychological health. The converse was true for the working-class lesbians in the study.

Ethnicity

There is a misconception that black and minority ethnic communities are more homophobic than white communities because of certain faith beliefs (Fish, 2006). Reflect back on Chapter 1 where we discussed religious views and sexuality and concluded that intolerance of sexual diversity can be a feature of any religious faith and was a particular feature of religious fundamentalism regardless of ethnicity. It is useful to note that there exists a range of support groups and organisations in the UK particularly for lesbian, gay and bisexuals from black and minority ethnic communities, such as NAZ project (**www.naz.org.uk**) and Safra Project (**www.safraproject.org**). The UK Black Pride organisation (**www.ukblackpride.org**) organised its first gay Black Pride festival in the UK and won the 2007 Black Lesbian, Gay, Bisexual and Transgender Community Award for Community Development.

Lesbian and gay parenting

Lesbians and gay men can become parents through co-parenting, donor insemination, surrogacy, fostering and adoption (Cooper, 2004). Some lesbians and gay men, on the other hand, have children from previous relationships when they identified as heterosexual. Fostering law and policy within England, Wales and Northern Ireland rejects any discrimination of potential foster carers based on their sexual orientation (Department of Health, 2002c). The Adoption and Children Act 2002 in England and Wales allows unmarried couples, including lesbians and gay men, to adopt jointly. Prior to this lesbians and gay men could only adopt as single people. Lesbian and gay families are becoming more accepted and the number of approved lesbian and gay carers for fostered and adopted children has been increasing over the last 20 years (Hicks, 2005a). Progress towards positive recognition has not been easy and continues to be challenged. For example, Catholic adoption agencies campaigned recently to be exempt from the Equality Act 2006 that prohibits discrimination in the provision of goods and services to lesbians, gay men and bisexuals, by continuing to disallow lesbians and gay men to adopt (Wintour et al., 2007).

A large part of social work policies and practice with lesbian and gay parents has been based on stereotypical and discriminatory assumptions such as concerns about children experiencing, social and psychological abuse and trauma (Skeates and Jabri, 1988), inappropriate gender role models and the risk of sexual abuse (Hicks, 1996). Many lesbian and gay parents have been denied custody of their children or visiting orders following the break-up of heterosexual relationships and a greater proportion of lesbian mothers have lost custody of their children in comparison to heterosexual mothers (Lamb, 1999). Many fostering and adoption applications have been rejected on the basis of sexual orientation alone (Hicks, 2005a). When lesbians and gay men have been successfully approved as carers, it has been in relation to short-term fostering as opposed to adoption and it has involved a disproportionate number of disabled children. Many lesbian and gay carers have felt that they have been used by the social welfare agencies as a 'last resort' (Hicks, 1996, p.15). Policies have not encouraged positive relationships between social workers and lesbians and gay men. For example, Section 28 of the Local Government Act 1988 (which was finally repealed in 2003) made it illegal for local authorities to promote lesbian and gay relationships and labelled lesbian and gay families as 'pretend' families. Slowly however, there have been positive changes, such as lesbian and gay carers being more open about their sexuality during the application process and expecting social workers to address their needs in an anti-discriminatory manner. However, the service received by lesbians and gay men is inconsistent, with only some areas, mainly inner cities, such as Manchester City Council, pioneering progressive and supportive practice, by producing guidance for social workers (Hicks, 2005a).

ACTIVITY 2.6

Case study

Myra and Marcia are lesbians who have been together for ten years and both are of African-Caribbean heritage. Myra comes from a working-class background and works as a support worker in a residential unit for looked-after children. Her partner Marcia comes from a middle-class background and works as a co-ordinator of a sexual health project for young people. They are both in their late 30s, and have a good network of friends, who are mostly lesbian and gay. Myra and Marcia have some contact with their respective families, particularly their sisters who live close by. Six months ago Myra had read an article in a national newspaper suggesting that local authorities now welcome applicants from different backgrounds, in terms of race and sexual orientation, for fostering and adopting children. After lengthy discussions Myra and Marcia decided that they would like to become adoptive parents and have undertaken the training course offered by their local authority. The next stage is their assessment by the social worker from the Fostering and Adoption Team. You are on placement in this team and have been invited by the social worker allocated to Myra and Marcia to undertake a joint assessment with her.

As stated earlier, social workers have been and continue to be discriminatory in their assessments of the suitability of lesbians and gay men as carers. Reflect back on your reading so far, particularly on heterosexism, and write down what you think are the main issues that need to be considered if you are going to work with Myra and Marcia in a positive and anti-oppressive way.

Comment

Social workers have a powerful and influential role in such an assessment and much of the bad practice is based on heterosexist attitudes that insist *upon the superior 'nature' of the two-parent heterosexual model* (Hicks, 2005a, p.43). We have therefore decided to highlight what we feel are some best-practice guidelines that challenge these attitudes, some of which you may have identified yourself when reflecting on this case study.

- The aim of the assessment is about the potential carers' ability to provide good enough childcare. Lesbians and gay men should not be scrutinised more than heterosexual people. The issue of risk is not about sexual orientation but about the standard of childcare practices which concern all applicants. Everyone should be offered a fair and adequate assessment as children have the right to good placements.

- Social workers need to use research to inform their assessments with lesbians and gay men. Pervasive and inaccurate views, such as, children of lesbians and gay parents are at more risk of sexual abuse and experience impaired social and psychological development through being exposed to inappropriate gender and sexual identity roles can be challenged by research studies. See 'Research summary' below for an overview of some of the key research within this area.

- The role of sexuality in an assessment is important for all applicants, including heterosexual people (Brown, 1998). In their assessments of lesbians and gay men, social workers have tended to either ignore sexuality and feel they are being non-discriminatory by treating lesbian and gay couples like heterosexual couples, or they have focused on sexuality to the exclusion of all else (Hicks, 1997). Sexuality is an important aspect of everyone's identity and needs to be discussed within the context of people's childcare abilities.

- Lesbian and gay carers do have some different issues to heterosexual carers, which are usually generated by heterosexist attitudes towards same-sex relationships. Social workers need to be aware of this impact and be prepared to talk through specific issues as part of the assessment. For example, how to 'come out' to professionals, schools, birth parents, and how to cope with the possibility of their child(ren) being bullied. There also needs to be recognition that lesbians and gay men may offer particular skills and experience in terms of dealing with discrimination and living in family networks that do not fit into the traditional heterosexual mould (Brown, 1998).

RESEARCH SUMMARY

Over the last 20 years a significant amount of research studies have been undertaken comparing children with lesbian mothers and children with heterosexual mothers. Susan Golombok and Fiona Tasker have researched a range of aspects with children, such as gender identity (Golombok et al., 1983), personal and social development (Tasker and Golombok, 1997; Golombok et al., 1997) and the development of sexual orientation (Golombok and Tasker, 1996). Within their comparative studies they have found no significant differences or difficulties between the two groups of children in any of the areas researched.

RESEARCH SUMMARY *continued*

With regard to the areas of sexual abuse, Fergusson and Mullen (1999) have brought together the findings of eight different research studies, which suggest that heterosexual men account for 97.5 per cent of the sexual abuse of girls, 78.7 per cent of the sexual abuse of boys and 92.5 per cent of the sexual abuse of children overall. Lamb (1999) suggests that based on statistics lesbians and gay men present a very low risk of sexually abusing children.

Regarding parenting ability, systematic studies to date do not provide any reason to believe that lesbians and gay men are any less suitable or less able than heterosexuals to be adoptive or foster parents based on their sexual orientation (Lamb, 1999; Hicks, 2005a). It is not sexual orientation that is an indicator of parenting ability (Golombok, 2002) but factors such as parenting skills, knowledge of children's needs and development, and attitudes towards discipline. Hicks (2006) argues that foster-care and adoption practice might learn from the new forms of intimacy, care and parenting developed by lesbians and gay men. (See 'Further reading').

Transgender people

'Transgender' is a term used to include a range of diverse people who challenge the sex and gender division of men and women. The social groupings under this umbrella term include cross-dressers, drag queens and kings, intersexed people and transsexuals. (For a definition of each please see the 'Glossary'.) As you can see from the detailed definitions, the diversity of transgender people is immense, ranging from men who identify with their birth gender and dress in women's clothing through to transsexuals (men and women) who surgically alter their bodies to change their birth gender. In Western societies the belief in a binary sex/gender system tends to put pressure on transgender people to identify either as male or female. This system invalidates and silences their experiences of their identity as possibly something more fluid or less divided.

RESEARCH SUMMARY

In some societies there is recognition of people who identify as neither male nor female, for example, the hijras in India, the kathoey in Thailand, and the mak nyahs in Malaysia. The deities within Hinduism have ambiguous gender and can change sex, and within the oral teachings of Buddhism four sexes/genders have been referred to.

Source: Fish (2006)

Up until recently it has been difficult for transgender people to form political alliances with lesbians, gay men and bisexuals, in order to organise themselves against the discrimination and oppression that they experience. Transgender people, and in particular transsexuals, have been accused of supporting as opposed to challenging rigid sex/gender stereotypes. Transsexuals awaiting surgery often have to conform to the stereotype of the gender they are realigning to in order to prove to the psychiatrists that they will be able to psychologically cope with the operation (Fish, 2006). Through the lives of transgender people and the establishment of queer theory, there is much more recognition that transgender people are challenging the social construction of the sex/gender system. Recent legislation such as the Gender Recognition Act 2003 helps to challenge discrimination as it gives transsexual people the right to change their gender on their birth certificate and marry and adopt a child with someone of the opposite sex.

Queer theory

Queer theory is a perspective on sexuality that was developed mainly by lesbian and gay writers/theorists, during the emerging HIV/AIDS crisis in Western societies. The term 'queer' is an attempt to positively reclaim a derogatory use of the word and is an inclusive label referring to gay, lesbian, bisexual, transgender and any other sexualities and sexual practices that challenge the dominant sex/gender/sexual identity system (Richardson, 2000). It could refer to a 'queer' heterosexuality. One of the aims of queer theory is to analyse or deconstruct the separation, referred to as a binary division, between heterosexuality and homosexuality (Scott and Jackson, 2006). It argues that this division puts heterosexuality at the centre and homosexuality on the outside as the 'other'. Heterosexuality's normality depends on homosexuality being 'other', that is its 'unnatural' opposite. Queer theorists argue that the division is not natural and can be challenged. This challenge or destabilising of heterosexuality can be done through an acknowledgement that all sexual identities are fluid, changeable and a matter of choice. The terms 'lesbian' 'gay' and 'homosexual' are rejected because of the way that they consolidate and support the binary division between heterosexuality and homosexuality. The 'naturalness' of other binary divisions such as men and women, feminine and masculine that support fixed sex/gender/sexual identity system are also challenged. The aim of destabilising the 'naturalness' of these divisions:

> is not to assimilate into, or even seek to reform, the current sexual system, but rather to challenge and transform it in such a way that heterosexuality is displaced from its status as privileged, institutionalised norm.

(Richardson, 2000, p.43)

For further critical debate on queer theory refer to Richardson (2000) (see 'Further reading').

Sexuality – a pleasure and a right

It is important to recognise that sexuality is not only about the exercise of power and the oppression of others. Sexuality is an integral part of our identity and involves positive aspects such as our desire for contact, intimacy, emotional expression, pleasure, tenderness and love, and its full development is essential for individual, interpersonal, and societal well-being (Weeks, 2003). However, for some people there are barriers to attaining these positive aspects within their lives, and in the main the barriers can be linked to oppression and the denial of their sexual rights. The World Association for Sexual Health in 1999 adopted a 'Declaration of Sexual Rights' (which is summarised in the last chapter) to promote a healthy sexuality for all individuals and societies in the world, in terms of their sexual rights being defended, recognised, respected and promoted (WAS, 2006). Sexual rights embrace human rights and therefore should be based on freedom, dignity and equality of all human beings (WAS, 2006).

C H A P T E R   S U M M A R Y

This chapter has taken you through a detailed consideration of heterosexuality, enabling you to demonstrate your understanding of its construction and effect on 'other' sexual orientations. You should feel confident to be able to iden-tify and give some examples of the way other social divisions impact on sexuality. A key learning point from the chapter is that there are various forms of sexuality and it is not necessarily a unified whole. Weeks (2003, p.40) states:

> *there are in fact many sexualities...class sexualities...gender-specific sexualities...racialised sexualities and there are sexualities of struggle and choice.*

FURTHER READING

Donnellan, C (2005) *Sexuality and discrimination*. Cambridge: Independence.

A useful and accessible resource book covering the main issues regarding lesbian, gay, bisexual and transgender people.

Fish, J (2006) *Heterosexism in health and social care*. Basingstoke and New York: Palgrave.

A comprehensive book that uses theory and research to explore in detail the issue of heterosexism within health and social care services.

Hicks, S (2006) Genealogy's desire: practices of kinship amongst lesbian and gay foster-carers and adopters. *British Journal of Social Work*, 36: 761–776.

An article that considers the challenge and contribution presented by lesbian and gay men carers to the practice of foster-care and adoption.

Nagel, J (2003) *Race, ethnicity and sexuality: intimate intersections, forbidden frontiers*. Oxford and New York: Oxford University Press.

A well-documented book that explores the intersection between ethnicity and sexuality.

Richardson, D (2000) *Rethinking sexuality*. London: Sage.

An accessible book that details recent feminist and queer theoretical debates around issues of sexuality.

Chapter 3

Sexuality, young people and social work

A C H I E V I N G   A   S O C I A L   W O R K   D E G R E E

This chapter will help you to meet the following National Occupational Standards.

Key Role 1: Prepare for and work with individuals, families, carers, groups and communities to assess their needs and circumstances.
- Work with individuals, families, carers, groups and communities to help them make informed decisions.
- Assess needs and options to recommend a course of action.

Key Role 2: Plan, carry out, review and evaluate social work practice, with individuals, families, carers, groups, communities and other professionals.
- Respond to crisis situations.

Key Role 4: Manage risk to individuals, families, carers, groups, communities, self and colleagues.
- Assess and manage risks to individuals, families, carers, groups and communities.

It will also introduce you to the following academic standards as set out in the social work subject benchmark statement:

3.1.1 Social work services and service users.
- Explanations of the links between definitional processes contributing to social differences (for example social class, gender and ethnic differences) to the problems of inequality and differential need faced by service users.

3.2.2.3 Analysis and synthesis.
- Assess human situations, taking into account a variety of factors.

Introduction

In this chapter we are focusing on sexuality and young people and will be exploring the influences on the way young people learn to be sexual and begin to develop their own sexual identities. We will be building on discussions we have had in the previous chapters regarding the impact of social divisions on sexual development. It is argued that adults are challenged by young people's sexuality because it is not on the whole about developing long-term relationships or about reproduction and therefore it:

> ...makes adults admit that sex may be purely about play and pleasure.

> (Risman and Schwartz, 2004, p.277)

Introducing young people

Who are young people?

As you will appreciate, using chronological age to define a 'young person' is problematic due to the influences of social and cultural factors on the process of ageing as well as the diversity of subjective experiences. It is argued that the period of 'youth' is becoming longer in Western societies due to the earlier onset of puberty and the increasing number of years young people are involved in formal education (Hunt, 2005). We are focusing in this chapter on young people in terms of their developing sexual awareness, becoming sexually active and developing a sexual identity on the road towards sexual maturity. To this purpose we will be viewing young people as being, in the majority, between the ages of 11 and 18. Although the chronological age span for this group is small, the developmental changes and growth are significant. It must be remembered also that the term 'young people' has a tendency to assume homogeneity, where in fact the people who are included bring with them a range of differences in terms of gender, ethnicity, class, disability, sexual orientation and age.

Views of young people

ACTIVITY **3.1**

Write down all you know about young people and reflect on where you acquired your knowledge.

Comment

Your view or knowledge of young people will come from a range of different sources, such as personal or professional contact or from your own personal experience of having been a young person. Your knowledge may come from what you have read in the media or from social work books and articles. The more diverse the sources of your knowledge are, then the less likely your views of young people will be based on stereotypes. Young people attract a great deal of public and media attention in Western societies for issues which are distressing and problematic for all concerned. Negative stereotypes of young people are then created based on certain high-profile issues which in turn fuel discriminatory attitudes. Social workers may develop distorted perceptions of young people because contact is instigated only when things are difficult. For example, teenage pregnancy, youth offending, gang membership, substance use, high risk-taking behaviours/actions, depression, self-harm, homelessness, non-attendance at school or school exclusion are all issues on which social workers work with young people. It is important to recognise that these issues statistically are the exception not the rule.

Young personhood – a period of challenges

Young personhood is a period in a person's life that has many challenges and is probably the most difficult stage in relation to growth and development. For example, puberty presents challenges through major physical changes in a person's body, such as menarche (that is, first menstruation) for young women and spermarche (that is, first ejaculation of semen) for young men. This change is seen as very significant, as it is an indication that the young person is now capable of reproduction. As well as the onset of fertility there is also a period of rapid physical and intellectual growth (Crawford and Walker, 2003). It is worth noting that a period of young personhood of any significant length, often referred to as adolescence, is for the most part a Westernised construct. However, this change from child to adult is recognised in most cultures, but the period is briefer. For example, in certain cultures girls can be married at the age of 12 (Beckett, 2002). Although the biological changes are commonly identified and referred to as the major influences on a young person's development in adolescence, it must be recognised that cultural and social factors have at least an equal, if not greater, influence and significance.

RESEARCH SUMMARY

Psychosocial challenges in becoming an adult

A young person experiences the following significant psychological and social challenges:

- *adjustment to being a sexually mature adult developing which involves a sexual identity, sexual orientation and sexuality;*

- *developing sexual and non-sexual peer relationships;*

- *developing a personal sense of identity;*

- *acquiring a personal set of values and ethical system, a personal ideology;*

- *increasing responsibility for one's own behaviour and achieving socially responsible behaviour;*

- *achieving emotional, psychological and financial independence from parents and other adults;*

- *preparing for committed sexual relationships and parenthood.*

Source: Dogra et al., (2002, p.84)

Although throughout our lives we are constantly re-evaluating who we are, many theorists claim that forming a new identity is a theme that is particularly central for young people (Beckett, 2002). The development of our sexuality is an intrinsic part of our identity as a whole and for young people the experience of a new sexual awareness requires a substantial revision of their sense of self (Crawford and Walker, 2003). It is important to recognise however, that although issues relating to sexuality are a key developmental challenge for young people, the development of a sexual identity is not a fixed entity that starts and finishes in this part of our life course.

Social construction of young people's sexuality

In Western societies young people's sexuality is constructed as either problematic or non-existent (Shucksmith, 2004). These two conflicting aspects cause a dilemma. The problematic issues, presented within a discourse of risk, include commencing sexual activity at an early age, sexual (over)activity, pregnancies, sexually transmitted infections and the issue of the age of consent (Hunt, 2005). There is also the recognition that young people need to be protected from sexual abuse and exploitation. Sexual activity amongst young people often provokes anxiety from adults who feel that it is their responsibility to regulate and protect young people from sexual risks and danger. The dilemma is that in order to address some of these issues there needs to be a positive recognition of the existence of young people's developing sexual awareness and sexuality. Professionals engaging with young people about the issues of sexuality can encounter difficulties and criticism as 'sex education' is a hotly contested and *highly politicised area of social policy* (Hockey and James, 2003, p.144). There is very little material and guidance to ensure that young people learn how to have positive, fulfilling and safe sexual relationships (Batchelor and Raymond, 2004). Much of the neglect surrounding young people's sexuality can be connected to a tension between a young person's developing sexual awareness and the notion of childhood innocence. It is believed therefore that limiting access to information about sexuality can somehow protect a young person's innocence and purity (Hockey and James, 2003). Here again there is a dilemma, as Western societies are becoming increasingly sexualised and there are more and more sexualised images of children and young people (Andrews, 2006). For girls and young women in particular there is pressure to adopt gender-specific sexualised behaviour at an earlier age (Shucksmith, 2004). It could be argued that in relation to sexuality the boundary between childhood and adulthood is being continually pushed downwards and challenged by an adult concept of sexuality. A good example is the child beauty pageants phenomenon (see **www.universalroyalty.com** for information). There appears to be little room for young people to talk about and develop their ideas about their own sexuality. A recent Ofsted report found that young people felt that many parents and teachers were not very good at talking to them about sensitive issues, such as sexuality. Young people wanted to talk about feelings and relationships and not just be informed of the biological facts (Ofsted, 2007).

A developing sexuality – influences and diversity

Our sexual knowledge and awareness are gained from different sources such as our families, peers, education, religion, media and our own experiences. When considering the influences on the sexual development of young people you may want to reflect back on the 'nature versus nurture' debate that was introduced to you in Chapter 1. There are obviously a range of biological, psychological and sociological influences which are inter-related. For example, let us consider the sexual activity of masturbation. When touching their genitalia girls and boys become aware of physical sensations before they begin to understand about their sexuality, and with their developing sexual awareness may go on to enjoy masturbation. Becoming sexualised individuals therefore has a biological component but it is the social responses that young people receive whilst enjoying a sexual activity such as masturbation that will be significantly influential in terms of giving meaning to their experience. Although masturbation is a sexual activity that is the most popular and practised by the majority of people regardless of gender, age, ability, class or ethnicity, it has been subjected to regulation over the centuries through medical discourse (Hawkes and Scott, 2005). In the nineteenth century masturbation was viewed as extremely damaging to both physical and mental health whereas today it is associated with 'normal' sexual development. Social responses reflect this history, ranging from acceptance through to regarding masturbation as dangerous (Hawkes and Scott, 2005). The type of social responses experienced by children and young people will therefore influence how they experience and learn about their developing sexuality. The perception of their sexuality is therefore socially constructed.

> *Masturbation is the most significant source of orgasmic sexual pleasure for young people. While the promotion of masturbation remains controversial masturbation is a physically safe sexual practice that becomes an integral component of the sexual repertoire of most adults.*

(Smith et al., 2004, p.104)

As social workers we can ensure that young people learn about the issue of privacy in relation to masturbation whilst reinforcing that the activity is positive and acceptable as opposed to negative and shameful (Andrews, 2006).

For the rest of this section we are going to consider the influences of various social divisions on young people's sexual experiences. Although we will be considering gender, sexual orientation, class and ethnicity separately, we trust that you will realise that in real life they interact with each other. This complex interrelationship makes for a range of diverse experiences in terms of young people and their sexuality. We will be returning to some of the themes and issues we examined in the previous chapter when considering the influence of various social divisions on heterosexuality.

Gender

To recap, gender is the social division that involves the hierarchical relationship between women and men, and heterosexuality is the institutionalised form of that relationship (Jackson, 2006). The dominant versions of gender, that of femininity and masculinity for women and men respectively and heterosexuality, are interrelated, playing a significant role in the development of a young person's sexual identity. In other words, to be regarded as a 'real' young man or a 'real' young woman involves *displaying a recognisable heterosexuality* (Renold, 2007, p.281).

Young women

The development of young women's sexuality and the negotiations of their first sexual experience are fraught with conflict and confusion. Gender for young women involves conforming to the dominant traits of femininity within a heterosexual context. This involves an expectation that young women will be sexually passive within a loving and committed relationship (Lindsay, 2005). Young women who show that they have sexual knowledge or engage in sexual activity outside of a committed relationship put their femininity at risk

(Hockey and James, 2003). For example, young women can be referred to as 'easy' or a 'tart' by their male peers who share information amongst themselves about which young women have and will participate in sexual activity. Young women's sexuality is controlled by their sexual reputations which are constructed for them by their male peers. Young women who are aware of this maintain a sense of empowerment by knowingly adopting stereotypical feminine responses whilst being able to engage in sexual relationships.

> *I have to let him make the first move, not appear too keen, so that he can feel as if he's in control; I don't want to seem easy, so keep my sexual feelings to myself.*

> (Ussher, 2005, p.29)

Young women may find that protecting their reputation conflicts with their sexual health needs. For example, many young women find it difficult to carry condoms because they may be perceived as 'sluts', which would compromise their femininity (Hockey and James, 2003). Others find it difficult to insist on condom use in a sexual relationship because it implies that the relationship is temporary, which places *a young woman's sexual reputation in danger* (Thomson, 2004, p.102). This is linked to another aspect of femininity referred to as the 'romantic discourse' which involves attracting and holding onto a male partner and any engagement in sexual activity confirms the intimacy and seriousness of the relationship. Confusingly for young women they are often put in a position of control by being made to feel responsible for the arousal of (young) men's sexual urges and for negotiating safer sex. Both of these themes we return to in later chapters on sexual violence and HIV. Young women regard their first experience of heterosexual sexual intercourse as a gift to their male partner, or a strategy to keep the relationship with their male partner, or something to get over with as quickly as possible, reflecting a lack of sense of self, power and pleasure (Lindsay, 2005). Often in relation to identity *a woman's knowledge of who she is cannot be separate from her relationship to an individual man* (Stoltenberg, 2004, p.41). The other dominant factor regarding young women's sexuality is their relationship to their bodies. Women of all ages are made to feel concerned about their body shape and other aspects of their physical appearance. It is argued that the value of a woman is measured by her attractiveness, which in turn is essential to her femininity (Best, 2005). Young women are encouraged to constantly improve their appearance and view their bodies as existing for the pleasure of others. If young women feel that they do not fit the 'norm' physically it can make them feel sexually and socially unattractive, resulting in insecurity and isolation. This can lead young women to do dangerous things to change their appearance. For example, eating disorders are experienced predominantly by young women (Anorexia Nervosa and Related Eating Disorders, Inc., 2005), and there is currently a growing trend for young women who have diabetes to take too much insulin in order to lose weight (www.cnn.com/2007/HEALTH/conditions/06/17/diabetes.bulimia. ap/index.html accessed 3/07/07). The way that female beauty and femininity are socially constructed in our society is particularly oppressive and harmful to young disabled women. The discourses that construct female beauty in terms of 'bodily perfection' also construct young disabled women as unfeminine, unattractive and asexual (Best, 2005).

Young men

Masculinity does have a profound and negative influence on the development of young men's sexuality. Although unlike young women, they do not have to solely rely on their sexuality as confirmation of their gender, being (hetero)sexually active is a valued way of demonstrating their masculine identity.

ACTIVITY 3.2

Masculinity and male sexuality

How do you think the dominant traits of masculinity will affect the way a young man may express himself sexually?

Comment

Masculinity, like femininity, is socially constructed, shaped by heterosexuality and varies across cultures. You will have come up with a range of different ways that masculinity moulds male sexuality and influences how young men should act and express themselves sexually. We highlight the following points.

- In direct contrast to femininity's romantic discourse, the dominant traits of masculinity make up a predatory discourse where young men are expected to be sexually active, have many sexual partners, and treat young women as sexual conquests to be talked and bragged about (Holland et al., 1998). A young man expressing any aspects of the romantic discourse such as talking about relationships and feelings is ridiculed by his peers and often referred to as 'gay' or 'girly'. The predatory discourse puts young men under a lot of pressure to engage in sexual activity and pursue sexual experience for its own sake. Their first heterosexual sexual experience is about becoming a man and enjoyment.

- Young men obtain their self-worth and status from other young men. In the process of male bonding young men both recognise and reinforce each other's masculinity and in turn learn how to achieve and maintain their positions of power. It is the fear of not measuring up to their peers that drives young men's compliance to the norms and expectations of being 'manly and masculine' (Plante, 2004), which can often result in a conspiracy of silence around unacceptable sexual behaviour such as sexual violence and harassment.

- As with young women, young men are faced with conflicting and contradictory situations that they have to negotiate. For example, the sexual development of girls/young women is focused on more than the sexual development of young men due to the visible physical development in terms of puberty of girls/young women. Research concludes that girls/young women are therefore (hetero)sexualised more than young men and will know how to be a 'girlfriend'. Becoming a 'boyfriend' for boys/young men is not 'taught' and therefore involves trying to make sense of sexuality in a masculine way. Young men fear displaying 'feminine' traits and define their (hetero)sexuality through sex talk, sexual fantasy, misogyny, sexual harassment, antigay behaviour, and policing and shaming others who do not conform (Renold, 2007). The other aspect to this dilemma is the assumption that 'real' young men 'naturally' know everything in terms of sexuality, which makes it difficult for them to ask for help in relation to sexual health matters, for example, how to use a condom (Blake, 2004).

41

Young men and young women

We would conclude that the dominant traits of femininity and masculinity 'trap' young women and young men, limiting exploration of their sexuality. All young people have the potential to experience and express the positive traits of each gender. For example, young men should be encouraged to express their emotions and young women should be encouraged to express their autonomy. However, at the moment heterosexuality is not made up of a balance between femininity and masculinity. Research suggests that 'male-in-the-head' discourse which revolves around male desire and (hetero)sexual penile penetration drives the behaviours of both young women and young men (Holland et al., 1998). Currently heterosexuality is a form of masculinity from which femininity is constructed. Challenges to the dominant constructions of gender and heterosexuality are however on the increase from disabled heterosexual people (see discussion in Chapter 6), progressive heterosexual people, gay men, lesbians and transgender people.

RESEARCH SUMMARY

Challenging femininity?

Research was undertaken with a group of lesbians and heterosexual women of mixed ethnicity and class aged between 17 and 24 years of age on the issues of sexual desire and first sexual experiences. The young lesbians tended to feel less constrained by gender roles within their sexual experiences/relationships but less free to talk generally about their feelings of desire for fear of hostility or discrimination. It was the opposite for the young heterosexual women. A young lesbian in the study says:

> I feel I can take the initiative, and be dominant, and be active, whereas in straight [heterosexual] relationships I've had, ah, I never felt that was allowed, or was okay, or I would be seen as masculine if I did.

(Ussher, 2005, p.29)

For the young heterosexual women the first sexual experience/relationship confirmed for them their adult womanhood whereas for the young lesbians it confirmed their sexual identity.

Source: Ussher (2005)

Sexual orientation

Many psychological theories of personality and identity development (for example Freud and Erikson) have tended to equate 'normal' development and sexual maturity with heterosexuality, reinforcing prejudice towards people who identify as lesbian, gay or bisexual (Davies, 1996). Our earlier discussion on gender highlighted how masculine and feminine ideals are synonymous with heterosexuality. There is obvious pressure from family, peers and society to identify as heterosexual, and the question is how we support young people who feel they are somehow 'different'.

Case study

You are on placement in a young person's residential home and have been allocated as a key worker for Sajjad, who is 15 years of age. Sajjad is popular among his peers, likes making everyone laugh and loves playing football. Sajjad is not attending school for the next few weeks following exclusion for fighting with other lads and you have noticed that he is becoming withdrawn and spending a lot of time in his own bedroom. During one of your chats with him he says that he got involved in the fight because some other lads in his class had called him gay, as he had had an erection when he was hugging a lad last week after scoring a goal. He goes on to say that he does really like this particular lad and has strong feelings for him. Sajjad admits he is confused and frightened and wants to know what to do.

How would you support Sajjad?

Comment

There are a range of strategies that you could employ to support Sajjad but your starting point is accepting his confusion, validating his feelings and being there to listen to him, discussing his doubts and fears about his sexual identity. Young people who feel 'differently' about themselves fear rejection from family and friends. Acceptance from a significant other, such as you as his key worker, is a valuable basis on which to build confidence. It is important that you proceed at his pace and do not hurry or push him into a particular sexual orientation. Sajjad may want to try a range of sexual relationships out for himself and the issues that you will be working with are common to all young people who are developing their sexuality, such as trust, respect, self-esteem, responsibility and safety. You do need, however, to recognise that there are additional difficulties for young people who may feel that they are lesbian, gay or bisexual created by heterosexism, which can result in isolation, self-hatred and low self-esteem. It is important that work with Sajjad includes identifying positive images and role models in relation to a gay identity as well as enabling him to develop skills in challenging prejudice effectively. A supportive network needs to be created for Sajjad which will also involve you working with the residential home and the school in terms of challenging any heterosexism and homophobic bullying.

Development of lesbian, gay or bisexual identity

For some theorists the process of developing a lesbian or gay identity is viewed in terms of stages (see Davies and Neal, 1996, for discussion of different theories of lesbian and gay development). We present one theory in the following research summary.

Developing a lesbian, gay or bisexual identity

The following stages make up the development process.

- **Sensitisation** *where the young person begins to sense that he/she may be different to others and becomes aware of sexual feelings that are different to the ones experienced by others of the same gender.*

RESEARCH SUMMARY *continued*

- *Identity* confusion where the young person experiences sexual feelings towards others of the same gender whilst also experiencing a sense of stigma surrounding lesbian and gay behaviour. The young person's confusion will be increased by the lack of or inaccurate information about same-sex relationships and sexuality.

- *Identity* assumption where the young person begins to take on a lesbian or gay identity and is able to come out, at least, to close friends.

- *Commitment* where the young person makes a commitment to having a romantic and passionate sexual relationship with someone of the same gender and is also able to disclose to family and other important people.

Source: Coleman and Hendry, (1999)

Young people come to know about their sexual orientation in different ways. For example, some will have known about their lesbian, gay or bisexual sexual orientation from early childhood, others will have assumed that they were heterosexual until they started experiencing sexual feelings for people of the same gender, others may feel that their sexual orientation is more fluid and changeable depending on whom they feel romantically attached to at the time, and others may feel confused about their identity through into adulthood. This diversity is precious and must be the factor that dictates which theories or parts of theories are relevant. It must not be assumed that the above theory implies that in order to develop a lesbian, gay or bisexual identity young people have to go through all the identified stages. It might be helpful to consider the stages as examples of tasks and issues facing young people who may be lesbian, gay or bisexual (Coleman and Hendry, 1999).

Developing a lesbian, gay or bisexual identity is made more complex by the 'assumption of heterosexuality' where people are presumed to be heterosexual unless they state otherwise. A major task therefore facing young lesbian, gay and bisexual people is the process of 'coming out'. It is a continuous one in that it needs to be undertaken in every new situation with new people if the assumption of heterosexuality is going to be challenged. For some young people 'coming out' to family, carers and friends can be a relief and the reactions can be reassuring and supportive. For other young people 'coming out' is frightening and demoralising, resulting in hostility and rejection from significant others (Coyle, 1998). Research has found that lesbian, gay and bisexual young people have higher rates of self-harm, suicidal thoughts and suicide attempts connected to experiences of harassment and discrimination related to their sexual orientation compared to heterosexual young people (Warner et al., 2004).

> [I]t is a sad indictment of our society that people are driven to kill themselves because they cannot see a future as lesbian, gay and bisexual people.

> (Davies and Neal, 1996, pp.137–8)

These findings support and highlight the need for strategies that raise awareness of the vulnerability of lesbian, gay and bisexual young people and the need to develop support strategies

Homophobic bullying

One such strategy is the legal obligation on schools to prevent bullying of pupils because of their sexual orientation or perceived orientation (DfES, 2000; Warwick and Douglas, 2001). Bullying can involve verbal, physical or psychological abuse. Homophobic bullying is not only experienced by young people in schools who are lesbian, gay or bisexual but also by young people who do not conform to ways of behaviour that are traditionally associated with their gender, for example young men not matching the masculine ideal and young women not being feminine enough. Research shows that homophobic bullying increases truancy, self-harm and suicide rates by young people, damages self-esteem and lowers educational attainment (Stonewall, 2007).

Class

Most research in Western societies regarding social class, sexuality and young people focuses on sexual activity at an early age and unplanned pregnancies (Lindsay, 2005). Young people from working-class backgrounds compared to middle-class young people are more likely to engage in heterosexual sexual intercourse under the age of 16 and less likely to use contraception. Consequently young working-class women are more likely to get pregnant and to proceed with the pregnancy, as opposed to middle-class young women who if pregnant are more likely to seek a termination (Lindsay, 2005). The majority of the research presents a *deficit model* of young parenthood (Coleman and Hendry, 1999, p.112) by focusing on the negative aspects such as isolation, poor parenting, absent fathers, lost opportunities and ruined futures.

ACTIVITY 3.4

Can you think of any positive aspects of young parenthood?

Comment

The main problem with the deficit model of young parenthood is that it does not take account of the diverse experiences of young people. For example, some young mothers receive a lot of emotional support and validation from their own mothers, from whom they develop the skills and confidence to become effective parents (Coleman and Hendry, 1999). A large number of young fathers do have contact and establish a role in the upbringing of their child(ren) (Speak, 1997). For many young women being a mother is an opportunity to make the transition out of a damaging family home life, create a new start and for some act as the catalyst to go back into education (Shucksmith, 2004). The important aspect here is to represent all views and recognise that for some young people parenthood will be negative but for some it will be positive.

Ethnicity

A young person's experience of their developing sexuality will be influenced by their ethnicity. Much of what we know, however, is about the influences of white ethnicity on sexuality as very little has been published about the experiences of people from black and minority ethnic communities in the UK (Wight and Henderson, 2004). Although black and minority ethnic communities are very diverse there is a tendency to stereotype and generalise experiences.

RESEARCH SUMMARY

Researching young people's sexuality and learning

During research on issues of sexuality, young people from black and minority ethnic backgrounds (African-Caribbean, Pakistani and Somali) felt that only white identities were represented in school sex and relationship education.

There's nowt about me in sex education. It's all White (Jo).

It's (sex education) not really aimed at us...Pakistanis. It's like more for White kids (Ruby).

Source: Hirst (2004, p.121)

Teachers agreed that the needs and experiences of black and minority ethnic students were not represented, justifying the situation on the grounds that most Muslim students excluded themselves from the sessions on faith grounds. This was found to be incorrect, as the male Muslim students only participated in the aspects of the sessions they enjoyed, which were the videos. The female Muslim students could not access the sessions because they were facilitated by a male teacher and were delivered in a mixed gender group. Both male and female Muslim students stated that their faith permitted their participation in sex and relationship education sessions.

Everyone who isn't a Muslim thinks that we don't do it 'cos of our beliefs and 'cos we don't allow being in sex education lessons. But you're wrong there, very wrong (Javed).

Source: Hirst, 2004, p. 121

Young people from the Indian, Pakistani and Bangladeshi communities are often negotiating conflicting influences of family, community and Western society. Discussions of sex and sexuality are culturally taboo so young people may not have the opportunity to talk about these issues with parents or carers (Patel-Kanwal, 2004). They have to rely on their friends and the media for information, which often results in misinterpretations and the reinforcement of myths and stereotypes. There are other pressures such as sexual activity outside of marriage bringing shame on a family, making it particularly important for young people who are being sexually active not to be discovered. This is particularly important for women who are viewed as responsible for ensuring that moral values are passed on from generation to generation (Patel-Kanwal, 2004). Young people for whom marriages are arranged or facilitated by their families are perceived as not needing any sex and relationship education until they marry. Young people in this situation can feel excluded from receiving any information about their developing sexuality. As with people from the white ethnic communities, there is an assumption that young people will be heterosexual in orientation. It is a major challenge for lesbian, gay and bisexual young people from black and minority ethnic communities to express their sexuality openly and confidently (Patel-Kanwal, 2004). Although many of these issues may to a lesser or greater extent be similar for white young people, the significant difference is the experience of racism for young people from black and minority ethnic communities. Racism is often combined with social and economic deprivation, creating barriers to obtaining appropriate and relevant sexual health information, support and services. Families and communities are vital in enabling young black people to challenge and cope with racism, therefore ostracisation because of an issue of sexuality is devastating.

There is a perception from Indian, Pakistani and Bangladeshi communities that the dominant 'British' culture has a more open and liberal approach towards sexuality. This has prompted some parents from these communities to become more open to young people's issues of sexuality and to be able to adopt a supportive and facilitative role (Patel-Kanwal, 2004). An example is from a case discussion within *Community Care* where a Bangladeshi young woman of 15 years of age was being supported by her family to have her child and marry the 17-year-old father whom she loved (Thompson and Siddiqui, 1999). Another example of change is the Safra Project (see www.safraproject.org) which was set up as a resource by and for lesbian, bisexual and transgender women who identified as Muslim culturally and/or religiously. Its aim is to empower, challenge discrimination, promote diversity and make service provision more accessible.

Young people's experience of sexuality

As young people are often 'spoken for' we felt that it was important to include a small sample of the voices of young people on their thoughts and experiences of sexuality which have been taken from a variety of research studies.

RESEARCH SUMMARY

Voice of the young person

Safe sex is as pleasurable an experience as actual penetration. Oral sex, just things like touching somebody's else's body in a very gentle way. Kissing. Appreciating one another's bodies. I think it's just as much fun, if not more. (young woman, 18)

(Thomson and Holland, 1998, p.73)

When she kissed me, I felt as if my whole life had flashed in front of me, and I knew I was a lesbian.

Source: Ussher (2005, p.30)

It's like in sex education, you either have sex, as in, with a willy inside ya, or you don't. Well it's not true, there's all sorts goes on between that. (Angela)

Source: Hirst (2004, p.120)

I just feel that because I really like her and she likes me, you shouldn't have sex if you don't want to. A boy should have a girlfriend if he likes her, not for the sake of having one. (Damien, aged 14)

Source: Martino and Pallotta-Chiarolli (2001, p.72, cited in Lindsay, 2004)

RESEARCH SUMMARY *continued*

Yeah, it was quite a good experience. I thought I'd done all right, like – never doing it before. I was quite pleased really. (young man, working class, aged 18)

Source: Holland et al. (2003, p.87)

The girls would usually sit down and talk about make-up and the boys would usually play football...and the boys would say like 'you look nice, what make-up is it?' And the girl would say 'oh yeah this and this. You're a good football player'...we'd meet each other half-way yeah. It's nice to know that you can talk about something and she would talk about you as well. (Alan aged 14)

Source: Frosh et al. (2002, p.116)

Sexuality, young people and social work practice

Social workers will need to work with young people on issues of sexuality in a range of different settings and contexts. Before considering specific issues it would be helpful to say something about the social work role.

Social work role

Although we will not be considering issues of sexual violence in relation to young people, either as 'victims' or as 'perpetrators' in this chapter, however, it is important to recognise that for some young people sexual violence will be/has been part of their sexual experiences and influences how they view their sexuality. Working around issues of sexuality with these young people will necessarily bring up a range of additional complex issues and possibly negative emotions. It is useful to note that sexuality and in particular sexual activity amongst young people is a site of pleasure and danger, in that it can involve love, intimacy and fun, and also it can involve coercion, risk and abuse (Lindsay, 2005). We would argue that the social work role is about enabling young people to achieve sexual well-being by upholding their right to have *egalitarian, free and safe sexual lives* (Lindsay, 2005, p.85).

Corporate parenting

For many young people who are 'looked after' the state assumes the formal role of corporate parenting to provide care and support. The Children Act 1989 states that the local authorities in England in their role of corporate parents of 'looked after' children and young people have duties to address the issues of sexuality (Department of Health, 1991). It is only relatively recently that policies and training for staff have begun to ensure that sex and relationship education sessions for young people who are 'looked after' have taken place. Research has found that issues of sexuality were minimally addressed by residential staff and usually only as a response to direct questions as opposed to setting up any group or individual discussions (Corlyon and McGuire, 1999). 'Looked after' young people are a diverse group with a range of different needs. However, due to their emotional and psychological vulnerability, they can be more at risk of engaging in unsafe sexual practices particularly at an early age. Young people who have personally experienced rejection and feelings of insecurity, loneliness and low self-esteem can view sexual relationships as a way of feeling loved and valued. This particular group of young people often have more sexual health needs, in terms of information and support regarding relationships, but these needs tend to go unmet. In a recent Green Paper focusing on the lives of children and young people in care, it is recognised that the social work role as corporate parent needs to be strengthened, particularly to address the issue of teenage pregnancies (DfES, 2006).

Sex and relationship education

As an aspect of the social work role is an educative one, it is important that you are aware of some of the issues in relation to sex and relationship education, as it forms part of the context in which young people gain knowledge and information about their sexuality. There is a range of legislation that governs what and how sex education is delivered in schools in the UK (see www.avert.org/legislation.htm for a useful summary). The main guidance for sex and relationship education emphasises the need to ensure that young people learn the value of family life, marriage and stable and loving relationships for the nurture of children (DfEE, 2000). Despite this recognition of relationships outside of marriage, research highlights a lack of or silence around lesbian, gay or bisexual relationships, concluding that schools tend to support the institution of heterosexuality as the 'norm' (De Palma and Atkinson, 2006). This silence was fuelled initially by Section 28 of the Local Government Act 1988 (referred to in Chapter 2) leaving a legacy of neglect in relation to same-sex relationships, despite government policy directing schools to address homophobic bullying (DfEE, 2000). Another issue is that sex and relationship education tends to focus on women's sexual health issues, alienating many young men in the process (Buston and Wight, 2006).

ACTIVITY 3.5

What do you think are some of the consequences for young people if the sex and relationship education they are receiving is dominated by heterosexuality and marginalises young men?

Comment

You will have come up with a range of consequences and we would like to highlight the following points:

- Young people who identify as gay, lesbian or bisexual will feel disregarded. It is important for positive self-esteem that difference is recognised and validated. The Children Act 1989 guidance states that the needs and concerns of young gay men and women must be recognised and approached sympathetically (Department of Health, 1991). Young people who are unsure about their sexual orientation would not feel safe to explore their thoughts and feelings within the heterosexist culture of sex education.

- Young men not only feel marginalised from sex education but also from sexual health services for young people which tend to focus on young women's needs in terms of contraception, abortion and pregnancy. This marginalisation reinforces the idea that women are responsible for men's sexuality, and in turn encourages young men to involve or continue to involve themselves in high-risk behaviour. Young men are not encouraged to engage with their sexual behaviour and emotions in a responsible and positive way.

- Feeling included in sex and relationship education is important as research has found that young people who learn about sexuality mainly from school (as opposed to family and friends) are more likely to delay starting a sexual relationship and more likely to use contraception when they do (Wellings et al., 2001).

RESEARCH SUMMARY

Young men and sex education

Research was undertaken with 18 young men, between the ages of 14 and 16 years, exploring their views of an inclusive sex education programme in which they had participated. The young men, aged between 14 and 16 years, were all white except for one young man who described himself as Chinese. The majority of young men felt that the programme had given them an awareness of young women's perspective on sexual issues. They felt that they had learnt how to communicate with young women and were more aware about the issues of coercion and force in relation to sexual activity. Many of the young men said that they would change their sexual behaviour by engaging in more discussions with young women about sexual issues, being prepared to wait if their partner did not want to engage in sexual intercourse, and not pressurising or forcing a young woman to engage in sexual activity.

> *...makes you realise that the girl doesn't always want to do it and that you shouldn't really pressure them. (Kenny, 14 years old)*

(Buston and Wright, 2006, p. 145)

Source: Buston and Wright (2006)

Age of consent

The Sexual Offences Act 2003 states that the age of consent for all individuals regardless of sexual orientation is 16 years. However, the law does not intend to prosecute mutually agreed sexual activity between people of a similar age between 13 and 15 years of age unless it involves abuse or exploitation. Children 12 years of age and under cannot legally give their consent to any form of sexual activity (Home Office, 2004c). A research study found that 26 per cent of women and 30 per cent of men had sexual intercourse before the age of 16 (Wellings et al., 2001).

Case study

You are on placement in a school as a student social worker and are approached by Lisa, who is 13 years of age, who tells you that she is being taunted by some young women who used to be her close friends. They are calling her names such as 'slag' and 'slapper'. In exploring the reasons for this name-calling Lisa proceeds to tell you that she has had sex with a young man, Peter, who is the same age, and with whom she has fallen in love. Peter has since 'dumped her', talked to all of his classmates about her and Lisa feels that everyone in the school knows about the fact that she has had sex with him. Lisa is also worried that she may be pregnant because she had believed Peter when he had told her that he did not need to use a condom as it was her first time. Lisa says that she feels 'stupid' and only agreed to have sex with Peter because he threatened to 'dump' her for someone else who would. However, she says that she is desperate to get back with Peter as she is in love with him. You are the first adult she has confided in.

- *What are your initial thoughts about this situation?*
- *What do you think about Lisa and Peter's ages in relation to them being sexual with each other?*
- *What do you think are Lisa and Peter's sexual health needs?*

Comment

Although Lisa and Peter are under 16, because they are of similar age it would be highly unlikely that there would be a prosecution. The important issue would be to establish that they were both able and competent to make their own decisions about engaging in sexual activity. This assessment would be based upon their overall level of development in terms of understanding, knowledge and skills to make informed choices about sexual relationships. You may like to consider the question about whether Peter's threat to 'dump' Lisa is a form of exploitation.

With regards to Lisa and Peter's sexual health needs, under the Sexual Offences Act 2003 young people still have a right to confidential advice on contraception, condoms, pregnancy and abortion even if they are under 16 years of age (see the following research summary for details). Professionals giving sexual health advice without parental knowledge or consent are not committing an offence if it is in the young person's best interests in terms of protecting the young person from sexually transmitted infections and physical harm, preventing pregnancy and promoting the young person's emotional well being (Myers and Milner, 2007). Therefore as the student social worker involved in this situation you would be able to take on the role of discussing and addressing both Lisa and Peter's sexual health needs.

RESEARCH SUMMARY

Gillick competence

The case of Gillick v West Norfolk and Wisbech Area Health Authority (1983 and 1985) laid down criteria for establishing whether a child or young person could consent to medical treatment irrespective of their age. These criteria became widely referred to as the 'test for Gillick competence' after the name of a mother who contested the decision of the health service to provide contraceptive advice to her daughter (under 16 years of age) without her parental consent or notification. A child/young person under 16 is deemed 'Gillick competent' if they are able to:

> demonstrate sufficient maturity and intelligence to understand and appraise the nature and implications of the proposed treatment, including the risks and alternative courses of action.
>
> *(Wheeler, 2006, p.1)*

The courts will however overrule the wishes of 'Gillick competent' young people if the decision is not in their best interests; for example, if a young person refused to consent for treatment whilst suffering from anorexia nervosa (Brammer, 2007).

One of the Law Lords responsible for the Gillick judgment, Lord Fraser, also came up with additional guidance to the 'Gillick competency' criteria which must be applied specifically in a situation where children/young people are to receive contraceptive advice. Most agencies offering information, advice or services to young people about their sexual health have adopted the guidelines as a basis for best practice.

The Fraser guidelines (Surrey County Council, 2007) require that the professional is satisfied that:

- the young person understands the professional's advice;
- the young person cannot be persuaded to inform their parents/carers;
- the young person is likely to begin, or to continue having, sexual intercourse with or without contraceptive treatment;
- unless the young person receives contraceptive treatment, their physical or mental health, or both, are likely to suffer;
- the young person's best interests require them to receive contraceptive advice or treatment with or without parental consent.

Sexual health needs of young people

Sexual health needs of young people are frequently discussed using a medical discourse emphasising sexually transmitted infections and unplanned pregnancies. We do not want to minimise these issues, as statistics show that they increasingly continue to be part of young people's sexual health needs (see www.statistics.gov.uk/cci/nugget.asp?id=721). However, this medical discourse tends to narrowly define the responses to young people in terms of advice and treatment. As student social workers it is important to regard sexual health in a holistic sense by recognising the impact of social and emotional factors on a young person's sexual health. In the previous chapter we identified some 'non-medical' issues around sexual health when we considered ways of working positively with a group of young women around the issues of sexuality. Other factors influencing the sexual health needs of young men have also been highlighted earlier. We do not want to repeat the issues already discussed but would reiterate that sexual well-being is about embracing sexuality in its fullest sense and recognising its interrelationship with other social and emotional factors.

ACTIVITY 3.7

What social and emotional factors impact on a young person's sexual health?

Comment

We have identified the following factors which we feel impact on a young person's sexual health.

- Marginalisation and exclusion have a powerful impact on a young person's sexual health. As we have seen issues in relation to gender, sexual orientation and ethnicity can create barriers in accessing sexual health services. Young people with learning difficulties are more often than not seen as needing to be protected from sexual information and relationships as opposed to being sexually active in their own right (Douglas-Scott, 2004). There is little recognition that their sexual desires and needs are similar in range and variety to the rest of the population. Their sexual health needs need to be addressed in order that they can become sexually empowered in terms of their own sexual relationships and to be more informed regarding the risk of sexual abuse and coercion. Further issues relating to sexuality and disability will be explored in Chapter 5.

- Issues such as substance use, mental ill health and homelessness impact on young people's vulnerability and self-esteem, which affect their sexual health. For example, young people who are already disadvantaged by poverty, excluded from education and living in care are at most risk of unplanned parenthood (DfES, 2006). Pregnancy and childcare can further isolate young women who find accessing support in order to continue with their education difficult due to lack of knowledge of services, being too intimidated to ask about services or failing to qualify for services.

Sexual risk

Working with young people around issues of sexuality and sexual health involves working with the concept of risk. Risk is subjective and influenced by a range of social, cultural and psychological factors. There is however, a difference between 'being at risk' resulting in a negative outcome such as sexual violence, and engaging in 'risk-taking' where someone is choosing to be involved in risky activities.

- **Risk-taking and safer practices** Developing an awareness of sexuality is a major aspect of a young person's development towards autonomy, independence and finding out who they are.

For many young people, sexual activity is not a problem in itself, but is more likely to be used as a way of finding an answer to problems about identity.

(Shucksmith, 2004, p.12)

The perception of risk differs and can complicate and even prevent the take-up of safer practices. Parents, carers and professionals may perceive sexual risks primarily in terms of infections and pregnancies. Young people may do so too, but will have other risks competing with these such as the risk to their reputation. Although young people are consulted in terms of sexual health promotion, much of the sex and relationship education, driven by adult concerns, tends to sanitise safer-sex discussions and mainly focus on condom use (Shucksmith, 2004). The issue regarding reputation is complex and firmly linked with identity development. For example, a young man who does not know how to use a condom may not try to find out because of the risk to his reputation and as a consequence will engage in unsafe sexual activity. We also discussed earlier how protecting their femininity can conflict with young women's use of condoms. The focus on condom use presupposes planned sexual activity, communication and the power to negotiate types of sexual practice. The reality of first-time sexual intercourse particularly at a young age involves limited communication and speed as well as many young people being caught up in the notions of romance and spontaneity. (See Chapter 6 on HIV for further discussions about the complexities of safer sexual practices.) The social work role of engaging young people in discussion regarding safer sexual practices is important as it increases the likelihood that they will become involved in informed positive risk-taking. The different perceptions on risk shows that sexual health promotion is not solely about advice and treatment and must take account of social, cultural and psychological factors. The perception of risk should also be extended to young people's emotional well-being when exploring their sexuality. Many young people will initially experience short-lived, intense and passionate sexual relationships, where they will need to be able to manage 'traumatic' endings (Moore and Rosenthal, 1998). It is important that young people are given the emotional time and space to recover from these endings as managing this process effectively will benefit young people in terms of their growth and maturity (Coleman and Hendry, 1999). We therefore need to be respectful and acknowledge the significance of young people's sexual relationships and provide them with support, skills and knowledge to enable them to gain control in their lives and relationships.

- **Sexual violence**

It is important to appreciate that working with young people on issues of sexuality may prompt discussions and disclosures of sexual violence. In Chapter 7 we detail the provisions under the Sexual Offences Act 2003 for the protection of children/young people from sexual offences. We also refer you to other Acts that guide the work of the social worker in terms of sexual violence against children/young people and provide a 'Further reading' list that will be useful.

C H A P T E R   S U M M A R Y

This chapter has introduced you to some of the key issues and debates in relation to young people and sexuality. You should be able to demonstrate your understanding of the different influences of the various social divisions on young people's sexual experiences and be able to apply that understanding of difference to your social work practice with young people. A key learning point from this chapter is that young people have to negotiate complex issues around their sexual development and are continually balancing who they feel they are or want to be with what is expected of them. You should feel able to engage positively and sensitively with young people on issues of sexuality and be able to offer constructive support through your social work practice.

FURTHER READING

Burtney, E and Duffy, M (eds) (2004) *Young people and sexual health*. Basingstoke and New York: Palgrave Macmillan.

A good comprehensive book which includes an international section as well as exploring the range of diversity found among young people and their sexual experiences.

Carr, A (2002) *Avoiding risky sex in adolescence*. Oxford: The British Psychological Society and Blackwell Publishers Ltd.

A useful practical guide which can be used in a range of situations when working with young people on issues of safer sexual practices.

Coleman, JC and Hendry, LB (1999) *The nature of adolescence*. 3rd edition. London and New York: Routledge.

Chapter 6 covers a range of issues in relation to young people and sexuality.

Chapter 4
Sexuality, older people and social work

Introduction

There has been a tendency to see sexuality as the prerogative of young people and incompatible with ageing. This, together with the silence surrounding the issues of sexuality in relation to older people, is slowly being challenged. This chapter will introduce you to the main debates and discussions as well as linking the issues to social work practice.

Introducing older people

How old is older?

For the purpose of this chapter older people will be defined as people who are 65 years and over. There are obvious problems using chronological age in defining the word 'older' (Crawford and Walker, 2004) but it is consistent with the definitions used predominantly by health and social care provision and the National Service Framework for Older People (Department of Health, 2001b).

The diversity of older people

Society tends to view older people as a homogenous group with similar needs, expectations and lives. Language such as 'the elderly' encourages the ageist attitude of 'lumping together' older people, who in reality are a diverse group reflecting the range of different social divisions. The one exception is gender, where there is a predominance of women within the older population, giving rise to the term 'feminisation of old age' (Hunt, 2005, p.201). Examples of the diversity of older people can be seen in the number (175,000 and rising to 1.7 million over the next 15 years) of older people from black and minority ethnic communities (www.praie.org), and the number (600,000) of older people identifying as lesbian, gay or bisexual (www.ageconcern.org.uk). Older people are represented in terms of class with poverty and low income continuing to affect a substantial proportion of older people (Crawford and Walker, 2004). In relation to disability older people are over-represented (Crawford and Walker, 2004). Although our discussions in Chapter 2 recognised the significant impact social divisions have on sexuality, existing research tends to focus on younger people. Whilst there is recognition of the impact of gender on sexuality in later life, there appears to be no UK research studies on the impact of ethnicity (Gott, 2005). Also sexuality is assumed to be a luxury when issues such as class, poverty and ageing are discussed (Gott, 2005). The diversities of our personal biographies, histories and experiences stay with us as we grow older and influence our experiences of ageing and our sexuality.

Sexuality and older people

The context

When considering sexuality and older people, it is impossible to ignore the influence of ageism. The term 'ageism' in relation to older people was first defined by Butler (1969) to refer to the stereotyping, prejudice, discrimination and oppression people experience because they are old. Ageism has a number of dimensions and aspects, operating on an individual as well as societal level. It is frequently experienced by older people together with other prejudices and discrimination based on ethnicity, gender, class, disability and sexual orientation. As we are arguing that ageism plays an important role in the perception and construction of older people's sexuality, we need to consider how.

ACTIVITY 4.1

What do you think are some of the commonly held assumptions about older people's sexuality? What ideas are these assumptions based on?

Comment

The most commonly held assumption in Western societies about older people is that they are asexual (Gott, 2005). This is based on the belief that older people cannot and do not enjoy sex and are no longer interested in being sexually active (Sherman, 1999). Support for this belief comes from a dominant view that sexuality is equated with youth, and in turn youth is equated with physical attractiveness and beauty. Physical attractiveness and beauty are assumed to be the trigger to sexual desire. These interrelated ideas and assumptions conspire to make sexuality and sexual activity in later life the subject of humour, ridicule and disgust (Butler and Lewis, 1986). For example, an older man who shows any sexual interest is frequently referred to as a 'dirty old man' (Walz, 2002). Another dominant aspect of sexuality is how heterosexuality and reproduction are presented as the norm. This has a particular effect on older women because of the way female sexuality is more closely related to reproduction than male sexuality. Older women's sexuality is constructed as 'out of place' or 'impure' because of the fact that generally older women are no longer able to reproduce (Bildtgard, 2000). Older women are portrayed as sexually unattractive and may lose their sense of femininity as they age (Hinchliffe and Gott, 2004). This assumption of asexuality could be viewed as the dominant discourse in relation to later-life sexuality. As we explore further the construction of older people's sexuality a more complex picture will emerge.

RESEARCH SUMMARY

In 2006 Dr Rashbrook, a 62-year-old child psychiatrist, became the oldest woman in Britain to have a baby. Her baby boy was conceived through IVF using a donor egg. Dr Rashbrook stated that parenting is not about age but about the ability to meet a child's needs.

Source: news.bbc.co.uk/1/hi/health/5160142.stm

It is worth noting at this point that old age and sexuality share a common feature, in that they are both socially constructed. What is meant by 'old' and in particular 'too old' is defined by society. The research summary above is a good example of how currently society's biomedical capability starts to challenge the definition of 'too old' to reproduce. However, the language of ageing, unlike the language of sexuality, does not differentiate between the physiological and the social. Wilson (2000, p. 7) states that in gerontology there is

> *no equivalent of sex and gender to distinguish between biological and social ageing…this lack of a word for the socially constructed characteristics of later life leaves a gap in the language of conceptualisation that makes it very easy to think of biological and social ageing as the same thing.*

(p.7)

The exclusion

Failure to recognise older people's sexuality manifests itself in the three areas of policy, practice and research. In relation to policy the National Sexual Health Strategy (DoH, 2001c) does not make reference to sex or sexual health in later life. The National Service Framework for Older People (DoH, 2001b), whilst discussing issues of rooting out age discrimination, person-centred care and the promotion of health and active life in older age, fails to make any reference to sexuality. In practice health and social care professionals predominantly disregard issues of sexuality in relation to older people. This is particularly prevalent amongst staff working in residential and nursing care homes (Bowman et al., 2006). Within the area of sexuality research older people are often excluded. The National Survey of Sexual Attitudes and Lifestyles in 1991 and its subsequent follow-up survey in 1998 included no one over the ages of 59 and 44 respectively (Gott, 2005). Both were fundamental pieces of research that were to inform the National Sexual Health Strategy (DoH, 2001c). These decisions to exclude older people are reinforced and justified by the commonly accepted belief that older people have little interest in issues of sexuality and seldom engage in sexual behaviour (Levy, 1999). Exclusion, marginalisation and discrimination are all interlinked and have a real effect on older people's lives whereby they are denied opportunities and resources (Bytheway, 2005). This dominant view of asexuality which leads to exclusion, disregard and disapproval can be internalised by many older people. Older people can then view themselves as sexless and unattractive and feel ashamed of any sexual interest or desire (Levy, 1999). In effect for some older people the social disapproval will be sufficient for them to present themselves as asexual. When any problems regarding sexuality arise they are then concealed, giving rise to misery, fear and suffering at best and possibly perpetuating further problems at worst (Oppenheimer, 2002).

The importance

So why is sexuality important for older people? Foucault (1988) claimed that sexuality is the prime site in which identity is inscribed, and that to strip sexuality of its significance or to silence it is to do damage to the very notion of being human. Influential human growth and development theorists such as Freud and Erikson, although recognising the centrality of sexuality in the development of self and identity in childhood and young adulthood (see Crawford and Walker, 2003) are silent about sexuality in old age. The broader definition of sexuality that we discussed in Chapter 1 presents sexuality as an intrinsic part of what makes us what we are as individuals whether or not we are sexually active. Sexuality is central to our identity and sense of self and contributes to our 'personhood' (Kitwood, 1997, p.7). As well as the crucial link to identity there is a small but growing body of recent research that links sexuality to quality of life issues in terms of physical and psychological well-being (Hinchliffe and Gott, 2004; Gott, 2005).

Attitudes of health and social care professionals

ACTIVITY 4.2

Case study

You are on placement in a multidisciplinary older person's team and are asked by your supervisor to arrange a home visit to assess an older woman, Iona Williams, who is 82 years of age and whose partner died 18 months ago. She has been referred by her GP who states that she is not coping very well emotionally, which is impinging on her ability to look after herself. During your visit Iona starts talking about the things she is struggling with and states that she is particularly missing the sexual relationship she had with her partner.

- *How do you think you would feel at this point?*

- *What do you think your attitude towards what Iona is saying would be?*

- *Do you think that your feelings and attitude would be an advantage or disadvantage in enabling her to talk further about how she feels about her sexuality?*

Comment

People's attitudes are an important part of how aspects of society are constructed. Bowman et al. (2006, p. 158) undertook a literature review of research focusing on attitudes regarding sexuality and older people. They concluded:

> *that the medical and nursing profession appear to have an often rather negative attitude of later-life sexuality (unlike most studied groups of older people themselves), despite their professional bodies having implemented clear guideless to combat ageism.*

This would have a particular impact on older people within residential and nursing care services. Also with the multidisciplinary approach to older people's care this finding has implications for social workers, particularly in relation to anti-discriminatory and good social work practice.

The social construction of older people's sexuality

The question we need to ask ourselves at this point is whether the assumption of asexuality gives us the whole picture regarding the social construction of older people's sexuality. In other words, are there any other competing discourses? In Chapter 1 you considered ways in which discourses contributed to the social construction of sexuality. The four ways of 'representation', 'silence/absence', 'proliferation' and 'address' will now be explored in relation to older people's sexuality using research studies from the field of health and social care.

Representation

In what ways are the issues and aspects of older people's sexuality represented? Although the sexuality of older people has been recognised for some considerable time (Hendricks and Hendricks, 1977), research over the last 20 years has been dominated by quantitative studies focusing on sexual behaviour and technique. (See Gott (2005) in 'Further reading' for a comprehensive review of this research). The focus has been very narrow, presenting older people's sexuality in purely biomedical terms and quantifying sexual activity in terms of *which older people do it and how often?* (Gott, 2005, p.55). As well as quantifying sexual activity the research has also highlighted certain sexual problems that can arise with the ageing process, referring to these problems as 'dysfunctions', which are seen as curable. A good example which has had disproportionate attention is 'erectile dysfunction', *an inability of the male to achieve an erect penis* (National Institute of Health, 1992, p.2), which is cured with Viagra. What is interesting for us to note here is that although the likelihood of erectile dysfunction increases with age, neither is it the most distressing of sexual problems older men experience nor does it necessarily affect sexual desire or pleasure. In fact there is growing research to show that older men experience less difficulty than younger men in adjusting to erectile dysfunction and continue to have satisfactory sexual relationships (Bortz et al., 1999; Moore et al., 2003). We would argue that this emphasis on erectile dysfunction reflects a dominant discourse that penetrative vaginal heterosexual intercourse is the only normal and desirable way of expressing ourselves sexually. A central aspect of this discourse is the dominance of male sexuality and in particular the notion that the central responsibility for the sexual act is based on the ability of the man to perform. This reinforces the notion of a passive female sexuality and contributes to the view that women's sexuality in its own right is invisible. This is particularly problematic for older women who are already fighting invisibility due to ageing. The debate around Viagra and sexual dysfunction is a powerful one involving large drug companies and the medical establishment (Loe, 2004). It reinforces a narrow definition of 'normal' sexuality and constructs a medical model of older people's sexuality. Discourses that are medical and/or health related are the most powerful and influential in the social construction of sexuality (Weeks, 1986). Sexuality in later life is also quite often represented within the context of problems such as illnesses and other health-related issues. This will be discussed further when considering 'proliferation'.

Silence/absence

In what ways are issues and aspects of older people's sexuality absent or invisible which indicates that they are unimportant, shameful or do not exist? What must be acknowledged in this area is the dominance of silence or absence of most aspects of older people's sexuality. We discussed earlier examples of the exclusion of older people's sexuality from policy, research and practice. The voice of the older person struggles to be heard in sexuality research. Many researchers believe that older people do not want to talk about sex and sexuality because of the era they were brought up in where sexuality was not discussed. Not only has this justified excluding older people from research studies but also when older people have been included they have more often than not been given self-administered questionnaires (Gott, 2005). When older people's sexuality is represented there is an assumed homogeneity where older people are all assumed to be heterosexual (Wilton, 2000). The other area of relative silence is in terms of research-based evidence on which to develop policy and practice in relation to the sexual abuse of older people (Jeary, 2004). This issue will be returned to later.

Proliferation

Is excessive attention paid to issues and aspects of older people's sexualities, which gives the impression that they are extremely important? When older people's sexuality is discussed in research it tends to be within the context of sexual activity and/or as a problem. There is a concentration on sexual problems in two ways: firstly in relation to sexual dysfunction and secondly in relation to expressing sexuality within the context of experiencing dementia, chronic illnesses and disabilities. In this latter situation it is the older person's sexuality that is viewed as the problem. We would not want to be critical of these issues being researched and discussed but there are so many aspects of older people's sexuality where there is a silence which in turn creates an imbalance in how sexuality in later life is being portrayed. Proliferation is a powerful way of establishing norms and creating oppressive stereotypes.

Address

Who is the research intended for and who is being targeted? Most of the health and social care research into sexuality and older people is presented in a biomedical way. The effect of this is first, it assumes that the readership is interested only in a medical viewpoint of the sexuality of older people, and second, it constructs and supports a medical model of older people's sexuality (Katz and Marshall, 2003; Gott, 2005).

Building a viewpoint of older people's sexuality

ACTIVITY **4.3**

Take the main points from each of the four areas discussed above. What viewpoint(s) of older people's sexuality do they construct?

Comment

It appears from our analysis that the themes of silence and invisibility dominate older people's sexuality. If it is recognised, discussion tends to be narrow, biological and within the context of heterosexual sexual activity. This constructs a narrow definition of what is 'normal' sexuality for older people and in the process excludes many older people's experiences. Older people's sexuality within the field of health and social care is frequently seen in the context of other challenges such as illness, dementia and residential care. This has the effect of problematising the older person's sexuality itself as opposed to discussing the challenges facing an older person in their struggle to continue to be able to engage in sexual expression. It could be argued that a lot of the recent research successfully challenges the view of an asexual later life, but it is also in danger of creating another stereotype of the 'sexy oldie' (Gott, 2005, p.23). The combination of the importance of sexuality, its link to healthy ageing, and the availability of Viagra can put pressure on older people to feel that they should be sexually active as often as possible. Replacing one stereotype by another does not help older people to express and share experiences of their sexuality. It is argued that Viagra has done a disservice to older people because it has assumed that sexuality through the life course should be ideally unchanged and youthfully defined (Loe, 2004).

The voice of the older person

We would argue that the two dominant constructs of older people in terms of their sexuality, that of 'asexuality' versus 'the sexy oldie', do not help to develop knowledge that is credible and meaningful to a diverse population of older people. Obviously these social constructs are powerful and we have argued that they influence the experience of older people in very real but oppressive ways. There is a complex interrelationship between how society constructs dominant discourses, how these discourses influence the experience and behaviour of people and how in turn people's experiences and behaviour can end up supporting the dominant discourses by reflecting them. For this cycle of perpetuation to be broken, and for other discourses to compete, it is important for the voice of the older person to be heard. The views and experiences of older people do not feature in the main debates around their sexuality. However there are a small number of qualitative studies (see Jones, 2002 and Gott, 2005 in further reading) that capture the diversity of experiences of sexuality of older people and begin to challenge the dominant discourses that we have highlighted.

Older people's experiences of sexuality

So what is known about older people's experiences of sexuality in terms of desires, relationships, identities, acts, beliefs and behaviours? Older people experience and express their sexuality in a range of different ways. These differences are important to recognise and reflect the diversity that exists in society in terms of different types of relationships, sexual orientation, sexual practices and sexual desires.

RESEARCH SUMMARY

Research in Norway and Sweden has identified older people establishing lasting sexual relationships in which each partner continues to live in their own home. The relationship has been referred to as 'living apart together' (LAT) and has been seen by 'single' heterosexual older people as an alternative to marriage. The research has suggested that older women are particularly favourable towards a LAT relationship as opposed to cohabiting or remarriage because it allows them to maintain autonomy and personal control over their lives. LAT relationships for older people are more likely to have been preceded by divorce or widowhood.

Source: Borell and Ghazanfareeon Karlsson (2003)

Older people's experiences of their sexuality depend on their life histories and biographies. Everyone's sexuality is shaped by their personal biography, which is influenced by society's discourses. Expressing your sexuality is influenced by past experiences and meanings that continue to be important as you age. From this you will conclude that older people are not that dissimilar to the rest of society when it comes to experiences of sexuality. However, it is worth mentioning a positive and liberating finding that has emerged from some of the more recent qualitative studies. Hinchliffe and Gott (2004) found that older people are redefining what constitutes being sexual by embracing a much broader definition of sexuality. They are challenging the narrow definition of sexual activity and placing more importance on the diversity of sexual expression.

> *As you get older you act differently and you adjust to your age, but I consider that a cuddle is sex...intercourse does not take place as much...but the desire to love someone is there, and love, it takes a different form...(Male participant, aged 73)*

> (Hinchliffe and Gott, 2004, p.604)

Sexuality and older people: social work practice

As we saw from the case study of Iona Williams, issues of sexuality can be raised by older service users at any time and in any context. As sexuality is part of people's identity it follows that it will be of significance in many different contexts. Therefore it would be impossible to list social work situations where you may be needed to work with an older person or older people around issues of sexuality. We therefore propose for the remainder of the chapter to concentrate on particular areas where we feel issues of sexuality and social work practice converge.

Older lesbians, gay men and bisexuals

We would like to start off by challenging the assumption that all older people are heterosexual. In 2002 Age Concern launched its Opening Doors Conference which brought together for the first time older people, statutory service providers, voluntary organisations and representatives of government to begin addressing the needs of lesbians, gay men and bisexuals as the population ages (www.ace.org.uk/AgeConcern/openingdoors.asp).

Who are older lesbians, gay men and bisexuals?

Older lesbians, gay men and bisexuals are not a socially cohesive group and reflect the diversity of society in terms of disability, ethnicity and class. Recognising this diversity is an important starting point and

> *the development of sexual identity will vary from one person to another, reflecting past and current experiences. There are many ways of being a lesbian or gay man as much as there are many ways of being an older person.*

> (Pugh, 2005, p.210)

Older lesbians, gay men and bisexuals will have experience of marriage, parenthood, grandparenthood, heterosexuality, lesbianism, being gay and being bisexual. Some older people will have been lesbian, gay or bisexual all their lives and other older people will have changed their sexual orientation during their lives. Some older people will have been open about their sexuality all their lives, others will have kept their sexuality a secret or partial secret, and other older people may have started recently to become open or more open about their sexuality. The differences are never-ending and practitioners need to recognise that the diversity will be reflected in the different ways older people are lesbian, gay or bisexual.

Invisibility and oppression

Despite the diversity, invisibility and oppression are common experiences for older lesbians, gay men and bisexuals, as a result of ageism and heterosexism. Whilst recent legislation such as the Civil Partnership Act 2004 and the Equality Act 2006 help to promote a climate of rights and anti-discrimination with regard to different sexualities, older people will have lived through times when 'homosexuality' was illegal and viewed as a mental illness. Some will have experienced prosecution and medical intervention as a result (Fenge, 2006). Some older lesbians will have been judged as unfit mothers and with the aid of social work reports will have lost custody of their children based on their sexual orientation. It is only since the late 1980s that there has been the slow development of positive attitudes towards lesbian mothers (Brown, 1998). The impact of this type of oppression will ensure that many older lesbians, gay men and bisexuals continue to keep their sexuality invisible for fear of further discrimination. However, recent findings suggest that there are increasing numbers of older lesbians, gay men and bisexuals who are disclosing their sexual orientation for the first time in later life (Herdt and Beeler, 1998), and that their visibility will increase in years to come as people who have lived in more liberal times retire (Lavin, 2004).

Sexual orientation – what difference does it make?

ACTIVITY 4.4

Reflect back to the case study earlier in the chapter concerning Iona Williams. Did you make any assumptions about the gender of her partner? Would the issues she is facing be any different if she were a lesbian as opposed to identifying herself as heterosexual?

Comment

If we say that the issues facing Iona Williams are no different whatever her sexual orientation we risk contributing to the view that older people are a homogenous group. We would also be doing Iona Williams a disservice as our assessment of her situation would be unlikely to consider the impact of heterosexism on her life. We would not have an understanding of the social context of her life and the challenges she has had to face. There are obviously common issues that are experienced by many older people regardless of gender, ethnicity, sexual orientation, class or disability, such as frailty, loss of significant people and ageism. However, in order to undertake anti-oppressive practice we would maintain that it is imperative to consider the impact of heterosexism on the lives of older lesbians, gay men and bisexuals.

The impact of heterosexism

We have highlighted the following examples of the impact heterosexism may have on older people's lives.

- **Mental health** Many older lesbians, gay men and bisexuals feel guilty and ashamed of their sexuality, leading to low self-esteem, increased social isolation and poor mental health such as depression, anxiety and suicidal thoughts (D'Augelli et al., 2001). Mental health issues have a significant impact on people's ability to cope with the challenges of ageing.

- **Social isolation** Invisibility and discrimination can take place in many ways. For example, older lesbians, gay men and bisexuals may feel excluded from leisure and support services offered by the gay communities because of ageism, and in turn feel excluded from leisure and support services offered by older people's communities because of heterosexism (Pugh, 2005; Fenge, 2006). Many of the gay networks in terms of leisure and support tend to be in urban areas and access for older people living in rural areas or for older people who are experiencing transport/mobility difficulties may increase their sense of isolation.

- **Exclusion** There is a risk that partners may be excluded from an older person's support network and care, and if not recognised as the main carer will themselves be excluded and miss out on important support services such as respite care (Sale, 2002).

RESEARCH SUMMARY

The Lesbian and Gay Carer Network was founded, as part of the Alzheimer's Society, in 2000 by Roger Newman, whose partner David was diagnosed with dementia in 1992. They had been together for 30 years. David spent six years in a residential home before his death in 2000. Roger Newman stated that in order not to feel excluded he had to educate staff about the nature and significance of their relationship and that he should be regarded as David's next of kin (Sale, 2002).

- **Positive impact** Research shows that many older lesbians, gay men and bisexuals have developed strength, tenacity and wisdom whilst enduring stigma and oppression. This has led to expertise in developing social networks, using community resources and taking care of themselves (Allen, 2005). Support networks are mainly made up of friends who provide mutual support, enjoyment and lack the obligatory expectation and demands of family/relative type support networks (Pugh, 2005). The lack of relatives within these networks may be due to the fact that support has been withdrawn due to disapproval of the older person's sexual orientation. However, these positive friendship networks are a direct challenge to the negative and powerful stereotyping of older lesbians and gay men being lonely, sexless, unattractive and depressed (Fenge, 2006).

Empowering social work practice

ACTIVITY 4.5

The impact for the service user of heterosexism can be a sense of disempowerment. What things could you do in your practice as a social work student to enable an older lesbian, gay man or bisexual to feel more empowered?

Assessment A useful starting point is not assuming anything about an older person's sexual orientation and being aware that many older lesbians, gay men and bisexuals will not necessarily be open about their sexuality to a social worker. Social workers need to be open to all possibilities and be able to develop ways of discussing and validating same-sex relationships without putting pressure on the older person to come out about their sexuality. A good example of this would be phrasing carefully many of the standard questions asked at the beginning of an assessment about relationships and next of kin, so that the person feels included. An open and inclusive question may be along the lines of 'Please tell me about all the relationships that are or have been important in your life'. Good social work practice is not about placing the onus on older lesbians, gay men and bisexuals to disclose their sexual orientation. It is about providing an open and supportive environment where service users feel they can come out if they want without fear of judgment. Due to the overwhelming assumption of heterosexuality within our society it is important to note that coming out is not a one-off event but a continuous process that happens when older lesbians, gay men and bisexuals face new situations with new people. Coming out is therefore an exhausting process and many older lesbians and gay men may decide to come out on a need-to-know basis (Pugh, 2005). When older people are involved with social workers they are generally in a state of vulnerability and crisis. The social worker needs to be able to sensitively encourage older people to be open about their sexual orientation so that the assessment of need can be open and honest and be a true reflection of the important aspects of a service user's life. An assessment based on partial information can itself only be partial (Bayliss, 2000).

Service provision Research has shown that many older lesbians, gay men and bisexuals feel that the services on offer would not be appropriate or they fear non-acceptance because of their sexuality (Langley, 2001). This issue of inappropriate services is particularly pertinent to day, intermediate and long-term nursing and social care services, as well as sheltered housing. The role of the social worker in this situation is to advocate on behalf of the service user by ensuring that services are at the very least 'gay friendly', inclusive and welcoming of all service users regardless of their sexual orientation. This can be done on two levels, firstly on a 'frontline' level of sexuality awareness training for staff and other service users, and secondly on a policy level where organisations such as care homes and housing associations recognise the existence of older lesbians and gay men and their need for an inclusive environment (Sale, 2002). The dilemma for the social worker is whilst encouraging the older person to be open about their sexual orientation at the assessment stage of the care management process he/she cannot guarantee a positive response at the service delivery stage.

ACTIVITY 4.6

Case study

Two older women live in a private residential care home. They had moved there together when one of them became a wheelchair user after having a stroke. They had been sexual partners for 50 years but had hidden their sexual orientation from the staff of the care home. The non-disabled partner is referred to a community mental health team for her 'disruptive behaviour' after a member of staff had found the women together in the disabled partner's bed. Staff had made fun of the women but also felt that the non-disabled woman had taken sexual advantage of the disabled woman, who they felt was vulnerable. The situation has been allocated to you as the social worker in the team in the area. What would you do?

Comment

You will have come up with a range of suggestions on how to support the two women. This case is based on a real situation (Smith, 1992) and the outcome was that both women were given positive acknowledgement of their sexuality and life together by the practitioner involved. The latter tried to change the attitudes of the staff in the care home but failed. The two women were moved to another care home where their relationship was validated and they were given a shared room with a double bed. Despite having been open about their sexuality for years, many older lesbians and gay men are forced to hide their sexuality when they need care because they fear homophobic attitudes from care staff and other service users (Sale, 2002). The issues of nursing and residential care services in relation to older people and sexuality generally will be returned to again later in the chapter.

Imaginative and empowering responses to the needs of older lesbians, gay men and bisexuals could also involve the use of the direct payments scheme which has been extended to older people (DoH, 2001d). It is an opportunity for service users to take control and create packages of care that are more appropriate in enabling them to continue to live in the way they choose. Developing and strengthening service users' existing networks can also be empowering, such as enabling older lesbians, gay men and bisexual service users to be in touch with available gay support groups and networks. This does however require the older person to be comfortable about being open about their sexuality.

Within this section we have addressed some of the issues that have particular relevance for social work with older lesbians, gay men and bisexuals. The remaining sections are issues which are relevant to all older people regardless of their sexual orientation.

Psychosocial changes

Like most people in society, older people experience changes. It is the psychosocial changes as opposed to the biological ones which have the biggest impact on older people's sexuality. Some changes will be directly linked to a specific life crisis such as death of a partner and others will be more difficult to identify such as the influence of oppressive attitudes and assumptions. Many psychosocial changes in an older person's life can pre-empt social work intervention. Therefore it is important that you are aware of the links between these factors and possible changes in relation to an older person's sexuality.

Oppressive social attitudes

As stated earlier, ageist attitudes towards sexuality in later life can have a psychological impact where older people cease to view themselves as sexual and desirable, and in turn lose the motivation to express themselves sexually (Reed et al., 2004). The impact of oppressive attitudes cannot be underestimated and can affect the way that care services are delivered. An older person's existing sexual relationship is often perceived as asexual as their dependency and frailty increases. For example, older people often experience a lack of privacy and opportunity to maintain an existing sexual relationship, whilst for example, living in residential or nursing care, or having carers into their home (Reed et al., 2004).

Availability of sexual partners

Life events bring about gains and losses in social relationships. The lack of a sexual partner for older people can either be a choice or it can be a force of circumstance. Although for many older people their lack of a sexual partner will be due to their partner having died, it must not be assumed that this is the case for all older people. Some older people may have separated from their partner and some older people may never have had a partner. For some older people it is the lack of opportunity to find a sexual partner and as older women outnumber older men, this becomes an increasing problem for older heterosexual women. It also must not be assumed that because an older person appears not to have a sexual partner that he/she is asexual. As we discussed in the first chapter sexuality is part of our identity and does not disappear if we do not have a sexual partner.

Health issues

Although health issues such as heart disease, diabetes, arthritis and incontinence can impact on an older person's sexuality, it does not necessarily mean that a person cannot express themselves sexually. Health issues are linked to dependency, frailty and disability, all issues which society feel are incompatible with the sexualised ideal of youth, beauty and fitness. The important issue is the ability of the person to adjust to their illness and continue to express themselves sexually. Research has found that for women health factors are of little significance in explaining the development and/or maintenance of sexual interest and activity in old age and that it has more to do with body image (Fooken, 1994). Expressing sexuality through physical appearance remains an important goal for older women, although it is recognised that there are challenges that make this difficult to achieve (Gott, 2005).

Sexual health needs of older people

Sexual health is a state of physical, emotional, mental and social well-being related to sexuality (WHO, 2002). It is an interrelationship between health and social care factors and a concern for all professionals. Older people's sexuality should be validated by professionals who need to be aware that sexual expression is vital for self-esteem, self-acceptance and general well-being. This is of particular importance in later life when other sources of support and well-being might have been lost or reduced. We have identified a number of sexual health needs which we feel are relevant to older people.

- Older people need professionals to view sexuality in a broad and inclusive sense so that all aspects of sexual expression are validated. It is unhelpful if aspects of an older person's sexuality are measured and judged by the 'norm' of heterosexual sexual intercourse.

- Older people need to understand the changes and influences on their sexuality as they age. They need to be given accurate information and be encouraged to share issues and concerns. Older people need professionals who understand the effects of society's attitudes on older people themselves. Groupwork may be a powerful way of older people sharing their experiences and challenging society's oppressive attitudes.

- Professional workers need to be aware of 'triggers' to sexual health issues, such as onset of physical illness or death of a partner, which may impact on an older person's sexual identity, sexual feelings and sexual activity. Professional workers should sensitively instigate discussion and not wait for the older person to bring up issues. Older people need information about how, for example, physical illness, disability, and the effects of medication could affect sexual feelings and desires.

- Older people do engage in sexual behaviours which place them at risk of sexually transmitted infections (STIs) and HIV. Sexual health promotion is particularly youth focused and older people do not feel encouraged to seek the services of the genitourinary medicine clinic. Many older people feel that they do not receive enough information about STIs and HIV (Gott, 2005). Similarly, with sexual problems many older people fear the attitudes of their GP, or feel that sexual problems are a normal part of ageing, or lack knowledge about appropriate services. (See Gott, 2005, in 'Further reading'.)

Nursing and residential care services

The sexuality of older people is a neglected area that has received insufficient attention in terms of care home practices. We considered the impact of this neglect earlier in relation to the case scenario of two older lesbians. The National Minimum Standards (DoH, 2002a) for care homes for older people provide a broad regulatory framework on issues such as privacy and dignity, dying and death, social contact and activities and protection from abuse. They do not specifically address older people's sexuality. Apart from a good practice guide published by the charity Counsel and Care (Clarke et al., 2002), no other publications exist addressing the issue. There is a danger therefore that without any clear guidance care homes will differ immensely in their care practices, leaving care staff in the powerful role of facilitating how the sexuality of older people should be expressed. There is a lack of knowledge and experience amongst care staff of working with older people on issues of sexuality and attitudes tend to be restrictive and stereotypical (Low et al., 2005). There is still a predominance of the view that old age is, or should be, asexual, particularly when combined with frailty, disability and vulnerability. This inhibits and discourages older people from expressing or discussing their sexual needs and desires (Gott, 2005). We feel that care practices should be solely guided by the National Minimum Standards (DoH, 2002a) involving privacy, dignity and protection from abuse. Therefore an older person has a right to express their sexuality in whatever way they choose, within the context of their right to privacy, dignity and the right not to be involved in an abusive situation. Obviously every older person in a care home has these rights.

RESEARCH SUMMARY

Thirty-two care staff from a care home for older people with dementia were asked which sexual behaviours they found difficult to cope with. They listed 15 in total and could only reach an agreement of unacceptability for four of the behaviours. These four behaviours infringed the right to privacy, dignity and protection from abuse, for example, exposing genitalia in public. The judgment of what was inappropriate with the remaining 11 behaviours tended to reflect the staff's moral standpoint, for example, an older person spending a lot of time with someone else when one or both were married to other people, and gay and lesbian relationships. Other sexual behaviours that were disapproved of were behaviours that would be acceptable in a person's own home, for example, being sexual with a visiting partner. Other behaviours such as hugging could also be associated with friendship and may not necessarily have been meant in a sexual way.

Source: Sherman (1999)

Read the case of Hugh Taylor and Frances Evans (not their real names), both in their eighties, both widowed and in the early stages of dementia. They lived in a care home and started a romantic [sic] relationship. The case can be accessed via the web by going to **www.communitycare.co.uk** *then clicking onto 'advanced search' and typing in* a romance in the twilight *and then pressing Enter.*

What learning do you take from this case?

Comment

This case shows very clearly the important role of advocacy, negotiation, training, policies and procedures. The manager of the home demonstrated good practice in relation to advocating for the older couple and their rights, as well as negotiating with the relatives and other service users. The staff were provided with support through training and policies. The social work role could involve support for the manager, negotiating with the relatives or providing some of the staff support and training.

Sexual abuse

Sexual abuse is recognised as one of the categories of abuse that adults can experience which is identified in the 'No Secrets' guidelines to protect vulnerable adults from abuse (DoH, 2000). It is defined as *including rape and sexual assault or sexual acts to which the vulnerable adult has not consented, or could not consent or was pressured into consenting* (DoH, 2000, p.9). For further reference with regard to 'No Secrets' see Crawford and Walker (2004) and Johns (2005). Action on Elder Abuse helpline states that 3 per cent of reported abuse is sexual abuse and it was the only type of abuse where reporting rates have increased, which may be due to abusers seeking softer targets due to more recent rigorous protection of children (Kenny, 2004). As there is limited knowledge in terms of research-based evidence of the sexual abuse of older people we have decided to summarise the main points of a recent study.

RESEARCH SUMMARY

In the research study* of 52 cases of sexual abuse of older people between the ages of 60 and 90, the following findings were reported.

- *The range of sexual abuse older people experienced included sexual harassment, inappropriate touching perceived to have an unacceptable sexual element, extreme sexual violence, sometimes including the death of the victim, and necrophilia.*

- *The sexual abuse of older people took place in residential settings and in their own homes, where some were in receipt of community care services and others lived independently.*

- *The perpetrators of the sexual abuse included care service staff, other service users, and relatives. The majority of survivors were women and the majority of perpetrators were men.*

RESEARCH SUMMARY *continued*

- *Older people's vulnerability to sexual abuse was compounded by factors such as dementia, requiring assistance with intimate personal care, and being alone in a one-to-one situation with the abuser either in their own home or in their room within residential care.*

- *Only in the minority of the cases where the abuser was known to the older person, was the abuse followed up within the criminal justice system. Sexual abuse of an older person living in their own homes independently of any care services, tended to involve an unknown abuser. These cases were all dealt with through the criminal justice system.*

- *There was frustration from care providers about the number of 'unproven' sexual abuse cases they were left with after having suspected sexual abuse and having used the adult protection procedures.*

- *The study felt that what they had explored was the tip of the iceberg.*

*Research project directed at the University of Nottingham by Professor Olive Stevenson, funded by Nuffield Foundation (Jeary, 2004)

Attitudes towards older people and in particular their sexuality influences the way that sexual abuse is regarded. The research study found that there was an overwhelming ambivalence about acknowledging the sexual abuse of older people. The study also suggested that there was an ignorance and misunderstanding from residential staff about older people's capacity for sexual feelings and expression, which staff confused with sexual abuse. One example involved a developing sexual relationship between a man and a woman in a care home and questions were raised about the woman's capacity to consent. Although the issue of consent is of utmost importance, many of the staff in the home felt that the issue was used as a diversion from having to manage the relationship and a justification for stopping the relationship. Nothing was recorded on the residents' files in terms of either how they felt about the situation or about the assessment of capacity of the woman concerned.

The research study raises the following issues for practitioners.

- The effects of sexual abuse can cause an otherwise independent older person to seek the help of care services. Practitioners within the care services must be prepared to be able to support the older person emotionally and practically, particularly if there is a criminal investigation. The older person's need for any help regarding personal care must be handled with extreme sensitivity.

- Unusual behaviours and reactions from older people who have difficulties in communicating or memory loss, need to be explored by social care staff. For example, a sudden unwillingness to undress together with looks of anxiety may be clues to sexual abuse.

- All health and social care staff need training and support with regard to sexual abuse and older people in relation to procedures and information about sexual abuse itself, how to recognise it and its effects on older people. There have been cases where domiciliary care staff have found a situation of sexual abuse and their immediate reaction of making the older person more comfortable has in effect destroyed vital evidence.

- Staff need support to work in situations where the sexual abuse is 'unproven'. Staff can feel powerless and at times may feel they are colluding with the situation.

C H A P T E R S U M M A R Y

This chapter has introduced you to some of the key issues and debates in relation to older people and sexuality. As well as being able to demonstrate your understanding of the social construction of sexuality and ageing, you should also feel able to identify the key role played by discrimination and oppression in the dominant discourses that influence the way the sexuality of older people is perceived. A key learning point from this chapter is that older people's sexuality reflects the diversity that exists in society in terms of how sexuality is experienced and expressed. You should feel able to begin to engage positively with older people on issues of sexuality and know that you have the basis to challenge the oppressive views of others whilst undertaking an advocacy role.

FURTHER READING

Fenge, L (2006) Promoting inclusiveness: developing empowering practice with minority groups of older people – the example of older lesbian women and gay men. In Brown, K (ed.) *Vulnerable adults and community care*. Exeter: Learning Matters.

An overview of social work practice and role in relation to older lesbians and gay men.

Gott, M (2005) *Sexuality, sexual health and ageing*. Maidenhead and New York: OUP/McGraw-Hill Education.

A good comprehensive book which covers the main theoretical debates with regard to older people's sexuality as well as looking at the sexual health promotion services.

Jones, RL (2002) 'That's very rude, I shouldn't be telling you that': older women talking about sex. *Narrative Inquiry*, 12(1): 121–42.

This is a good example of research that finds out about older people's experiences of sexuality.

Chapter 5

Sexuality, disabled people and social work

ACHIEVING A SOCIAL WORK DEGREE

This chapter will help you to meet the following National Occupational Standards.
Key Role 2: Plan, carry out, review and evaluate social work practice, with individuals, families, carers, groups, communities and other professionals.
- Interact with individuals, families, carers, groups and communities to achieve change and development and to improve life opportunities.
- Support the development of networks to meet assessed needs and planned outcomes.
Key Role 3: Support individuals to represent their needs, views and circumstances.
- Advocate with, and on behalf of, individuals, families, carers, groups and communities.
Key Role 6: Demonstrate professional competence in social work practice.
- Manage complex ethical issues, dilemmas and conflicts.
- Contribute to the promotion of best social work practice.

It will also introduce you to the following academic standards as set out in the social work subject benchmark statement.
3.1.1 Social work services and service users.
- The social processes that lead to marginalisation, isolation and exclusion and their impact on the demand for social work services.
- The nature of social work services in a diverse society.
3.2.2.3 Analysis and synthesis.
- Assess the merits of contrasting theories, explanations, research, policies and procedures.

Introduction

This chapter will discuss the issues of sexuality in relation to disabled people. We will be considering the social construction of disabled sexuality and the influences of the social and medical models of disability. We will not however be going into any depth about the specific nature of the different types of impairment, and we encourage you to read other sources in the Learning Matters series for information about mental health (see Golightley, 2006), physical impairment (see Crawford and Walker, 2004) and learning difficulties (see Williams, 2006). Many of the issues we discuss in other chapters are also relevant as disabled people can be young, old, affected by HIV, experience sexual violence and do have sexual rights.

Introducing disabled people

Terminology

Within this chapter (and throughout the book) we use the terms 'disabled people' or 'people who are disabled' to emphasise that people are disabled by society rather than by a medical or other condition. This is not to diminish the reality of the physical and emotional trauma that people may experience but rather to highlight the way society's structures are designed to service the needs of people who are not disabled. These views will be considered in more detail later on in the chapter. The terms are also used by the British Council of Disabled People (see www.bcodp.org.uk) as well as being widely adopted by government health and social care policy.

Who are disabled people?

The Disability Discrimination Act 2005 builds on and extends earlier disability discrimination legislation, principally the Disability Discrimination Act 1995, and defines a disabled person as someone who has a physical or mental impairment that has a substantial and long-term adverse effect on her/his ability to carry out normal day-to-day activities. The definition also includes people experiencing mental illness, people with learning difficulties who are disabled, and people living with HIV, cancer and multiple sclerosis from the point of diagnosis (Department for Work and Pensions, 2005).

The diversity of disabled people

There is a tendency for all disabled people to be grouped together and regarded as a homogenous group by policy-makers, service providers and by non-disabled people. Language such as 'the disabled' is offensive, discriminatory and denies individuality and diversity. The differences amongst disabled people can be seen firstly in relation to their ethnicity, age, gender, class and sexual orientation and secondly in relation to their impairments (Molloy et al., 2003). As can be seen from the Disability Discrimination Act 2005 there is an immense diversity in the types of impairment people experience. People have different relationships to their impairments in terms of how their lives are affected and how society responds, which means that disabled people will all experience a range of different issues around their sexuality. In the UK there are estimated to be 10 million disabled people as defined by the Disability Discrimination Act 2005. The majority of people acquire their impairment during their working lives with only $1^3/_4$ million people having congenital impairment. Five million disabled people are of working age but they are five times as likely as non-disabled people to be out of work and claiming benefits. Thirty-three per cent of people over the age of 55 have impairments. The majority of impairments are not visible, with $2^1/_2$ million people having mobility impairment, half a million people using a wheelchair and over a million people having a learning difficulty (Northampton County Council, 2006). In relation to social divisions disabled people represent:

> ...the same degree of diversity as the general population. The assumption that because people share the characteristic of disability, they share other similarities [is] resented by disabled people.

(Molloy et al., 2003, p.163)

> **RESEARCH SUMMARY**
>
> *A qualitative research was undertaken with a group of disabled people to explore the complex interrelationship between disability, ethnicity, age, gender and sexual orientation. Following are a sample of the participants' views.*
>
> - *Some participants did not see themselves as disabled or regard being disabled as a pivotal aspect of their identity. This was particularly true for the lesbian and gay participants.*
>
> - *Many participants felt that being disabled affected their experiences of finding a sexual partner and forming relationships. South Asian women participants felt that being disabled had affected their chances of forming marriages and partnerships, whilst the lesbian and gay participants felt that society's negative attitudes towards sexuality and disability made it harder for them to be open and accepted by their families.*
>
> - *Some participants, namely the African, Caribbean, lesbian and gay participants, identified more with the concept of 'compounded' or 'multiple' disadvantage and gave examples of numerous incidents in education, at work and in their social lives where they felt they were discriminated against as a result of their ethnicity, sexuality and being disabled.*
>
> - *On the whole diversity amongst disabled people and within wider society was viewed positively by all the participants despite some of their personal narratives demonstrating that the interrelationship between disability and other social divisions made them more vulnerable to disadvantage and discrimination.*
>
> *Source: Molloy et al. (2003)*

The social construction of disability

In order to analyse and understand the issues regarding sexuality and disabled people we need initially to consider the way that disability is viewed and constructed in Western society.

The medical model of disability

The medical model has dominated society's perceptions of disabled people by presenting their disability as a personal tragedy. Medical discourse focuses on people's physical and mental impairments as the cause of functional limitations or disabilities which in turn prevent 'people with disabilities' from fully taking part in social, cultural, economic and political arenas of society (Hyde, 2000). This exclusion from particular aspects of society is regarded as the 'fault' of the person's specific disability, such as their inability to walk, and is individualised by being referred to as their personal tragedy (Best, 2005). Within this model people who are non-disabled are regarded as 'normal' and in turn construct disabled people as 'other' people who are physically and/or mentally 'abnormal' or 'deviant'. This process of 'othering' establishes disabled people as having *an inferior-stigmatised status* (Best, 2005, p.87). Consequently disabled people are viewed as dependent, helpless, deserving of pity and at times dangerous because of possible violent tendencies due to frustration with their disabilities (Best, 2005). In turn this view creates and supports the pervasive structural, cultural and personal oppression experienced by disabled people.

The social model of disability

The social model differentiates between 'disability' and 'impairment' to describe disabled people's situation and themselves respectively.

> *Disability is the disadvantage or restriction of activity caused by a society which takes little or no account of people who have impairments and thus excludes them from mainstream activity. Impairment is a characteristic, feature or attribute within an individual which is long term and may or may not be the result of disease, injury or congenital condition.*

> (Gradwell, 1997, p.8)

Proponents of this model argue that people are disabled by society rather than by their impairments. For example, stairs disable a person who uses a wheelchair as opposed to their inability to walk. Therefore the exclusion of disabled people from aspects of society is due to barriers on a structural, cultural and personal level of society that are rooted in prejudice and discrimination. These barriers can range from inaccessible working environments through to inadequate disability benefits and devaluing disabled people through negative images in the media and discriminatory attitudes from individuals. The social model firmly highlights that disability is a form of oppression that gives rise to distinct forms of social inequality, disadvantage and exclusion.

CRITICAL THINKING

Impairment and disability – the experience of disabled people

The social model has successfully challenged the ideas and views of the medical model by establishing discourses on the way in which social structures and processes construct disability. In order to establish these discourses the social model initially has had to ignore impairment and underplay the very real effects of bodily differences and painful medical problems (Shakespeare, 2000). Any discussion of impairment has been left to medical discourses. This strategy has particularly affected people with learning difficulties who are ignored or marginalised by the social model in two ways. Firstly there is a tendency to define impairment in terms of the physical as opposed to the mental functioning of the body (Chappell, 1998). Reference is frequently made to physical or sensory impairment to the exclusion of intellectual or mental impairment. Secondly the disability experienced by people with learning difficulties is largely perceived as having a predominantly biomedical cause (Goodley, 2001). There is a view that the split between impairment and disability does not help the development of a holistic understanding of the experiences of disabled people. Some theorists claim that impairment, like disability, should be viewed as socially constructed. This view challenges the binary division that places non-disabled people at the centre representing 'normality' and disabled people on the outside as the 'other' representing 'abnormality'. A task for the social model is to:

> look at impairment and the identity of the impaired person as something other than a deviation from the 'normal', able-bodied identity.

> *Source: Best (2005, p.106)*

The critical challenge is for the social model to be able to do this without diminishing people's embodied experiences of their physical, sensory and intellectual impairments.

Sexuality and disabled people

It is important that we have spent some time considering how contrasting perspectives influence the different ways that disabled people are viewed in our society as these same perspectives will also influence to a greater or lesser extent the perception and construction of disabled people's sexuality.

ACTIVITY 5.1

What do you think are some of the commonly held views about disabled people's sexuality? What ideas are these views based on?

Comment

We should not be surprised to find that owing to the differences amongst disabled people, there are some widely held but contradictory views. Disabled people are commonly assumed to be either asexual and innocent, or oversexed and dangerous (Best, 2005). These views or discourses are influenced to some extent by the person's impairment. For example, a person with a cognitive impairment or mental health issue is perceived as being oversexed whereas a person with a physical impairment is perceived as asexual. Society's response to these discourses has been to deny, regulate and control the sexuality of disabled people (Priestley, 2003). In order to analyse the ideas that these views are based on we will consider in more detail the way sexuality and disability are constructed in Western society.

The social construction of disabled people's sexuality

Analysing the social construction of people's sexuality is particularly complex when they experience *overlapping intersections of difference from the norm* (O'Toole, 2000). For example, in the UK a gay, black, disabled man will experience three sets of predominantly negative discourses about his sexuality linked to his three areas of difference from the norm, those of sexual orientation, ethnicity and disability. When these sets of discourses come together, or intersect, they interact with each other resulting in changing, or modifying or giving additional support to the discourses that construct a view of a person's sexuality. Therefore many of the discourses that you have been introduced to in previous chapters will have relevance to disabled people. For example, discourses involved in the social construction of young people's sexuality will affect young disabled people who will also be affected by the discourses involved in the social construction of disabled people's sexuality.

Asexual

Asexuality is a dominant discourse in relation to disabled people's sexuality, particularly impacting on people with a physical impairment (Milligan and Neufeldt, 2001) and is supported in three ways. Firstly disabled people are treated as children, due to their perceived dependency, passivity and fragility. This process of infantilisation associates disabled people with sexual innocence, asexuality and the need for protection from sexual abuse.

The difference between young non-disabled people, whose sexuality is also associated with these ideas, and disabled people of all ages is that the latter are perceived as being 'eternal children' (Shakespeare et al., 1996, p.162) who will never be sexual. Secondly as we are already aware the image of sexuality and in particular sexual attractiveness in Western society is associated with the young, fit and 'perfectly formed' body. People perceived as outside of this ideal, such as disabled people with a visible impairment are regarded as asexual or repulsive if seen being sexual (Bonnie, 2004). Thirdly there is a perception that disabled people will not be able to engage in 'normal' penetrative heterosexual sexual intercourse because of their impairment. As we have seen, equating sexuality with (hetero)sexual activity is a narrow but powerful view of 'normal' sexual expression and people who are unable or choose not to engage sexually in this way are often deemed as asexual or perverted. People with a cognitive impairment or mental health issue are perceived as having the ability to 'perform' (hetero)sexually but thought to have *limited social judgement, and therefore, lack the capacity to engage in responsible sexual relationships* (Milligan and Neufeldt, 2001, p.92).

ACTIVITY 5.2

How do you think the discourse of asexuality in relation to disabled people is perpetuated in society? Give some examples.

Comment

Silence is the main way that the discourse of asexuality is perpetuated. As you will know from previous discussions about older people's sexuality, silence or absence is a particularly powerful mechanism that creates 'invisibility', which implies insignificance or 'abnormality'. For example, disabled people are rarely included in theoretical or practical discussions regarding sexuality or have their sexuality represented in everyday life in terms of the media and popular culture (Bonnie, 2004). Silence can result in exclusion from health and social care services. For example, young disabled people are excluded from appropriate sex and relationship education and in some instances are discouraged from articulating issues regarding their sexuality and sexual needs (Choppin, 2005).

Oversexed

Being oversexed and presenting a threat or danger to others is another dominant discourse in relation to disabled people's sexuality, particularly impacting on people with a cognitive impairment or mental health issue (Priestley, 2003). This discourse has been perpetuated in society through proliferation, where excessive attention has been paid to perceiving sexuality in terms of deviancy (Bailey, 2000). Nursing and care staff focus their efforts on preventing people masturbating in public or dealing with allegations of sexual abuse, neglecting to also provide support for the development of loving sexual relationships (Priestley, 2003). People with learning difficulties have felt the impact of both of the dominant discourses being regarded as oversexed and a threat on the one hand and asexual and an eternal child on the other. This has led to a serious neglect and denial of their sexual needs.

Any signs of sexual interest or arousal were ignored, repressed or misunderstood...it was thought essential to keep [people with learning difficulties] in a state of ignorance about sex.

(McCarthy, 1999, p.53)

Although there have been developments in ways of working positively and effectively with people with learning difficulties in all aspects of their sexuality (McCarthy, 1999), support workers and parents can still perceive sexual activity as problematic before considering emotional and health needs (Disability Now, 2005). The 'oversexed' discourse has not only resulted in the denial of sexual needs but also given rise to the regulation and control of disabled women's sexuality through the practice of institutionalisation and the use of compulsory/'voluntary' sterilisation and contraception. This policy was known as 'eugenics', which involved preventing people who were perceived as 'less fit' from reproducing, such as women with learning difficulties, mental health issues or who were 'morally defective' (Priestley, 2003). (See Priestley, 2003 in 'Further reading' for a detailed account of the history of the eugenics movement.) The legacy of the eugenic policies of the nineteenth and twentieth centuries can be seen in the way that disabled women are often discouraged from becoming mothers by being advised that their impairment will result in their incapacity to parent or that their child may 'inherit their problem' (Hughes, 2004). As a result disabled women find that their reproductive rights are constrained through lack of appropriate sexual and reproductive health care, together with a social resistance to the concept of disabled women becoming mothers (Kallianes and Rubenfield, 1997).

Sexuality represented?

There is an assumption of heterosexuality in any 'positive' representation of disabled people's sexuality (Whitney, 2006). Five hundred thousand lesbian, gay and bisexual disabled people are estimated to be living in the UK (Rainbow Ripples and Butler, 2006), many of whom experience discrimination based on their sexual orientation from heterosexual disabled people and discrimination based on their impairment from lesbian, gay and bisexual non-disabled people (Fish, 2006). Many lesbian, gay and bisexual disabled people cope by trying to make an aspect of their identity invisible (Shakespeare, 1999). For instance, some disabled people will present themselves as heterosexual to become accepted within their personal social network and the wider disabled communities and others who do not have an obvious or visible impairment will present themselves as non-disabled to gain acceptance within the lesbian, gay and bisexual communities. Consequently disabled people engage with the process of 'coming out' on many aspects of their identity by coming out as disabled, coming out as sexual and for some coming out as lesbian, gay or bisexual (Shakespeare, 1999). As well as an assumed heterosexuality, disabled people's sexuality is overwhelmingly discussed in a limited and functional way. Whilst focusing on sexual technique and fertility issues, broader psychosocial aspects of sexuality in terms of emotions, relationships and identity are neglected and rarely represented (McCarthy, 1999).

As we have been discussing the main discourses that have made up the social construction of disabled people's sexuality, you will have noticed the influence of the themes of the medical model of disability. In particular the discourses have focused on people's impairment as the cause for not being able to benefit from a 'normal' sexuality. Representations of disabled people's sexuality that claim to be positive also tend to focus on people's impairment and limitations.

Experiencing disabled sexuality

The exclusion of disabled people from many aspects of our society means that they have very little control over the way they are defined and represented (Best, 2005). As we have seen from our earlier discussion it is non-disabled people's sexuality which is used as the 'frame of reference' for 'normality' against which disabled people's sexuality is defined, compared and represented. We felt it was therefore important to include disabled people's experiences and views of their sexuality by presenting some of the main themes recently highlighted by the disability movement.

Sexuality as a disability rights issue

> *Sexuality is often the source of our deepest oppression; it is also often the source of our deepest pain. It's easier for us to talk about – and formulate strategies for changing – discrimination in employment, education and housing than to talk about our exclusion from sexuality and reproduction.*

> (Finger, 1992, p.9)

Disability rights have tended to concentrate on discrimination in the 'public' sphere of life, with sexuality being ignored, marginalised and regarded as a 'private' issue. However, there is a growing recognition from disabled people that issues within the 'public' and 'private' spheres of life are interwoven and one cannot be tackled without the other.

> *For the first time now I'm beginning to believe that sexuality, the one area above all others to have been ignored, is at the absolute core of what we're working for...you can't get closer to the essence of self...than sexuality.*

> (Shakespeare, 2000, p.165)

Barriers to sexual expression

> *The problem of disabled sexuality is not how to do it, but who to do it with. The barriers to sexual expression...are primarily to do with society in which we live, not the bodies with which we are endowed.*

> (Shakespeare, 2000, p.161)

Disabled people are highlighting the importance of adopting a social model of disabled sexuality so that society's barriers to sexual expression can be identified and challenged. As we have already discussed, barriers for disabled people are created through their exclusion from many aspects of society.

ACTIVITY 5.3

What do you think are some of society's barriers that make it difficult for a disabled person to start a sexual relationship?

Comment

Disabled people state that they are excluded from most of the *socialisation processes that help teach and prepare people for love, sex and intimacy* (Davies, 2000). Some of society's barriers include:

- a denial of appropriate sex and relationship education;

- a lack of opportunity to meet potential partners through being denied access to work, education and social spaces;

- society's negative attitudes towards disabled sexuality;

- as a result of being systematically devalued and excluded, disabled people can have feelings of low self esteem which are not compatible with trying to start new and positive sexual relationships (Shakespeare, 2000).

'Normal' sexuality challenged

The struggle for many disabled people to conform to the conventional notions of gender and sexuality has prompted some to challenge the masculine and feminine ideal and the way that sexuality is expressed in Western societies. For example, some disabled men with visible physical impairment experience sexual oppression because their bodies represent inferiority, weakness and dependency (Best, 2005). This has resulted in some heterosexual men identifying more with their disability as opposed to their heterosexuality, resulting in a feeling of liberation in terms of how they dress, how they act and how they are sexually (Shakespeare, 2000). For some disabled people the limitations of their impairment have encouraged them to push the boundaries of how to be sexually active and to create alternative ways of giving and receiving pleasure.

> *If you are a sexually active disabled person and comfortable with the sexual side of your life, it is remarkable how dull and unimaginative non-disabled people's sex lives can appear. (Penny)*

> (Shakespeare et al., 1996, p.202).

Sexual pleasure

Discussion regarding sexuality and disability has tended to ignore the issue of sexual pleasure (Tepper, 2000). Disabled people are asserting the importance of sexual pleasure in their lives for enhancing intimate relationships and promoting their sense of physical, emotional and social well-being. This is an important assertion because often disabled people are assumed to be physiologically incapable of sexual pleasure or assumed to be more interested in their reproductive rather than pleasure capacity. As a result sexual well-being in the broader sense is ignored. It is important therefore that disabled people who are finding it difficult to access sexual pleasure are given the right support, advice and information.

Belonging and recognition

Disabled people's sexuality should not be *narrowly defined as a matter of sexual desire and physical entwining* (Shakespeare, 2000, p.166). Sexuality should be viewed broadly to include identities, relationships, desires, acts, beliefs and rights. This directly challenges the predominantly medical view of disabled people's sexuality. For example, for disabled people who are physically impaired there is a tendency to focus on the physical undertaking of sexual activity, whereas for people who are cognitively impaired or experience a mental health issue the focus tends to be around preventing pregnancy and sexually transmitted infections. Disabled people are highlighting that they need control over their bodies, feelings and relationships; access to representations, relationships and public spaces; and choice regarding their identities, lifestyles and experiences. These aspects would enable disabled people to achieve full recognition and a sense of belonging (Shakespeare, 2000).

These themes that have been identified by disabled people make up an alternative discourse. The social model of disability is influential in this discourse in challenging the medical model's emphasis on impairment and identifying society's barriers to disabled sexuality. However, this alternative discourse goes further as it also gives the sense that disabled people are not going to now become 'victims' of social oppression and are *resisting and exercising agency* (Shakespeare, 2003, p.148) by defining their experiences of sexuality for themselves.

Sexuality, disabled people and social work practice

Social work with disabled people takes place in different settings and for different reasons and any issues of sexuality will be wide ranging to reflect the diversity amongst disabled people. As we cannot cover all aspects of disabled people's sexuality we intend to give you an opportunity to consider some of the issues that you may find yourself working with as social workers. We start by considering some of the issues which will be relevant to working with all disabled people regardless of their differences.

General issues for social work practice

ACTIVITY 5.4

Use the discussions we have had so far in this chapter and undertake the following tasks.

- *Identify and write down the main issues that you think affect all disabled people's sexuality.*

- *What are the implications of the issues you have identified for social work practice?*

Comment

This exercise is a useful way to identify aspects and tasks of the social work role that would make up the basis from which to work effectively and sensitively with disabled people. We have identified the following three areas and would argue that together they make up a solid value base.

- We feel that it is essential for social workers to adopt the social model of disabled sexuality as it enables work with the service user to identify and address structural and social barriers to sexual expression. For example, many disabled people struggle to achieve the same level of privacy as non-disabled people as many aspects of their lives are monitored through the receipt of care packages or living in supported accommodation or residential care (Shildrick, 2004). This level of intrusion can have a detrimental affect on the development and continuation of sexual relationships. The social work role may involve working with other professionals such as support workers to explore ways that privacy could be assured at specific times.

- Social workers, whilst recognising the impact of structural barriers, must not neglect the role and impact of impairment on the lives of disabled people (Shakespeare, 2000). It is not possible for social workers to have in-depth knowledge about the physiological or emotional impact of every type of impairment on a person's sexuality. It is important therefore that social workers recognise that it is the service users who are the experts in relation to how the impairment impacts on their sexuality. Social workers need to be able to engage sensitively and empathically so that disabled service users feel able to share information that is particularly personal.

- Social workers need to be able to challenge and identify how oppressive discourses such as 'asexuality' or 'oversexed' influence care practices and service delivery. For example, assessments of need involving disabled people do not include issues of sexuality and care staff tend to ignore the sexual needs of disabled people or view their sexuality as problematic (Valios, 2001). Social workers need to recognise the negative effects these discourses can also have on disabled people's self image and self-worth (Shakespeare, 2003).

In order to give some coherency to the rest of this chapter we intend to discuss some specific practice issues separately in relation to people with physical impairment, people with cognitive impairment and people with mental health issues. By doing this we are not intending to suggest that the impairment itself is the main determining feature in relation to sexuality issues. However, we do maintain that the social response to disabled people's sexuality differs according to the type of impairment, which in turn influences the way disabled people's sexuality is constructed. This can then influence what issues of sexuality are raised within the social worker/service user relationship. We also need to point out that some disabled people experience more than one type of impairment.

Disabled people with physical impairment

The issues of sexuality vary enormously amongst disabled people with physical impairment and can be influenced to an extent by when in the life course the person acquired their impairment. For example, someone who acquires a spinal injury when they are in their thirties will generally experience a sympathetic response from society for their 'lost' sexuality

(Shakespeare, 2003). Research has found that people who acquire an impairment later in life experience difficulties in adjusting and integrating their impairment into their new self. This is particularly the case for men, who show lower levels of sexual satisfaction and body esteem in comparison with men who have been impaired from an early age (Kedde and van Berlo, 2006). Social workers need to be aware that in this situation the person will experience loss of their sexuality as they knew it and any current sexual relationship(s) will have to undergo a substantial readjustment. In contrast, a person with a congenital impairment or an impairment which was acquired at an early age would not be regarded by society as experiencing a loss in relation to their sexuality because of being perceived as asexual. In spite of this, studies have found that people who have been physically impaired from an early age integrate their disability into all aspects of their sexual development (Mona et al., 1994). Social workers need to recognise that although this group of disabled people may not have immediate loss issues, there may be issues around identity and asserting their sexuality.

ACTIVITY **5.5**

Case study

You are on placement as a student social worker at a resource centre for disabled adults with physical impairments. You overhear a debate between four of the service users about how direct payments can be used. Two of the service users are saying that they use the money to employ a personal assistant but that they are unclear about whether a personal assistant could be asked to provide various forms of assistance that they may need in order for them to be able to participate in sexual activity with their partners, such as undressing or help onto the bed. Everyone seems to be unclear and they ask you for your advice.

Make a note of some of the issues and dilemmas of asking for and providing this type of assistance, which is referred to as 'facilitated sex'. How would you respond to the group of service users in the case study?

Comment

Assessment of need under the NHS Community Care Act 1990 excludes issues of sexuality and sexual need and care packages reflect this by only providing assistance with aspects of daily living such as eating, washing, dressing, cooking and shopping. The availability of the direct payments scheme has given disabled people the freedom to employ their own personal assistants and specify themselves what assistance they need. Many disabled people define their sexuality and being able to express themselves sexually as a need and argue that if they require assistance with basic care needs then they will require assistance to participate in sexual activity. Much of the assistance includes routine tasks of helping someone undress ready for sexual activity or bathing someone after sexual activity, but can include requests to assist the disabled person to masturbate, accompany the disabled person to a sex club or negotiating prices and services of sex workers. The question is whether it is justifiable to exclude certain people from the expression of their sexuality if the situation could be alleviated through assistance. The issue of facilitated sex raises many legal, ethical and moral issues which are not easily solved. At the moment in the UK the situation is unregulated and allows disabled people the freedom to negotiate directly with their personal assistants and to employ only people who are comfortable with sexual issues and who are aware that they might be asked to provide sexual assistance. This freedom, however, offers no protection or guidance to the disabled person or the personal assistants with regard to professional boundaries and the possibilities of sexual exploitation and sexual abuse. Research suggests that training for personal assistants needs to be developed to include issues of sexuality along with a Code of Practice for Facilitated Sexual Expression (Bonnie, 2004, p.130) which could act as a framework for negotiations between disabled people and personal assistants (Bonnie, 2004). There is recognition that the issue of facilitated sex is morally complex but that the sexual needs of disabled people are more likely to be met if things are discussed in an open and frank manner (Earle, 1999):

> *Sebastian: You've got to be clear right at the beginning about what you want and what you expect from your carer. To me, sexuality must be treated the same way as any other thing.*

> (Earle, 1999, p.319)

(See Browne and Russell, 2005, in 'Further reading' section for discussion around the issue of professional boundaries and facilitated sex.)

Disabled people with cognitive impairment

ACTIVITY 5.6

Case study

You are on placement as a student social worker in a community learning disability team. You have been assisting Simon, a 35-year-old white British man, to move into community-supported accommodation following the death of his mother who had been his main carer. Simon has a 'mild learning difficulty' but is able to undertake his personal care needs. Simon is hoping through your support to become fully autonomous in all aspects of his daily life. On your last visit Simon started to talk to you about how he 'fancied men' and that he would like to start a sexual relationship with a man. He also mentioned that over the last few years he had tried to talk to his mother about sexual matters but she had refused to talk to him, telling him that 'such matters shouldn't concern people like you'.

What do you think are the main issues in relation to sexuality that need to be taken into consideration in terms of your social work involvement with Simon?

Comment

The government White Paper *Valuing People*, which outlines the strategy to facilitate people with learning difficulties to live full and autonomous lives within the community, states that:

> *Good services will help people with learning difficulties develop opportunities to form relationships, including ones of a physical and sexual nature. It is important that people can receive accessible sex education and information about relationships and contraception.*

> (DoH, 2001e, p.81)

There is clear recognition that issues of sexuality such as sexual relationships and sexual expression can be an important part of life for people with learning difficulties and that support services such as social workers have an 'enabling' role. We have identified some of the main issues that we feel need to be incorporated into this role if the support is to be effective and positive. You may have identified some of these issues when you were considering the case study of Simon.

- The value base we identified earlier which included adopting the social model of disability whilst recognising people's limitations in relation to their impairment, needs to underpin the enabling role. As well as identifying and challenging oppressive discourses regarding the sexuality of people with learning difficulties it is important to be able to offer non-judgmental and positive support around the choice of sexual orientation.

- Sexuality should be seen as a priority and reflected in the service user's person-centred plan. Practitioners should be proactive in offering service users opportunities to reflect on their needs in terms of sexuality and relationships (Abbott and Howarth, 2005).

- The person's level of knowledge regarding issues of sexuality needs to be established together with her/his level of cognitive impairment. This enables both the social worker and the service user to identify what sexual issues need to be discussed and how the information can be made accessible. Sexual issues can be divided into three broad areas. Firstly, basic sex education involving discussions around the biological aspects of sexual activity. It is important that this includes all sexual orientations. Secondly, safer sex which includes not only the prevention of sexually transmitted infections and pregnancy but also enabling the person with learning difficulties to develop an understanding of how to keep safe when engaging in sexual activities. It is important that people with learning difficulties learn to recognise their vulnerability and know what to do in situations of sexual abuse, coercion and exploitation. The issue of consent needs to be discussed together with the right to say 'no' to sexual activity at any time. Thirdly, relationships, which involves discussing how to achieve fulfilling and enjoyable sexual relationships. People with learning difficulties need to develop their skills of negotiation and be able to assert what they want in sexual relationships without becoming abusive themselves. This is a complex process as it involves being able to identify the power dynamics within a sexual relationship. In our case study Simon appears to have little knowledge of sexual issues so it would be useful to plan a series of sessions with him so that he is able to build up his awareness and understanding gradually. Information and accessible materials can be obtained from the local Family Planning Association (see **www.fpa.org.uk**). (See also McCarthy and Thompson, 2007, training pack for practitioners working with people with learning difficulties.)

- An important aspect of the enabling role is to ensure that other professionals, parents and significant others involved in the service user's support network are not creating barriers to the development of sexuality and sexual relationships. Work may have to be undertaken with other people if there is a degree of resistance or if there are discriminatory views being expressed in terms of gay, lesbian or bisexual relationships. Residential homes and supported living accommodation should have policies indicating that residents have rights to form sexual relationships and as a consequence care practices should support service users' privacy and access to private spaces. It is important that you are clear that you are there to support the service user's rights and that *your concern is protection through education, rather than vulnerability through ignorance* (Abbott and Howarth, 2005, p.54).

- People with learning difficulties like Simon in the case study who want same-sex relationships or identify as lesbian, gay or bisexual can have particular difficulties in feeling supported. Setting up support or social groups for this particular group of people may be a way of strengthening their support networks. (See Abbott and Howarth, 2005, in 'Further reading' for other ideas on developing support).

RESEARCH SUMMARY

Secret loves, hidden lives?

Research with nine women and 11 men with learning difficulties who were having or wanted to have same-sex relationships revealed the following issues.

- *Participants' accounts of coming out were dominated by a fear of rejection, in particular that they might as a result be asked to leave services or organisations that they valued.*

- *Many participants had felt, and some continued to feel, that there was something wrong with their sexuality.*

- *Nineteen out of the 20 participants reported being bullied or harassed as a direct result of their sexuality. Much of the verbal abuse came from close family members but many of the participants had experienced heterosexism from professionals.*

- *The support the participants felt they received from the lesbian and gay 'scene' was varied, with some participants feeling excluded or discriminated against because of their learning difficulty.*

- *Women's relationships with women remain more hidden than men's relationships with each other and the recruitment of women participants to this research study had been difficult.*

- *Being lesbian, gay or bisexual was an important part of the participants' identity and despite the barriers many of the participants' stories about their sexuality were strong and positive.*

I suppose my ultimate dream is to be with someone who I'm going to be with for the rest of my life, who I'm going to love and cherish for the rest of my life. (Stephen)

(Abbott and Howarth, 2005, p.27).

Source: Abbott and Howarth (2005)

Disabled people with mental health issues

On the whole sexuality issues are not well addressed by the mental health services because of two main factors (Took, 2004). Firstly the sexuality of mental health service users has been constructed as dangerous and 'antisocial' and responded to as behaviour that needs to be controlled and managed. This has resulted in a neglect of wider sexual health needs that concern people with mental health issues. Secondly the classification of 'homosexuality' as a mental illness up until 1992 has left a legacy of negative, hostile and discriminatory attitudes towards lesbian, gay and bisexual mental health service users (Took, 2004). The context of mental health, however, is changing with a shift of emphasis away from 'cure' to 'recovery' and encouraging service users to live with dignity, maximum self-determination and to the highest level of role functioning as possible. It is argued that the expression of sexuality and the establishment of intimacy is an important part of that recovery process (Cook, 2000).

Many mental health service users experience similar barriers to other disabled people in terms of their sexuality. The following are the main issues which we feel are important in terms of the implications for social work practice.

- Many mental health residential units lack privacy, which forces people to engage in sexual activity which is rushed, risky and degrading.

- Mental health service users often experience a combination of a lack of self-esteem and a lack of confidence as a result of internalising society's views about mental health and sexuality.

- Sexual health needs are ignored through lack of understanding, care and support from health and social care providers (Cook, 2000). For example, symptoms such as delusions, hallucinations and depression can make it difficult for people to form and maintain lasting relationships. Additionally antipsychotic medication has side-effects that can cause sexual disinterest and dysfunction (Gray et al., 2002). The combination of mental health issues and medication does not however remove the desire for sexual contact. The absence of self-worth, sexual health information, professional support and society's barriers means that many mental health service users struggle to practice safer sex (Cook, 2000).

- Many women mental health service users have a history of experiencing sexual violence which acts as a psychological barrier to forming satisfying sexual relationships (Cook, 2000).

- Lesbian, gay and bisexual people are not prone to mental health issues any more than heterosexual people but the discrimination that they experience within society can affect their mental health. Their emotional problems are exacerbated by the marginalisation they experience when using the mental health services (McFarlane, 1998). PACE is a London-based charity which promotes the mental health and emotional well-being of people who are lesbian, gay, bisexual and transgender. It works with mental health services to promote anti-discriminatory practices and the development of therapeutic support services (www.pacehealth.org.uk).

What do you think are the main implications for social work practice of these issues?

Comment

You will have identified many implications for social work practice with mental health service users in relation to issues of sexuality. We have identified the following issues.

- Sexual issues should be considered as part of a holistic approach to assessment and care planning.

- People should have access to general sexual health advice and information as well as specific information in relation to the impact of medication and mental health issues on sexuality.

- Therapeutic support that recognises and builds on people's strengths should be available to facilitate the exploration of issues of sexual violence and sexual orientation that may be acting as barriers to forming fulfilling relationships. The goal of any therapeutic support should be self worth and confidence.

- Social workers need to work closely with other professionals and encourage the development of clear written policies that protect service users from sexual harassment and sexual abuse whilst positively developing their sexual well-being.

Sexual violence

It is important to appreciate that working with disabled people on issues of sexuality may prompt discussions and disclosures of sexual violence. Disabled women, in particular women with learning difficulties, experience high levels of sexual violence in comparison with non-disabled women (McCarthy, 1999; Shildrick, 2004). Disabled people generally are offered the same degree of protection against sexual offences as non-disabled people under the Sexual Offences Act 2003 (see Chapter 7 for detail of the Act). Disabled people with a 'mental disorder' as defined by the Mental Health Act 2007 which includes people with a learning difficulty, however, are offered further protection within the Sexual Offences Act 2003. This group of people can be deemed to be unable to give consent to sexual activity because of a lack of understanding or that they have, through their vulnerability, been coerced into giving their consent by inducements, threats and deceptions (Home Office, 2004c). Disabled people are also protected by the 'No Secrets' guidelines (DoH, 2000) which we refer to in Chapter 4 about older people. These guidelines will be further strengthened with the implementation in 2008 of the Safeguarding Vulnerable Groups Act 2006.

C H A P T E R   S U M M A R Y

This chapter has introduced you to some of the key issues and debates in relation to disabled people and sexuality. You should be able to demonstrate your understanding of the influence of the medical model of disability on the social construction of disabled people's sexuality and the challenge presented by the social model of disabled sexuality together with the themes from the disability movement. A key learning point from this chapter is the recognition of the way that disability is yet another aspect of a person's identity that impacts on their sexuality and creates further diversity in terms of experiences. You should feel able to engage positively with disabled people on issues of sexuality and be able to identify ways that society's barriers can be challenged through social work practice.

FURTHER READING

Abbott, D and Howarth, J (2005) *Secret loves, hidden lives? Exploring issues for people with learning difficulties who are gay, lesbian or bisexual*. Bristol: The Policy Press.

Research with lesbian, gay and bisexual people with learning difficulties which highlights examples of good practice and contains practical recommendations for staff and services.

Brown, J and Russell, S (2005) My home, your workplace: people with physical disability negotiate their sexual health without crossing professional boundaries. *Disability and Society*, 20(4): 375–388.

Research study exploring how sexual well-being is facilitated or denied and the implications for professional boundaries.

McCarthy, M (1999) *Sexuality and women with learning disabilities*. London: Jessica Kingsley.

A comprehensive book looking at the issues of sexuality and women with learning difficulties.

McCarthy, M and Thompson, D (2007) *Sex and the 3Rs: Rights, responsibilities and risks*. Brighton: Pavilion Publishing.

A training pack for practitioners working with people with learning difficulties which focuses on issues of sexuality.

Priestley, M (2003) *Disability: a life course approach*. Cambridge: Polity Press.

Chapter 2 gives a comprehensive review of eugenics.

Shakespeare, T, Gillespie-Sells, K and Davies, D (1996) *The sexual politics of disability: Untold desires*. London: Cassell.

Pioneering research involving the stories of disabled people and their experiences of their sexuality.

Sexuality and Disability **www.springerlink.com/content/104972/**

A journal covering a range of issues focusing on sexuality and disability.

Chapter 6

Sexuality, HIV and social work

Introduction

The UK's first National Strategy for Sexual Health and HIV (DoH, 2001a) was launched to address the growing increase of sexually transmitted infections (STIs) and HIV. In 2004, £300 million was made available to the primary care trusts for sexual health services (DoH, 2004), and in 2005 the government made sexual health a priority for the National Health Service. Despite this the UK has the fastest-growing HIV epidemic in Western Europe and the Health Protection Agency statistics show a rise in poor sexual health generally (Terrence Higgins Trust, 2007). HIV is predominantly transmitted through sexual activity and the focus of this chapter will be exploring issues of sexuality in relation to HIV.

HIV – relevance for social work

The International Federation of Social Workers has an International Policy on HIV/AIDS (1990) and a Social Work Manifesto on HIV/AIDS (2000). In both documents it is argued that social workers are crucial to the fight against HIV and bring with them a commitment to social justice, an ability to work in a range of health and social care settings, as well as a psychosocial perspective on people and their issues. In relation to social work in the UK there has been no recent reference to HIV by the British Association of Social Workers, or any reference within the Requirements for Social Work Training (DoH, 2002b). Guidelines issued in respect of the preceding qualification to the social work degree, which we feel are still very relevant today, state that in relation to HIV social workers have a dual role, that of working in the area of HIV prevention and working with people living with and affected by HIV (Turner, 1992). Many local authorities provide specialist HIV support services and social workers (see **www.hants.gov.uk/HIVwhatweprovide.html** as an example).

HIV – basic facts and information

RESEARCH SUMMARY

What is HIV?

HIV stands for human immunodeficiency virus, which is a retrovirus that infects and gradually destroys a person's immune system. HIV infects a person's CD4 cells, which co-ordinate the immune system's fight against infection. Therefore a person with HIV has reduced protection against infection and cancers. It is a delicate virus that does not survive outside the body for long and is easily killed by air, heat, detergents and bleach. A person living with the virus can describe their 'status' as HIV antibody positive or HIV positive. It follows that a person who does not have HIV would describe their 'status' as HIV antibody negative or HIV negative. A person is tested for antibodies to the virus as opposed to the virus itself. It can take up to three months for antibodies to develop, which is known as the 'window period'. The obvious implications of this are that people may believe they have been infected but cannot take a test until antibodies develop.

What is AIDS?

AIDS stands for acquired immune deficiency syndrome and is used medically to refer to a collection of specific infections, such as cancers or pneumonia, that establish themselves in the body of someone whose immune system has been weakened by HIV. People therefore do not actually die from AIDS but from a particular infection(s). Although there is no cure for HIV, since 1996 there have been antiretroviral drug treatments which benefit many people by controlling and suppressing the onset of infections. HIV and its related infections are perceived much more as chronic conditions, as opposed to acute and life-threatening illnesses. Therefore the term AIDS is now very rarely used and it is more usual to talk of HIV-related infections or possibly advanced HIV infection. It is important to note here that the situation in low- and middle-income countries, such as sub-Saharan Africa, is very different, with no or limited access to treatments.

How is HIV transmitted?

If HIV is to be transmitted from one person to another, three conditions need to apply, that of presence/quality of HIV, quantity of HIV and a route of transmission.

Presence/quality

Firstly, the virus must be present in the body of an infected person, or in a contaminated body fluid or body tissue. The virus must be of a suitable quality to cause infection, that is, undamaged by heat, air or bleach.

Quantity

Secondly, there must be adequate quantity or high concentration of the virus present to cause infection. HIV may be present in many body fluids, but the only ones which constitute a risk for infection are blood, semen, vaginal fluids and breast milk. Body fluids such as saliva and tears do not contain HIV in sufficient concentration to be able to transmit the virus. It is important here to distinguish between HIV being 'found in' and being 'transmitted via' particular body fluids.

Route of transmission

Thirdly, HIV can only be transmitted and cause infection if it gets into the body via a route where vulnerable cells are plentiful. There are only four proven, substantial routes of transmission, which we have listed below.

- *Unprotected (no condom) penetrative sexual intercourse (vaginally or anally) with a person with HIV (male or female) leading to a transfer of sexual body fluids (seminal, vaginal, menstrual blood) from one person to another.*

- *Sharing unsterilised injection equipment which has been previously used by someone who is infected.*

- *From a mother who is infected, to her baby, which may happen during the course of pregnancy, at birth or through breast feeding.*

- *Injections or transfusion of contaminated blood or blood products. However, due to blood donor screening and heat-treating processes this risk has virtually been eliminated in the UK. Donations of semen (artificial insemination), skin grafts and organ transplants taken from someone who is infected also pose a risk of transmission.*

The three conditions, presence/quality, quantity and route of transmission, can be visualised as a 'chain' which must not be broken in any place if infection is to occur. In other words, if any one of these conditions is not present then the 'chain' is broken and the transmission of HIV from one person to another cannot occur.

Source: www.aidsmap.com

ACTIVITY *6.1*

Case study: what is a risk?

You are on placement as a student social worker at a mental health day centre. Three service users are having a heated discussion about how people 'catch' HIV. There is disagreement about whether or not oral sex is safe and one service user is becoming particularly anxious because she had read in a newspaper that someone had been infected with HIV after stepping on a used syringe. A fourth service user joins the discussion and says that he is not worried about 'catching' HIV because he is not gay. No one can agree and they ask you what you think.

Use the research summary you have just read and make some notes about how you would explain the ways that HIV is transmitted, listing any issues that you feel need to be taken into account when undertaking this type of work.

Comment

Your information needs to be clear and accurate and it is important to check the service users' understanding of what you have said. We have highlighted the following issues that need to be taken into account when working with service users around HIV transmission.

- There has been a tendency for people on the one hand to deny proven ways of transmission, such as unprotected penetrative sexual intercourse, and on the other hand perpetuate highly unlikely ways of transmission, such as stepping on a used syringe. This focus on a 'theoretical' risk, which is a risk that is possible in principle but highly unlikely in practice, can frequently be used by people to avoid looking at their own risk behaviour. In relation to the case study your role would be to try to avoid theoretical arguments regarding the risk of contracting HIV from stepping on used syringes and sensitively encourage the service user concerned to explore the basis of her anxiety and to refocus on her own sexual and drug-using behaviour.

- It is important that people understand that it is their behaviour that is the important factor in determining whether they are at risk of becoming HIV positive as opposed to what group they do or do not identify with. For example, a heterosexual woman places herself at risk of contracting HIV if she engages in unprotected penetrative sexual intercourse with a heterosexual man. The belief that identifying as heterosexual in some way protects people from contracting HIV not only fuels oppressive attitudes towards lesbians, gay men and bisexuals but also highlights the fact that people have not grasped the basic facts of HIV transmission. In relation to the case study you should be alerted to the possibility that the service user concerned is assessing his own risks based on the misinformation that contracting HIV depends on sexual orientation as opposed to sexual behaviour (Alcorn, 1997a, b).

- Any work with service users around HIV transmission needs to be explicit and precise, in order to enable people to assess risks for themselves. For example, statements such as 'having sex' or 'using heroin' are too vague and do not explain what is going on in terms of actual behaviour. 'Having sex' for some people may mean having a massage, kissing and cuddling, and 'using heroin' may mean smoking the drug. None of these specific behaviours would put a person at risk of contracting HIV. In the case study it would be essential to explore with the group of service users what they mean by oral sex and to present them with a range of different situational examples involving oral sex so they start to analyse the 'variations on a theme' for themselves. This type of approach encourages and empowers people to develop skills to assess risks for themselves in the future.

HIV – the social context

Reflecting on the previous case study you will have become aware that as we go beyond basic information we start to grapple with the complexities of HIV. It is important that we do not view HIV purely in medical terms but also analyse the way that cultural, structural, political and economic aspects of societies shape, influence and socially construct people's experiences of the virus.

Sexuality and HIV

Sexuality has become very significant in our culture and has pivotal place and function in our identity. It is therefore important to consider how sexuality was being perceived at the time AIDS/HIV emerged in Western societies.

Before sexual liberalisation

As you will recall from our discussions in Chapter 1, sexuality and in particular sexual behaviour has, since the beginning of Christianity, been perceived as needing regulation and surveillance. This role has been fulfilled by religion, the medicalisaton of sexuality and the state (Weeks, 2000). In the nineteenth century public health literature focused on outlining the norms of sexuality by defining what the difference was between 'normal' and 'abnormal' sexual acts and desires. 'Abnormal' or *disordered forms of sexuality* (Ryan, 2005, p.203), such as same-sex relationships, sexual relationships outside of marital heterosexual relationships and women working as sex workers, were all perceived as dangerous, a source of contagion and a threat to the social order (Ryan, 2005). Sexuality was something to be repressed and controlled, particularly if it was not linked to reproduction. There was a tension in the fact that not only was sexuality a way in which the population of a society could reproduce and grow, but it was also a potential threat to health and well-being (Foucault, 1973).

Sexual liberalisaton?

In the two decades leading up to the start of the AIDS/HIV epidemic in the early 1980s, sexuality had undergone rapid liberal changes in terms of attitudes and legislation. Legislative changes involving issues such as marriage and divorce, premarital sex, birth control and abortion, and same-sex relationships signalled a move to less harsh ways of regulating sexuality (Weeks, 2000). With homosexuality being partially decriminalised, people from lesbian and gay communities were living much more openly and women were challenging traditional gender roles. Although for some this sexual liberalisation was welcomed, for others it was perceived in the context of permissiveness and moral decline. It was a period of immense change and uncertainty for everyone where sexuality had become a public and dominant issue within society and politics (Weeks, 2000). This was the context within which AIDS/HIV first emerged, primarily affecting the male gay communities in America. For many people HIV/AIDS was the response to the perceived 'immorality' of the new sexual freedoms. The reactions were stigmatising and oppressive, and AIDS was referred to as the 'gay plague'. Gay men were perceived as having caused the syndrome through their sexual practices and for many it was confirmation that being gay was unnatural, dangerous and sinful (Dodds et al., 2004). This combination of sexuality, disease and death caused fear and panic and the belief that being gay was synonymous with AIDS. Gay identity has in effect been systematically linked to HIV/AIDS throughout the pandemic (Fish, 2006).

Social construction of HIV

The social construction of HIV/AIDS has always revolved around the risk of transmission of the virus. 'What is a risk?', 'who is a risk?' and 'who is at risk?' are questions that have dominated the HIV/AIDS discourses. We would like to give some consideration to how these questions have been answered.

Risk groups versus risk behaviour

The medical establishment and the media were both influential in the initial construction of HIV/AIDS as a disease that affected gay white men only. The construction of risk at this stage was very much perceived in terms of 'risk groups', and people outside of these groups were perceived as safe from HIV. This viewpoint served to perpetuate the misconception that the risk of contracting HIV had nothing to do with risk behaviour such as unprotected penetrative sexual intercourse but more to do with sexual orientation. This was later challenged by the number of reports of AIDS amongst people from black communities in America and in particular the increase of HIV/AIDS affecting people in African countries, where the route of transmission was and still is predominantly heterosexual. The perception of risk at this point started to change and everyone, regardless of their sexual orientation, was perceived to be at risk. HIV was now becoming associated with risk behaviour. Government response in terms of HIV policy and health education up to this point had been minimal. The realisation that everyone who engaged in risk behaviour could be at risk gave impetus to a general public health campaign. What in fact has transpired with regard to the spread of the virus is that it has been relatively contained within certain communities, such as gay men, people who inject drugs and people from African communities. The reason for this is that people choose their sexual and needle partners from within their own communities, exacerbating the spread of the virus within their own communities (Alcorn, 1997b). If it had been recognised by the government that communities who had been disproportionately affected by HIV would continue to be so, HIV education and care services could have been targeted properly to the areas of greatest need and risk.

The 'general population'

This realisation that HIV is a threat to everyone does nothing to lessen the stigma that certain communities experience. This view of groups is still pervasive and constructed in terms of a 'threat to others', meaning a threat to the 'general population'. This term refers to everyone who is not a member of, or associated with, a 'high-risk group', who are viewed not only as 'at risk of' HIV but also as 'a risk to' the 'general population' (Ryan,

2005). Deconstructing the term 'general population' in relation to HIV reveals that it unreservedly includes heterosexual men (Waldby, 1996). The position of heterosexual women depends on their 'sexual status'. For example, heterosexual women are included in the 'general population' if they are married, monogamous, virgins or act as guardians by adopting the role of *enforcers of safe sex practice* (Waldby, 1996, p.86). Exclusion for heterosexual women may happen if they are sex workers, sexually active, pregnant, partners of bisexual men or men who inject drugs or unable to negotiate safer sex (Waldby, 1996). It is important here to bring in the issue of ethnicity and to state that being a person from a black and minority ethnic community and in particular an African community would exclude you from the 'general population'. We highlighted in our discussions in Chapter 2 how the sexuality of black people is portrayed as dangerous and black female sexuality is viewed as a specific threat to white heterosexual men (hooks, 1992). It has often been suggested that the heterosexual spread of HIV in African countries is associated with deviant sexual practices, in particular anal intercourse (Richardson, 2000). Risk in relation to HIV is constructed on the notion of deviancy in which the 'general population' are perceived as 'normal' and 'safe'. This construction of deviancy reflects the power relations found within the social divisions of ethnicity, gender and sexual orientation. Therefore the white male heterosexual is constructed as 'normal' and people outside of this construction are seen as 'deviant' and 'a risk'. However, heterosexuality also has its boundaries of what is 'normal', as we saw earlier in terms of women and their 'sexual status'. Anal intercourse, promiscuous women and bisexual men can all claim to fit into a heterosexual context but within the discourse of risk and HIV would be viewed as unsafe, risky and constructed as *'deviant heterosexuality'* [or] *'queer heterosexuality'* (Richardson, 2000, p.136).

Discrimination and HIV

Although a wide variety of people in the UK have acquired HIV, men who have sex with men and people from black and minority ethnic communities, in particular people from African communities, have been disproportionately affected (National Aids Trust, 2006). The discrimination experienced by members of these communities on the basis of being HIV positive is compounded by the discrimination they already experience around their sexual orientation and ethnicity (DoH, 2005).

> HIV discrimination can be used to 'legitimise' other prejudices that may have become less acceptable.

> (Terrence Higgins Trust, 2001a, p.10)

Gay men/bisexual men/men who have sex with men

Men who have sex with men make up 75 per cent of new HIV infections occurring in the UK today (National Aids Trust, 2006). Heterosexism plays a significant part in shaping and constructing their experiences of HIV, particularly as heterosexuality is used to judge and police other sexual orientations. Consequently gay and bisexual men are often perceived as promiscuous, effeminate, diseased and engaging in 'degenerate' sexual activity (Dodds et al., 2004).

ACTIVITY 6.2

How do you think heterosexist attitudes may influence the way gay and bisexual men experience HIV? Give some examples.

Comment

Your examples should highlight the fact that heterosexism operates at all levels of society, that is, personal, cultural and structural. It is not simply a discrimination that is carried out by individuals against other individuals. It is important to recognise that all these levels are interrelated and make up the processes that influence the way people experience HIV and HIV-related discrimination. We have the following examples.

- Heterosexist attitudes are often internalised by gay and bisexual men, which result in feelings of low self-worth, guilt and shame. Consequently people feel unable or do not want to look after themselves. In relation to HIV this has implications of people not wanting to, seek support from friends and family, take up employment, practise safer sex, test for HIV and access treatment and care services (DoH, 2005).

- As well as the experience of actual discrimination, the fear of discrimination will also result in gay and bisexual men becoming isolated, unsupported and not accessing fully the range of HIV services.

- Due to the government's reluctance to fund explicit safer-sex campaigns targeted at gay and bisexual men, the majority of HIV prevention has been left to gay organisations. Young gay men have been particularly neglected due to the failure of schools to provide comprehensive sex and relationship education that is relevant to their experiences. This failure combined with hostility that some young gay men experience may account for their involvement in high-risk sexual behaviour and the subsequent rise in new HIV infections amongst young gay men (Terrence Higgins Trust, 2001a).

People from black and minority ethnic communities

The majority of new HIV diagnoses in the UK are acquired predominantly through hetero-sexual transmission. People from African communities account for 75 per cent of the new heterosexual diagnoses and twice as many women are infected as men. The majority of people will have acquired the virus before arriving in the UK from countries that are not only acutely affected by HIV but also experiencing war, conflict and poverty. The numbers of black and minority ethnic adults actually acquiring HIV sexually within the UK is still low (National Aids Trust, 2006). People living with and affected by HIV confront discrimination on many fronts such as within their communities, from the media and wider society based on their HIV infection, ethnicity and immigration status (African HIV Policy Network, 2006b). Although many African people will have come to live in the UK for a range of reasons such as work, education or to join family members, many of the discourses around HIV and African people are related to asylum seekers (Fortier, 2004). Similar to gay and bisexual men, people from black and minority ethnic communities' experiences of HIV are significantly shaped by discrimination, that of racism. We would like to highlight the following examples, and like heterosexism, racism also operates on all levels of society.

- Immigration policies cause particular problems for asylum seekers with HIV. The policy to disperse asylum seekers away from urban environments makes it probable that people will be living far away from specialist HIV services. A recent change has been that dispersal can be delayed on the recommendation of a doctor (African HIV Policy Network, 2006a). Failed asylum seekers or illegal immigrants are allowed to access HIV testing but have to pay for HIV treatment. People with HIV are not exempt from being deported and many asylum seekers may feel reluctant to reveal their HIV status or find out about it in case it counts against them during the asylum process (National Aids Trust, 2006). All these structural factors discriminate and deny people their human right to the best possible standard of physical and mental health.

- Discrimination can also take the form of reporting within the media where African people, and in particular asylum seekers, are portrayed as 'AIDS carriers' (National Aids Trust, 2006). Many people argue that the language of discrimination that was used for gay men at the beginning of the HIV pandemic is now being used about black people. This obviously fuels discrimination as well as fear of discrimination, which can deter people from accessing services. People from black and minority ethnic communities tend to seek HIV testing much later than white people, when they have already started to experience HIV-related illness. General prognosis at this stage is poorer because the HIV treatments are more effective when taken earlier (Weatherburn et al., 2003).

- There is stigma from within the black and minority ethnic communities towards people who have HIV, who risk being shamed, isolated and rejected by members of their community if their status is disclosed. HIV is linked with promiscuity and is often perceived as a gay issue. The invisibility of men who have sex with men within black and minority ethnic communities is also of concern in terms of accessing services and support. There are often tensions between sexual health and faith messages and the role of the church and mosques has been seen as very important in the fight against HIV (African HIV Policy Network, 2006b). HIV prevention is further complicated by the fact that any public sexual health messages targeted at black people can inadvertently fuel racist attitudes.

HIV and social work practice

Social work within the area of HIV is often regarded as specialist work. We would argue that as HIV has the potential to affect anyone, social workers in any context may find themselves working with somebody who is concerned or affected by HIV. We have decided to divide this section into two main areas of practice reflecting the dual role of the social worker which we highlighted earlier in the chapter. We are not attempting to cover all the issues but do want to make you aware of the main features of social work intervention within the area of HIV.

Social work with people living with and affected by HIV

Within this section we will be discussing the values and tasks of the social worker but will not be covering in any depth the issues faced by people living with HIV. These issues tend to vary enormously from person to person and to deal with the issues respectfully would demand more space than one chapter. We do encourage you however, to undertake your own research of the different issues using the resources in 'Further reading'.

Social work values

As we stated earlier, men who have sex with men and people from black and minority ethnic communities have been the people most affected by HIV. The discrimination they experience has a multiple dimension in that it is not only motivated by their HIV status but also by their sexual orientation and ethnicity (National Aids Trust, 2006b). Issues such as discrimination have been identified as barriers to accessing HIV services and information (DoH, 2001a, 2005). It is important that social workers recognise the combined impact on people's lives of racism, heterosexism and HIV discrimination. An anti-oppressive value base is crucial for the social worker to be able to give a sensitive and empowering service as well as being able to challenge discriminatory attitudes. Owing to the issues of fear, prejudice and discrimination the social work value of confidentiality is a key issue in relation to HIV. Although the whole issue around confidentiality and HIV is under consideration the current situation is that statutory agencies, which include local authorities, are legally obliged to maintain confidentiality with regard to HIV under the National Health Service (Venereal Diseases) Regulations 1974. Failure to comply can lead to criminal prosecution and disciplinary action. Any disclosure of a service user's HIV positive status should be strictly confined to those people who really must know in order to provide proper care and services, and this disclosure should be done only with the consent of the service user (London Borough of Waltham Forest, 2005).

ACTIVITY 6.3

Case study: HIV and confidentiality

You are on placement in a primary care trust team and you receive a referral from the GP asking you to visit a man called Winston Thomas, who is in his early sixties, living alone, and who is finding it difficult to cope. When you visit Winston he tells you that he is HIV positive and has been ill over the past two weeks with persistent diarrhoea and a chest infection. He is unable to cope at the moment with his cooking, washing and shopping and has no other support. He says that he would like some home care support in the short term, until he's well again.

Who needs to know about Winston's HIV positive status and why do they need to know?

Comment

You may decide that you have enough information with regard to Winston's symptoms and how they are affecting him to make a good assessment that will ensure his eligibility for support services. You therefore may decide that no one needs to know about Winston's HIV status. If on the other hand you decide that, for example, the support services manager or the individual support worker 'needs to know' about Winston's HIV status, then you have to ask yourself 'why'? The only reason why specific people may 'need to know' about Winston's HIV status is for the provision of proper care and services. For example, a known diagnosis of HIV may influence a person's eligibility or priority for a service or may give someone a 'better' service in terms of sensitivity and appropriateness. If this is the case then you would have to get Winston's informed consent. The number of people that 'need to know' should be kept to a minimum and they should be aware that they need to keep the information in strictest confidence. Local authorities will have their own policies on how to proceed in this situation (see website of London Borough of Waltham Forest as an example, which can be accessed on www.lbwf.gov.uk/index/care/adults-and-older-people/hiv-aids/hiv-confidentiality.htm). It is worth noting that your supervisor/practice teacher does not need to know in order for you to be able to discuss the situation in supervision. For example, you could discuss your assessment of Winston's situation without mentioning his HIV status, or if you wanted to discuss the issues around HIV and confidentiality you could engage in a general discussion. The important aspect to grasp here is the difference between 'needing' and 'wanting' to know. If you are involved in a situation where the argument for the 'need to know' about someone's HIV status is based on public health concerns and/or for the protection of others, then as a rule this comes from a misunderstanding of how HIV is contracted and needs to be challenged. For example, someone may argue that all professional workers have a 'need to know' someone's HIV status in order to 'take extra precautions' to avoid contracting HIV.

> In the strictest sense of the term, there are no people in the local authority who have an absolute 'need to know' that a service user or colleague have HIV infection or disease. This is because good, hygienic working practice is sufficient to protect staff from any minimal risk of infection...additionally, since the majority of people currently infected by HIV are so far unidentified – even to themselves – it would be imprudent to rely on knowledge of a person's infection as a basis of employing safe working standards. Good infection control procedures must be standard practice at all times...

(London Borough of Waltham Forest, 2005, p.2)

Social work tasks

Social work intervention with people living with HIV would involve tasks such as assessment of need, care planning and management, counselling, advocacy, mediation, and networking. As HIV-related illnesses can fluctuate it is essential that care needs are responded to flexibly and the option of direct payments may be favoured by the service user. Some care packages may be very complex in terms of health and social care needs, so that the service user may prefer that the social worker retains the care management role. Although assessments tend to focus on people's care needs and support, it is important to recognise that the assessment process can also bring up other issues related to HIV. Social workers need skills to work with a range of HIV-related issues such as sexuality, drug use, loss and bereavement, dying and death. We have considered in other chapters issues around sexuality, disability and low self-esteem which may be relevant for people with HIV who are adjusting to changes within themselves, their body image and their sexual relationships. The use of highly active antiretroviral treatment (HAART) which slows the progression of HIV disease has also extended the social work tasks into the area of helping people to normalise HIV (Pierson, 2002). This involves working with people to plan for their future and includes issues such as continuing with or taking up employment or education/training, continuing with or taking up social and sexual lives, and learning how to manage intricate treatment regimes (Furley, 2000). With this type of work it is particularly important for social workers to undertake the tasks of advocacy, networking and liaising with a range of other organisations on behalf of the service user. Knowledge of discrimination legislation is important and it is worth recalling from our chapter on disability that people living with HIV are defined as disabled from the point of diagnosis by the Disability

Discrimination Act 2005. The proposed Single Equality Bill putting all law on equality and discrimination in one Act and supported by practical guidance should be a welcome development for practitioners working with people with HIV (see www.communities.gov.uk/index.asp?id=1511211 for details of proposed Bill).

People living with HIV

People living with HIV in the UK will predominantly be living with a chronic and debilitating illness as opposed to living with a terminal illness. There are, however, people who cannot fully benefit from current treatment because they are unable to adhere to the complex regimes that are demanded by the HIV treatments due to lack of support and/or chaotic lives. Some people also receive 'late' diagnosis where it is discovered that they are HIV positive after they have become ill and may only partially benefit from treatment. Social workers therefore will be working with people living with HIV who are acutely, chronically or terminally ill. There could be a situation, however, where someone is HIV positive and well, who has children or carer responsibilities and wants to plan packages of care for when they may become ill. Although HIV is predominantly seen as an issue for adults, some social work will be with children and young people who are HIV positive. The focus of the work would be around sexual health issues and in particular how to manage the development of their sexual identity whilst growing up HIV positive.

RESEARCH SUMMARY

Children and young people with HIV

Owing to the success of medical treatments there are many more children living successfully with HIV. All young people who are HIV positive, either from birth or from engaging in risky practices, are like other young people exploring issues of their sexual identity in terms of engaging in impulsive behaviour, managing a range of conflicting emotions, responding to peer pressure and wanting to feel included. Much of the sex and relationship education tends to focus on how to avoid becoming HIV positive and responds inadequately to the particular needs of young people who are HIV positive. There tends to be an overemphasis on the young person's HIV status, neglecting the psychological and emotional aspects of their sexuality. Safer sexual practices are important for young people with HIV to adopt because of the way that other sexually transmitted infections can compromise their immune systems. It is essential that young people with HIV feel included in sexual health education and are encouraged to adopt safer sexual practices for their own sakes and not for the protection of others.

Source: Cincotta et al. (2006)

Social work and HIV prevention

The other social work role is in the area of HIV prevention, where we are going to consider two issues that we feel social workers can be involved with in the course of their work. The issues are 'safer practices' where we will be focusing on 'safer sexual practices', and 'HIV testing'. Obviously the discussions we have had in the previous section about social work tasks and in particular social work values will be relevant here.

Safer sexual practices – what is safer sex?

ACTIVITY 6.4

What does safer sex mean to you? Write down your thoughts and suggestions.

Comment

'Safer sex' means different things to different people, and is influenced by people's views of sexuality. There is a tension between the 'safer sex' messages that stress the 'don't do it', or risk-elimination approach, and the messages that stress the 'do it safely', or risk-reduction approach.

- **The risk-elimination model** stresses either abstaining from sexual activity or being sexually active within a long-term monogamous relationship. Apart from whether or not such advice is adopted, messages such as 'don't have sex with more than one person' is disempowering on two levels. Firstly on a practical level, it does not protect the person from HIV if the person they are having 'sex' with is either HIV positive or is themselves sexually involved with other people. It is unclear about what it means by 'sex' and does not give the person any advice on how to minimise the risk of HIV if they decide to have 'sex' with more than one person. Secondly on a constructive level, the discourse around monogamy in our society, particularly for women's sexuality, is one of regulation and control. In relation to HIV this language constructs non-monogamous women as 'deviant' and as a risk to others (Richardson, 2000). Consequently they are blamed and held responsible not only for contracting but also for spreading HIV.

- **The risk-reduction model** identifies risky sexual behaviour, such as penetrative vaginal or anal sexual intercourse, and then promotes ways of making the behaviour safer, such as using a condom. It does also suggest alternative and safer behaviours, such as non-penetrative sexual activity. The majority of sexual activities carry in themselves very little risk and from a biological point of view there is nothing simpler than safer sex. It is penile penetration of the vagina or anus that has been identified as the most dangerous sexual activity in relation to HIV (and other STIs), and it is also the sexual act that carries the most cultural and societal significance, particularly to heterosexual men.

  ...non penetrative sex may be regarded as immature, as 'not real sex', as no more than foreplay, as perverted or kinky, or even as sinful...adult masculine status is...bound to erection, penetration, ejaculation and/or proofs of potency – a situation often described as 'phallocentric' – and safe sex may therefore appear emasculating to heterosexual men.

  (Wilton, 2000, p.90)

Male sexuality defines 'sex' as penile penetrative sexual intercourse and has in turn determined the central message of HIV prevention campaigns as the promotion of correct and consistent condom use. The central message of 'condoms equal safer sex' (Scott-Sheldon et al., 2006, p.750) has narrowly linked safer sex to HIV ignoring that sexual activity has been risky for women for centuries in terms of unplanned pregnancies, health risks associated with contraception and abortion, and sexual violence (Richardson, 2000).

Safer sexual practices – barriers to adopting safer sex

Research tends to point to the fact that on the whole people are generally more aware of safer sex messages and have increased intention to use condoms, but continue to engage in unprotected 'sex' or use condoms inconsistently (Scott-Sheldon et al., 2006). There has been a huge change in the sexual behaviour of gay men in terms of increased condom use, which is particularly impressive as condoms were, prior to HIV, alien to gay culture (Wilton, 2000). However, there does appear to be a trend, particularly amongst young gay men, of inconsistent condom use when engaging in penetrative anal sexual intercourse (www.avert.org; see 'Further reading').

ACTIVITY 6.5

Case study: barriers to adopting safer sex

You are on placement as a student social worker attached to a leaving care project working with young people from the ages of 16 to 25 years. The group of seven young people who you are working with are diverse in terms of ethnicity, gender, class, disability and sexual orientation. You have picked up that quite a few of the young people are engaged in high-risk sexual behaviour. This has worried and puzzled you particularly as you have had discussions with all the young people about safer sexual practices and know that they have a good understanding of the risks. What do you think are the barriers that these young people face that have made it difficult for them to practice safer sex?

Comment

You will have identified a number of barriers that will have specifically affected these young people. We would like to highlight the following general issues.

- People need to have the power to negotiate safer sex within their sexual relationships. Many sexual relationships are unequal in terms of power, for example, sexual relationships between men and women, sex workers (in particular young people) and their clients. The lack of power can be a particular issue for heterosexual women who have to rely on the co-operation of their male partners in using male condoms.

RESEARCH SUMMARY

Negotiation of safer sex – an issue of power

Research has found that women who have high levels of power within their heterosexual relationships are five times as likely as women with low levels of power to report consistent condom use. These findings highlight the importance of discussing issues of power in safer sexual practices campaigns (Pulerwitz et al., 2002).

Research has highlighted that social class and employment are factors that can influence condom use amongst gay men. Gay men who were marginalised by unemployment, poor education and poverty were less likely to practise safer sex and use condoms consistently (Hope and Macarthur, 1998).

- Self-esteem, prioritisation of sexual health and access to sexual health services are all issues that are negatively influenced by social exclusion and discrimination. In turn these issues create barriers that prevent people from practising safer sex. For example, a young gay man who has experienced homophobic bullying and discrimination whilst in care may as a consequence develop a very low self-esteem. People with low self-esteem can in turn engage in high-risk sexual behaviour which reflects their uncaring attitude towards themselves (Terrence Higgins Trust, 2001b). Sexual health may not be a priority for people who are coping with a range of other serious issues such as poverty, home-lessness, relocation and dispersal. For example, a woman with children may prioritise their needs in terms of food and shelter, rather than refuse unprotected sex. Access to sexual health services can be problematic for people who are socially excluded. A good example is that of male prisoners who have difficulty in accessing condoms whilst in prison. It is widely recognised that men have sex with men in prisons and although condoms are 'officially' available they are not easily accessible. As a socially excluded and powerless group they are being denied the right to reduce their risk of harm (National Aids Trust, 2006).

- The safer-sex message has tended to adopt a single model of safer sex with its emphasis on condom use. This blanket approach does not necessarily work due to many reasons. Firstly, not all unprotected anal or vaginal sexual intercourse is unsafe. For example, if two people are in a long-term relationship and have both tested HIV negative they may decide to have unprotected sex with each other. They may also have agreed that if they become sexually involved with other people then it is this sexual activity that will be protected or will involve only other 'safer' sexual activities. This is an example of how complex 'safer' sex strategies have become particularly with gay men (Weatherburn et al., 2004). People do not relate to messages that do not reflect reality. Secondly, other safer non-penetrative sexual activities have only been encouraged when the HIV prevention messages have been aimed at gay men. Heterosexual men and women have been presented with one option of penetrative sexual intercourse with a condom. Feminists would argue that this takes no account of women's sexuality other than in terms of recipients of penetrative sex and is a missed opportunity to transform heterosexual sexual relationships by challenging the dominance of penetrative vaginal sexual intercourse (Richardson, 2000). Thirdly, condoms have come to be associated negatively with the lack of spontaneity, lack of enjoyment, lack of trust, and ironically HIV. Although most condom use is for men, the advertising has tended to target heterosexual women, ignoring the fact that many women are not in a position to insist on its use or that they would feel that their sexual reputation is threatened by carrying one. This is a theme we explored in Chapter 2 when discussing gender and the sexuality of young women. Many of the images encouraging people to use condoms are not representative of disabled people or older people based on the assumption of asexuality which we have explored in earlier chapters. Therefore groups who are excluded will not necessarily feel that the safer-sex message is applicable to them.

Safer sexual practices – what should the message look like?
Highlighting some of the problems people face in using condoms forces us to look at safer-sex messages in new ways. Let us consider for example how we would engage differently

with the group of young people in the last case study. A good starting point is to encourage them to talk about their sexual relationships and find out how they feel about their ability to negotiate when, where and how they engage in sexual activity. By doing this the young people will be talking about their perceptions of risk and the pressures they face to engage in high-risk sexual behaviour. Conversations about themselves, their identity and their sexuality are more likely to encourage their participation as well as developing an awareness of their social and personal context. Working with the young people to increase their self-esteem and negotiating power may enable them to participate in safer sexual practices. This is a difficult area in which to encourage change as young people are often involved in situations where they are powerless. If the young people feel that they do have some control in their sexual relationships then they could be encouraged to look more broadly at a range of ways other than penetrative sex that they could express themselves sexually. Condom use itself could be explored in terms of its meaning, practical use and developing responsibility for its use in young heterosexual men. The messages around condom use need to be exciting, fun and appropriate. Research has suggested that emphasising the sexual and sensual aspects of condom use could encourage people to use them promoting the message that *condoms plus pleasure equals safer sex* (Scott-Sheldon et al., 2006, p.753).

Testing for HIV

The other issue in relation to the social work role in the area of HIV prevention is around the issue of testing for HIV. The issue of testing is obviously very closely linked to safer sexual practices and it is important that social workers inform themselves of the issues involved so that they can offer effective pre-test and post-test support.

Testing for HIV – pre-test support

ACTIVITY 6.6

Case study: issues in pre-test support

You are on placement in a family support unit and you are supporting a young mother, Nadia, who has one child. On one of your visits Nadia expresses concern about a comment her partner made about his HIV status when she was visiting him in prison last week. Although he has not been tested Nadia explains that before he went into prison he injected drugs and they often engaged in unprotected sex. Nadia says that she is thinking of having an HIV test but wants to talk through things with you first.

List all the issues you feel should be covered in your discussion with Nadia.

What do you think personally are the advantages and disadvantages of having an HIV test?

Comment

The aim of pre-test support is to ensure that the decision of whether or not to undertake a test for HIV is fully informed. Confidentiality should be assured at the outset of your discussion and you need to ensure that the support you offer is non-directive. A useful exercise to undertake for yourself is to list what you think the advantages and disadvantages are of having an HIV test. This allows you to be aware of your own position regarding testing and enables you to identify any possible bias within the support you offer. We have identified the following issues that pre-test support needs to include to enable Nadia to reach a fully informed decision.

- Although Nadia has told you the reasons why she wants to undertake a test for HIV it is worth exploring her understanding of what constitutes risk behaviour and her understanding of unprotected sex. This type of discussion allows you to assess Nadia's knowledge of HIV in terms of its accuracy. Nadia may have limited knowledge of the HIV test and needs to be made aware that it tests for HIV antibodies which usually take up to three months to develop. It is also useful to encourage Nadia to identify what she thinks are the advantages and disadvantages for her of undertaking the test.

- Nadia needs to be encouraged to explore what it would mean to her to receive a negative test result. It would not guarantee that her partner is HIV negative and she may want to talk to him about continuing to have unprotected sex. Also the 'window period' for the development of antibodies means that many people are recommended to retake their tests again in three months.

- Nadia also needs to consider the implications of a positive result as often people state that they are undertaking a test to 'make sure they are ok'. This statement is indicative of someone unprepared for a positive test result. Issues that need exploring with Nadia are how she will cope emotionally, implications for her partner(s) and other significant people, who she would tell, implications for future behaviour and awareness of stigma and discrimination. Other issues would include practical and medical aspects of a positive result but at this stage it is important that Nadia is not overwhelmed by information that can be discussed in more depth at a later date if her test turns out to be positive.

- If Nadia decides to go ahead with the HIV test she may need some practical advice such as where she can go for the test and she may want to arrange to see you again when she has been given her results. In the UK the genitourinary medicine (GUM) clinic can be accessed on a self-referral basis and ensures complete confidentiality. If Nadia decides not to go ahead with the test then it may be useful to discuss with her ways she can practise safer sex when her partner comes out of prison.

Testing for HIV – post-test support

Although post-test counselling is provided by GUM clinic health advisors, Nadia may feel that she would prefer to talk to you about the implications of her test results if she decides to proceed with the HIV test. If Nadia's results are negative then the post-test support will involve reiterating some of the issues you discussed with Nadia prior to her test such as the possibility of having a retest and that a negative result does not 'protect' her from becoming HIV positive, or indicate the status of her partner. It is a useful time to explore with Nadia whether going through the experience of being tested has made her want to change her sexual practices with her partner and if so how she can do this. Obviously some of the difficulties of changing sexual behaviour and negotiating safer sex that we have discussed earlier may apply in Nadia's situation. If Nadia's results are positive then the post-test support will involve initially exploring some immediate concerns. In any situation like this it is important to establish whether the service user has received a 'late' diagnosis where they have been living with HIV for many years and have already started to develop HIV-related illnesses. This is an important factor to establish because if it is an early diagnosis then it may be helpful to reassure them that HIV in the UK can be managed quite successfully as a chronic illness as opposed to being viewed as a terminal illness. Nadia should be encouraged to express her feelings and fears at this stage and it is important to understand that she may be experiencing shock and therefore be unable to take in any advice or information. The other immediate issues that you will need to consider in terms of post-test support are exploring Nadia's support networks and talking through who she is going to tell in the short term. It would be a difficult dilemma for you if Nadia is unwilling to talk to her partner and is going to continue practising unprotected sex when he comes out of prison.

RESEARCH SUMMARY

Criminal prosecutions of HIV transmission

Although there has been transmission of HIV in the UK for over 20 years it is only since 2003 that there have been prosecutions of people in England and Wales under the Offences Against the Person Act 1861 for recklessly inflicting grievous bodily harm through transmitting HIV. Courts now consider that if someone knows they are HIV positive, is aware of the risk of transmission and passes on HIV through sex, they are potentially guilty of recklessly inflicting grievous bodily harm and to date there have been nine prosecutions resulting in eight convictions. Critics state the emphasis in sexual health work has quite properly been on individuals taking responsibility for their own sexual health and that the recent prosecutions shift the responsibility for sexual health onto others. There are other damaging effects such as people being deterred from testing for HIV through to people losing trust in the confidentiality of GUM clinics if there is a possibility of records being ordered to be submitted for court cases.

Source: For a fuller discussion of all the issues refer to National Aids Trust (2006a)

Future concerns for Nadia may include practical, medical and emotional support, what is available in terms of support services, how to look after herself, telling a wider network (family, friends, GP, work, dentist), coping with the emotional stress of possible isolation, rejection and stigma, and coping with her sexuality in terms of identity, feelings and relationships. It may be good practice to offer a series of support sessions to Nadia where this range of issues can be considered and coped with in a manageable way.

The issues we have highlighted in relation to pre-test and post-test support using the case study of Nadia will obviously vary in practice to a greater or lesser extent depending on the circumstances and social background of individual service users, their understanding of HIV and their reasons for considering testing. For consideration of the different issues that can be raised by people in different situations see the National AIDS Manual website in 'Further reading'.

C H A P T E R   S U M M A R Y

This chapter has introduced you to the basic facts of HIV which you have used to explore, analyse and reflect on the social, political and practice aspects of the virus. A key learning point from this chapter is recognising that HIV cannot be treated solely as a medical condition and many of the complexities that gravely impact on people's lives are interconnected with the way society views sexuality. You should be able to demonstrate your understanding of the way that society, sexuality and HIV combine to affect the experiences of people concerned, and living, with HIV. You should also feel able to engage in a useful and appropriate manner with people in relation to issues of HIV and sexuality.

FURTHER READING

Websites are the best way to keep up to date with the issues of HIV and the following are the ones which we feel are the most accessible and comprehensive.

www.aidsmap.com National AIDS Manual (NAM) is a community-based organisation working from the UK providing reliable and accurate HIV information across the world to HIV-positive people and to the professionals who treat, support and care for them. Particularly useful links, up-to-date reports and articles regarding HIV treatments.

www.aidsmap.com/cms/1006596.asp takes you directly to the AIDS reference manual.

www.avert.org AIDS Education and Research Trust, providing accessible information on all aspects of HIV. It has useful links to relevant annual reports, statistics, plus UK and global news and developments, as well as information targeted at young people.

www.naz.org.uk Naz Project London provides sexual health and HIV prevention and support services to targeted black and minority ethnic communities in London.

www.ncb.org.uk/hiv The Children and Young People HIV Network is a national network that brings together a wide range of organisations concerned with children and young people affected by HIV/AIDS.

www.tht.org.uk Terrence Higgins Trust (named after Terry Higgins who was one of the first people in the UK to die from HIV-related illness) provides a comprehensive range of information about HIV.

www.unaids.org Joint United Nations Programme on HIV/AIDS providing comprehensive information about the impact of HIV/AIDS in other countries.

Community Care (2007) HIV and AIDS information.
www.communitycare.co.uk/Articles/Article.aspx?liArticleID=103542&PrinterFriendly=true
(accessed 2/3/07)

Comprehensive guide to HIV/AIDS including facts and figures, how social workers can support people affected by HIV, asylum seekers and HIV, HIV research and prevention.

Miller R and Murray D (1998) *Social work and HIV/AIDS: Practitioner's guide*. Birmingham: Venture Press.

One of the few social work books addressing issues of HIV.

National Aids Trust (2004) *The needs of people living with HIV in the UK: A guide*. London: National Aids Trust.
www.nat.org.uk/download?rootDocumentId=99&eid=WVC6CAPDIQD4Y&WebDeck.ICO=true
(accessed 2/3/07).

Useful guide outlining the needs of people living with HIV.

Chapter 7

Sexuality, sexual violence and social work

ACHIEVING A SOCIAL WORK DEGREE

This chapter will help you to meet the following National Occupational Standards.

Key Role 1: Prepare for and work with individuals, families, carers, groups and communities to assess their needs and circumstances.

- Work with individuals, families, carers, groups and communities to help them make informed decisions.
- Assess needs and options to recommend a course of action.

Key Role 2: Plan, carry out, review and evaluate social work practice, with individuals, families, carers, groups, communities and other professionals.

- Respond to crisis situations.

It will also introduce you to the following academic standards as set out in the social work subject benchmark statement.

3.1.2 The service delivery context.

- The significance of legislative and legal frameworks and service delivery standards.

3.2.2.3 Analysis and synthesis.

- Assess human situations, taking into account a variety of factors (including the views of participants, theoretical concepts, research evidence, legislation and organisational policies and procedures).

Introduction

We can experience our sexuality in both negative and positive ways. Sexuality can be the source of some of our best and most exhilarating experiences as well as the source of our most damaging, abusive and violent experiences (Buckley and Head, 2000). The focus of this chapter is sexual violence, which as you will see is an umbrella term for a range of coercive sexual behaviours. We will be focusing our discussions around the 'victims' and survivors as opposed to the offenders and perpetrators of sexual violence. The chapter covers a range of aspects which we hope will help you to start to develop a critical perspective as well as enabling you to think about how you would be able to support people who are experiencing or have experienced sexual violence. Although we will be making reference to child sexual abuse, we do not intend to do so in any depth owing to the fact that it is too vast a subject to be considered wisely within the constraints of this chapter. The area of sexual violence is wide and complex and some issues are only given the briefest of introductions. We hope therefore that this chapter will generate your interest to undertake further research and reading and we offer an extended 'Further reading' section as a signpost for you to do this.

What is sexual violence?

Comment

We would argue that sexual violence is a term used to describe actual or attempted unwanted, coerced or forced sexual activity (including sexual acts, comments or advances) against a person by any person regardless of their relationship and in any setting (Krug et al., 2002). Sexual violence includes rape, assault by penetration, sexual assault, sexual harassment, prostitution, pornography, coercive/exploitative sex, trafficking/sexual slavery, forced marriage, female genital mutilation, voyeurism, flashing, obscene phone calls and sexual grooming (Sheffield, 2004; Home Office, 2004a, b,). Although the majority of this list is covered by the Sexual Offences Act 2003 it has not always been the case, which would suggest that the perception and definition of sexual violence are historically, socially and culturally constructed. We give an example of this in the following research summary.

RESEARCH SUMMARY

Rape within marriage

Legislation in relation to sexual violence has historically tended to reflect patriarchal heterosexuality. Before the twentieth century women were regarded as the property of their fathers until they married, upon which time they became the property of their husbands. Linked to this was the assumption that rape was a violation of a father's or husband's property rights. By definition a husband could not therefore rape his wife. A court ruling in 1954 found a husband guilty of 'indecent assault'. Prior to this a married woman had no right to refuse consent to any sexual acts with her husband. However, rape within marriage did not become a crime in the UK until 1991.

Source: Sheffield (2004) and Waites (2005)

Sexual violence – legislation

Within this section we are aiming to introduce you to the legislative framework regarding sexual violence by summarising the main points of the Sexual Offences Act 2003. We will also briefly refer you to other relevant legislation in relation to children, young people and vulnerable adults.

Sexual Offences Act 2003

The Sexual Offences Act 2003 is the result of the first major overhaul of the sexual offences legislation in England and Wales for more than a century. It was recognised that the sexual offences legislation up until this point had been a:

patchwork quilt of provisions ancient and modern that works because people make it do so, not because there is a coherence and structure.

(Home Office, 2000, p.ii)

The Sexual Offences Act 2003 claims to provide *a clear, modern framework to protect the public from sexual crimes* (Home Office, 2004a, p.1). It is divided into two parts, with the first part focusing on sexual offences and the second part focusing on sex offenders. The following is a summary of some of the key points of the Act in relation to sexual offences only (Home Office, 2004a, b).

Adults and children/young people

- Rape and sexual assaults are regarded as sexual activities that take place without the consent of one of the people involved. Consent is seen as the central issue in deciding whether a sexual offence has been committed. A person consents to a sexual activity if that person agrees by choice and has the freedom and capacity to make that choice. Giving consent is seen as an active process and where a person is threatened by violence, drugged, asleep or unconscious there will be a presumption that the person did not give their consent to the sexual activity. An important change is dispensing of the 'mistaken belief' clause, referred to as the 'rapists' charter' (Temkin, 1987), where a man who honestly believed that a person was consenting to the sexual act regardless of how unreasonable that belief was could not be convicted of rape. This has now been replaced with an onus on the defendant to show that the grounds for believing that the other person was consenting are reasonable.

- Rape is classified as penetration of someone's vagina, anus or mouth without their consent by someone's penis. It is worth noting that as rape involves penile penetration it can only be committed by men, but can be committed against women and men.

- Assault by penetration covers penetrating the anus or vagina without consent with an object or another part of the body (other than the penis) and is therefore gender neutral in terms of the perpetrator or 'victim'.

- Other offences include sexual assault, causing people to engage in sexual activity, giving someone a substance with the intent to make them engage in sexual activity and committing one offence (such as violence) with the intention of committing a sexual offence.

- Exposure, voyeurism, prostitution and trafficking people for sexual exploitation are also referred to within the Act.

Children/young people

- Another aspect to the consent issue is age. The legal age for a young person to consent to sexual activity whatever their sexual orientation is 16. Children aged 12 years and under can never legally consent regardless of circumstances as sexual activity with children of this age is never acceptable.

- Sexual activity with someone under the age of 16 is a criminal offence. However, when the offender is below 18 years of age the offences will carry a lower maximum penalty. Prosecutions will not take place regarding teenage sexual activity between two young people of a similar age unless it involves abuse or exploitation. Sexual activity is defined as:

all intercourse, other penetration or sexual touching of a child...of any part of their body, clothed or unclothed, either with your body or with an object.

(Home Office, 2004b, p.5)

- Children under 16 are further protected from adults causing, persuading, inciting or procuring them to engage in sexual activity including stripping or masturbation. Adults engaging in sexual activity in the presence of a child or causing a child to watch sexual activity, including images such as videos, webcams or photographs, are committing a sexual offence. It is also now an offence to meet a child with the intention of committing a sexual offence following 'sexual grooming', which can take place via the telephone or internet.

- Although the age of consent is 16 there are some situations where the Act extends its protection from sexual violence and exploitation to young people who are 16 and 17 years of age. For example, it is a sexual offence to be involved in prostitution and pornography with people aged up to and including 17 years. The latter are also protected from sexual violence and exploitation by family members and carers, as well as by adults who have been in positions of trust in relation to the children and young people. This includes workers from schools, youth service, care homes, health and social care, and the criminal justice system. This protection from adults in positions of trust extends also to people with learning difficulties and certain mental health issues.

For further information we would refer you to the Home Office website on sexual offences which also provides links to the guides to the Sexual Offences Act 2003 for adults, children and young people, and the Office of Public Sector Information website for a copy of the Act itself (see 'Further reading').

Other legislation

In addition to the Sexual Offences Act 2003 social workers have other legislation that informs their practices with regard to the sexual well-being of children, young people, and vulnerable adults. It is worth noting that existing legislation will be strengthened by the Safeguarding Vulnerable Adults Groups Act 2006 which is to be implemented in 2008. With regard to vulnerable adults social workers have the statutory guidance *No secrets* (DoH, 2000) which we refer to in Chapters 4 and 5. With regard to children and young people both the Children Acts 1989 and 2004 require local authorities/social workers to have a general duty to safeguard and promote the welfare of children in need and undertake child protection work to investigate and tackle harm to children, which would include sexual violence. The requirements of these Acts inform the statutory guidelines *Working together to safeguard children* (HM Government, 2006). We would like to briefly highlight two areas of sexual violence discussed in the guidelines that are not referred to in the Sexual Offences Act 2003, that of female genital mutilation and forced marriage. We would encourage you to refer to the guidelines themselves for further detail (see 'Further reading').

Female genital mutilation

Female genital mutilation is a collective term for procedures that include the removal of part or all of the external female genitalia, for cultural or other non-therapeutic reasons. The practice is medically unnecessary and has serious mental and physical health consequences that carry on into later life, such as difficulty in giving birth, infertility and even death. It has been illegal in the UK since the Prohibition of Female Circumcision Act 1985, and the Female Genital Mutilation Act 2003 strengthens the 1985 Act by making it illegal to take girls abroad to undergo genital mutilation. Female genital mutilation is traditionally practised in countries such as Yemen, Oman, Malaysia, Indonesia, United Arab Emirates and 26 countries in Africa. It is estimated from the number of women and girls who live in the UK who originate from these countries that about 74,000 women in the UK have undergone genital mutilation, with about 7,000 girls under 16 years of age who are at risk (LASSL, 2004). The procedure is usually performed on girls between four and 13 years of age, but it can be performed on babies or on young women before marriage or pregnancy. Although female genital mutilation may be part of a community's cultural or ideological beliefs and practices it is important to identify it as an abuse of human rights that discriminates particularly against girls and women (FORWARD, 2007a). Female genital mutilation does differ from other forms of child abuse in that the parents and adults involved believe that they have the girl's best interests in mind and it is a one-off act of abuse that is not repeated. However, other female siblings may be at risk (LASSL, 2004).

Forced marriage

A clear distinction must be made between arranged and forced marriages. In arranged marriages the choice of whether or not to accept the marriage arrangements made by the families remains with the two people involved. A forced marriage is one which takes place without the consent of one or both of the parties and there is some element of physical or mental duress (Foreign and Commonwealth Office et al., 2004). Young women from a wide variety of backgrounds between 13 and 30 years of age are disproportionately affected although it has been shown that 15 per cent of the 'victims' are young men (FCO et al., 2004). Forced marriages can take place within the UK or abroad but the extent of the practice is difficult to ascertain due to underreporting. However, in 2004, 250 forced marriages were reported to the Foreign and Commonwealth Office (FCO et al., 2004). Although the majority of forced marriages within the UK involve people from the southern Asian communities, it is practised in other countries within the Middle East, East Asia, Europe and Africa. It is argued that any child marriage is a forced marriage because of the child being unable to legally give consent to sexual activity (FORWARD, 2007b).

> *Child marriages must be viewed within a context of force and coercion, involving pressure...and children that lack the choice or capacity to give their full consent.*

(FORWARD, 2007b, p.1)

There is a clear link between female genital mutilation and child/early marriage in that communities who practise the former are also likely to support child/early marriages (FORWARD, 2007b). Forced marriages can involve children/young people and vulnerable adults and are recognised as a form of domestic violence and child abuse. We would argue that anyone who is forced into a marriage does not have the freedom or capacity to consent to sexual activity and is therefore a 'victim' of a sexual offence. Guidelines for social workers give more information about forced marriages and the way forward in terms of best practice (see 'Further reading').

115

Role of legislation

The law reforms in relation to sex offences claim to reflect changing social attitudes by, among other things, tightening up loopholes around sexual offences against children, relaxing oppressive restrictions against gay men and reforming the rape law (Batty, 2003). Attitudes towards sexual offences can still create injustice as in the situation of rape cases where conviction rates are as low as 5 per cent and women are frequently being blamed for 'getting themselves raped' (Bindel, 2007). It will be interesting to see as the law reforms become embedded whether the role of legislation can be to inform as opposed to reflect social attitudes.

Sexual violence – what do we know?

So far within this chapter we have considered the definition of sexual violence as well as how the legislation defines a sexual offence. It is useful at this point therefore to highlight some general information about sexual violence.

ACTIVITY 7.2

Write down all you know about sexual violence, such as how common it is, who perpetrates it, who tends to experience it. Whilst you are doing this reflect on the source(s) of your information and knowledge.

Comment

It is important to realise that the area of sexual violence is rife with myths, misinformation and inaccuracies. It is difficult therefore to develop an accurate picture of the prevalence of sexual violence and it is a crime that is underreported (Home Office, 2005). This can be for a range of reasons, the most common being that many survivors find it hard to talk about their experiences and also fear that they will not be believed. In the 2001 British Crime Survey 40 per cent of the women who had experienced rape had not told anyone (Home Office, 2005). Although statistics can be inaccurate we feel that if treated with caution they can give a picture or pattern of sexual violence, its perpetrators and survivors. To this end we have compiled the following research summary which we hope will give you information to reflect on when we consider some possible explanations of why sexual violence happens.

RESEARCH SUMMARY

The profile of sexual violence
The recorded rape and sexual assault statistics for all ages for 2005/06 are:

- *out of 62,081 recorded sexual offences, 63 per cent were rape and sexual assault, 20 per cent included, amongst other things, sexual grooming, trafficking for sexual*

---

*exploitation, abuse of trust, and abuse of children in relation to pornography and pros-
titution, and the remaining 17 per cent were miscellaneous sexual offences;*

- *92 per cent of rapes were against women and 8 per cent against men;*

- *88 per cent of sexual assaults were against women and 12 per cent against men
  (www.homeoffice.gov.uk/rds/pdfs/100years.xls).*

*The cross-government action plan on sexual violence and abuse presents the following
profile of sexual violence.*

- *The majority of 'victims' of sexual violence are women (23 per cent of women and 3
  per cent of men experience sexual assault and 5 per cent of women and 0.4 per cent of
  men experience rape) and children of both sexes (21 per cent of girls and 11 per cent
  of boys experience some form of sexual abuse).*

- *The majority of rape and sexual assault takes place in domestic settings with over half
  of the rapists being current or former partners and a further third being known to the
  'victims'. Similarly the majority of child sexual abuse is committed by someone known
  to the child.*

- *Sexual violence is massively underreported by 'victims' of all ages and gender. Levels of
  reporting for rape and sexual assault are particularly low if they take place within a
  pattern of domestic abuse (Home Office, 2005). Two out of ten rapes are reported, one
  out of the 20 rapes reported result in a conviction (Kelly et al., 2005) and one out of
  the ten convicted rapists have their convictions overturned or sentences reduced on
  appeal (Cook, 2004).*

- *Sexual violence is more likely to be experienced by people who are in vulnerable positions. For example, children who are disabled, missing, looked after or from families
  experiencing domestic violence are more likely to experience sexual violence, as are
  adults who are disabled, involved in prostitution or who have been abused as children.
  Young women who use alcohol unsafely are also vulnerable to sexual violence.*

- *The majority of perpetrators of sexual violence are men, with about 5 per cent being
  women. Perpetrators come from all backgrounds but research estimates that one-third
  of sexual offences are committed by young people under the age of 18 years (Lovell,
  2002). (See Erooga and Masson, 2006, in 'Further reading' as a comprehensive text on
  children and young people who engage in sexual violence.)*

Source: HM Government (2007)

Sexual violence – why does it happen?

In order to explore some of the reasons why sexual violence occurs it is useful as a starting
point and in keeping with the general thread that has woven its way throughout this book
to consider the social construction of sexual violence. In order to do this we will primarily
be focusing on the experience of sexual violence in the UK, and in particular rape and

sexual assault. Although we will be concentrating primarily on the experiences of adults, reference will be made, if relevant, to the sexual violence experienced by children.

Social construction of sexual violence

As highlighted in the last research summary, men and boys are raped and sexually assaulted and women can be perpetrators of sexual violence. However:

> *most perpetrators are male and most victims are female. It is both a consequence and cause of gender inequality.*

> (HM Government, 2007, p.iii)

So how is sexual violence presented within our society? 'Common knowledge' relating to rape and sexual assault is often based on myths and misinformation. It is argued that the 'rape myths' are so widely believed that they have a direct impact on the *willingness of juries to convict in cases of rape* (Office for Criminal Justice Reform, 2006, p.4). Although there are many myths relating to sexual violence (see Kelly, 1988, in 'Further reading' for a full critical exploration of the myths) we would like to consider the ones which we feel significantly contribute to the views or discourses on sexual violence. Many people believe that sexual violence is committed by a stranger. For example, language such as 'sex-starved maniac', 'evil monster' and in particular 'paedophile' constructs male sex offenders as 'other' men, different and separate from 'ordinary' men. We have referred in earlier chapters to this process of 'othering' as a way of stigmatising people as 'abnormal' or 'deviant'. As you are already aware, the majority of perpetrators are men who are known to their 'victims', many of whom are partners or family members (HM Government, 2007). Therefore it could be argued that 'othering' protects 'ordinary' men and prevents us from looking critically at the roles that male sexuality and masculinity play in the perpetration of sexual violence (Kelly, 1996a). When 'ordinary' men are called to account for their abusive and violent sexual behaviour a couple of other powerful myths contribute to the construction of a different discourse. These myths revolve around the claims that women 'cause' or 'ask for' sexual violence and men have 'uncontrollable sexual urges' once sexually aroused (Rape Crisis, England and Wales, 2006). These myths are interrelated in that women are blamed both for 'leading men on' and for men's inability to stop 'being sexual' when there is no consent. This discourse has been referred to as the male sexual drive discourse (Holloway, 1984).

RESEARCH SUMMARY

Sexual assault research

As part of their 'Stop Violence Against Women' campaign in 2005, Amnesty International commissioned a poll of 1,096 randomly sampled adults aged 18 and over about their attitudes towards rape and sexual assault, particularly in relation to whether women were to blame for the sexual violence. Although overall the results suggested that people felt that women were not to blame, there was a disturbingly large proportion of the sample that felt women were partially or totally responsible for being raped or sexually assaulted.

The following percentages of the sample felt that women were partially or totally responsible for being raped or sexually assaulted in terms of the following specific behaviour:

- *34 per cent if women were acting in a flirtatious manner;*

- *30 per cent if women were drunk;*

- *25 per cent if women were wearing 'provocative' clothing, particularly if combined with drinking alcohol;*

- *10 per cent if women had had a number of sexual partners;*

- *37 per cent if women failed to clearly communicate that they did not want to be involved in the sexual activity.*

Older people and people from working-class backgrounds tended to be overrepresented within the above percentages. Gender did not seem to influence attitudes except that more men than women felt that 'provocative' clothing held women responsible for sexual violence.

Source: Amnesty International UK (2005)

Male sexuality, masculinity and heterosexuality

ACTIVITY 7.3

Reflect on your reading of earlier chapters and in particular discussions that we have had about masculinity and heterosexuality. What do you think are some of the elements that may make up the 'male sexual drive discourse'?

Comment

The male sexual drive discourse has its origins in the naturalist approach that we discussed in the first chapter of this book which argues that the heterosexual male role is to pursue and procreate. Sexual activity is seen as a force of nature and is primarily a male performance. Men are viewed as active and dominant, always ready and wanting sexual activity. Women are passive and submissive, always responding to meet men's sexual needs, not their own. Within this particular discourse male sexual urges are perceived as natural and compelling and men are expected to behave in a forceful and aggressive way to satisfy their sexual needs. Women are made to feel responsible for male sexuality, in particular the arousal of male sexual urges, and feel pressure to yield to men's demands in terms of sexual activity (Gilbert et al., 1999). Sexualised male aggression is then viewed as a 'natural' response to being aroused as opposed to a type of sexual violence. This discourse also helps to perpetuate particular myths such as women enjoy sexual violence and women routinely make false accusations about rape and sexual assault (McCarthy, 1999). The belief in the male sexual drive discourse and its interrelationship with the myths of sexual violence have also had a powerful impact in law cases where they have been used by defence lawyers to justify acts of rape (Phillips, 2000).

Feminist theories on sexual violence

Feminism has a long history of campaigning against sexual violence dating back to the late nineteenth century, where men's use of prostitutes, men's sexual abuse of children and men's 'right' to rape their wives were challenged (McCarthy, 1999). Feminism highlights the fact that adult sexual violence is gendered, maintaining that it is predominantly perpetrated by men against women. The analysis goes beyond the individual level of viewing sexual violence as something that solely occurs between a man and a woman in isolation from the rest of society. It states that the way society constructs the concepts of what it is to be masculine and feminine within a heterosexual context perpetuates and sanctions adult sexual violence within Western society (Gough and McFadden, 2001). In our discussions on heterosexuality in Chapter 2 we considered the social division of gender and the way that the inequality between men and women is supported by the masculine and feminine ideal. We identified that men had access to different types of power which controlled and oppressed women (Abbot, 2006). Feminist analysis identifies male sexual violence as a type of power which controls and oppresses women as opposed to being about 'sex' and sexual activity with women. For example, women fear rape above any other crime (HM Government, 2007). This fear can restrict and control women's movements and their capacity to fully involve themselves in different work and leisure activities. Women who do not conform to the feminine ideal or challenge male power can be threatened by sexual violence (Gough and McFadden, 2001). Through its analysis of sexual violence feminism has argued for recognition of a connection between the different types of sexual violence, referred to as *a continuum of sexual violence* (Kelly, 1988, p.27). Therefore sexist jokes, pornographic images, sexual harassment, sexual assault, domestic violence and rape are all connected by the same discourse involving the way female sexuality is portrayed and controlled by male sexuality under a patriarchal system. The argument is that men who use pornography perceive women and in particular women's sexuality in the same way as men who rape. From this particular patriarchal perspective men are entitled to engage in sexual activity as a right and a way to establish their masculinity and power. Female sexuality is a commodity to be taken, dominated or owned (Sheffield, 2004).

RESEARCH SUMMARY

Sexualised violence against women on film

Sexualised violence against women on screen is not new and has frequently in the past been a theme of horror or 'thriller' type films. There is, however, the emergence of a new genre of horror films that are particularly dehumanising and misogynist, known as 'gorno' (derived from a combination of 'gory' and 'porno') or 'torture porn'. Although they show both men and women being dismembered, it is the violence against women in the films that shows extreme graphic violence and sex simultaneously. There appears to be a wider trend of depicting women as highly sexualised prey in fashion magazines, advertisements and television series. A newly released film called Grindhouse *(Quentin Tarantino/Robert Rodriguez) has a character called 'Rapist Number One' which can be bought as an action figure for children.*

Source: Cochrane (2007)

What are your views about the possible connection between sexual violence and pornography?

Comment

There is much contradictory evidence as to whether there is a causal link between pornography and sexual violence. Some argue that there is a substantive link between the use of and exposure to pornography and sexual coercion towards women (Women's National Commission, 2005). Pornography means *the graphic depiction of women as vile whores* (Dworkin, 1981, p.200) and is a debasing, degrading and violent depiction of predominantly female sexuality. Many feel that the connection is obvious as the majority of sexual violence such as rape and sexual assault is towards women (Women's National Commission, 2005). We would argue that although the connection may not be a 'causal' one, the existence of pornography does little to challenge attitudes and misconceptions around sexual violence through its relentless support for the objectification of women's bodies and its portrayal of women enjoying sexual violation.

Criticisms of feminist theories on sexual violence

As feminist theories have tended to concentrate on the link between masculinity, sexual violence and men, there has been an apparent neglect of theory to account for women perpetrators. Although the number of women offenders is low, theories of sexual violence must not fall into the trap of viewing masculinity and femininity as fixed and 'naturally' associated with men and women respectively (see Kelly, 1996b, in 'Further reading' for a discussion on developing a feminist analysis of sexual violence perpetrated by women). Masculinity and femininity must be viewed as socially constructed and therefore offering a potential for challenge and change. Black feminism has also criticised the analysis for its neglect of race and the difficulty faced by black women in speaking out about their experiences of sexual violence by black men. This 'conspiracy of silence' (Hill Collins, 2000, p.158) can be due to loyalty to the black communities, a fear of and protection from the racism of the law enforcement agencies. Gay men who find themselves 'victims' of sexual and domestic violence have found it difficult to relate to the feminist analysis, although some of the references to power and control can be useful (see Vaughan, 2000, in 'Further reading' for a discussion about theory that may be helpful to gay men).

Despite the criticisms, feminism has contributed enormously to our understanding of sexual violence. It has challenged the myths and misinformation to such an extent that it has given women who experience sexual violence the courage and voice to speak out and tell their stories. The linking of sexual offences to power, control and violence has enabled a critical attack on adults who have tried to argue that paedophilia is a sexual orientation (Kelly, 1996a). Networks of support including rape crisis centres, women's refuges, sexual assault centres, survivor groups for women and men who have experienced child sexual abuse have all started from small beginnings to now feature prominently in the consultation of guidelines, policies, training and action plans supporting and in response to the recent legal reforms around sexual offences.

Sexual violence – social work practice

Covering all aspects of social work practice within the area of sexual violence is something that cannot be achieved in this chapter. We have therefore decided to concentrate on one case study involving the issue of rape and will highlight a range of practice issues that we hope will be useful in other situations. We would argue that a woman or man would not be referred to a social worker based solely on the reason of being raped. Social work involvement would already be taking place for other reasons, as we highlight in our case study below, or the rape might have brought to people's attention other issues that warrant social work involvement. An example would be if an older woman reported to her general practitioner that she had been raped and through discussion it was also revealed that she was struggling to cope with caring for her partner who had dementia. In this situation a referral would be made requesting an assessment of need under the NHS Community Care Act 1990. It is important to recognise therefore that the social worker needs to be able to deal not only with the issue that triggered the referral, in our example the older woman's struggle to care for her partner, but also with the issue of her being raped.

ACTIVITY 7.5

Case study

You are on placement in a multidisciplinary team which provides services for disabled children. For the last few months you have been supporting Bella Wilson, who is the mother of two severely disabled children aged eight and ten. Bella is 45 years old, white and comes from a working-class background. Bella has sole responsibility for the day-to-day care of her children as her husband works away from home on the oil rigs for many months at a time. On one of your support visits you arrive at Bella's house to find her in a very distressed state. After a considerable length of time she tells you that one of her husband's close friends, Tony, who she has always regarded as a friend of the family, had arranged to take her out a couple of weeks ago to 'cheer her up' and give her a bit of a break. Bella said that they had had a lovely relaxed time with no emergency phone calls from the babysitter. At the end of the evening she decided to invite Tony back to her house for a coffee. Back at the house Tony had tried to kiss her and she pushed him away. He then pulled her onto the sofa and raped her. Bella said that she had not fought back because she did not want to wake and upset the children. Bella says she does not know what to do.

Write down what you would do to support Bella in this particular situation.

Comment

As discussed earlier in this chapter, a lot of information about sexual violence is based on myths and misconceptions. A crucial starting point for your work with Bella is to encourage her to talk about the detail of what happened and to identify any 'rape myths' that may exist in her account or narrative. This is important as 'rape myths' can act as serious barriers for women in seeking, accessing and accepting support (Ward, 1995). For example, Bella may feel that she caused, provoked or deserved to be raped and that the rape was in some way her fault. You will need to sensitively challenge this common yet powerful myth by asserting with Bella that whatever she wore or said or however she acted is never a justification for the rape. Bella's response may be further complicated by the fact that the rapist is a family friend. She may be unaware that the majority of rapes are planned and carried out by someone who is known to the survivor (Rape Crisis, England and Wales, 2006). Many women worry about not being believed, which is exacerbated further by particular myths. For example, if a woman does not sustain any bruising then she is accused of not struggling enough and doubt is raised about whether the rape took place (Rape Crisis, England and Wales, 2006). Working effectively with Bella requires you not only to identify and challenge the 'rape myths' but also to believe her narrative of events. It is argued that in order to work effectively with rape survivors the worker needs to adopt a feminist perspective which challenges a medical model of rape and *acknowledges the conditions that cause and condone rape* (Foley, 1996, p.172). Building on this basis of working you would go on to discuss with Bella specific practical and emotional support issues.

Practical and emotional support issues

We are going to summarise the main practical and emotional support issues that need to be discussed with women and men who have been raped. It is important to bear in mind that both types of issues are interrelated and cannot be dealt with as a 'checklist'. The core helping skills of listening, attending, probing, challenging, empathy, acceptance and genuineness are crucial here for effective intervention (Parker and Bradley, 2003).

Practical support issues

Practical support issues initially involve personal safety, reporting the rape and medical care. It is important to check that the person is physically safe. This is usually an issue if the social worker is contacted immediately after the rape has happened. Nonetheless the person is unlikely to feel safe particularly if she/he has been raped by someone who knows where she/he lives and/or with whom she/he is likely to have future contact. It is the person's choice whether or not to report the rape and it may help the decision-making if the social worker explains what is likely to happen if the rape is reported. It needs to be pointed out that in order for forensic and medical evidence to be collected the rape needs, if possible, to be reported within 72 hours and the person ideally should not have washed or changed clothes. The person still has the right, however, to report the rape if it happened a while ago, or if evidence has been destroyed through washing and changing clothes. A person should be encouraged to have a medical check for internal injuries and sexually transmitted infections but be reassured that this does not mean that the rape has to be reported. It is essential for the social worker to ascertain what specialised services exist in the local area as these can affect the way that procedures are undertaken in terms of medical examinations and reporting the rape plus the type of short- and long-term support offered to people. If specialised services are available then the support needed does not have to be solely provided by the social worker. A large part of the practical support from the social worker will then be locating, liaising, advocating and accessing services on behalf of the person concerned, which in turn will strengthen their support network. Another practical support issue involves the social worker reassessing a person's situation and being able to provide additional care services whilst the person is going through the crisis. For example, in our case study you could arrange for Bella to receive additional services to support her in looking after her children.

Emotional support issues

Emotional support issues involve both the immediate feelings that a person experiences as well as considering any long-term support that might be needed. Initially the difficulty for many people is finding coping strategies to deal with extremely strong emotions as well as making decisions about what to do and who to tell. As in our case study the social worker may be the person best placed at this stage to offer the initial emotional support. There is no 'right' way to feel after being raped and people experience a range of different emotions. For example, people can feel anger, shame, fear, guilt, numbness and denial and go through changes in their behaviour such as difficulty in concentrating, inability to sleep and irritability. Other common feelings are a lack of control, helplessness and worthlessness and the experience can significantly change their relationships with others. The important point at this stage is to encourage people to talk about their experience and be accepting of their emotions. People who have been raped will need emotional support to tell other people, in particular partners and significant others, and in turn these people may also require support in order to deal with their own feelings and to be able to provide support for the survivor. As with the practical support issues it is useful if the social worker can find out what exists in terms of emotional support such as short- and long-term counselling as well as support groups.

RESEARCH SUMMARY

Specialised rape and sexual assault services

One of the first Sexual Assault Referral Centres (SARCs) opened in Manchester in 1986 as a national response to the appalling way women survivors of rape were treated by the police. The centres are designed to meet the needs of the survivors and the criminal justice system by providing crisis intervention in respect of a recent sexual assault. The services include prompt and immediate availability of forensic examinations, medical care and follow-up tests, assistance with reporting the attack to the police, and short-term counselling. There are variations between centres in terms of what they actually provide themselves and what they co-ordinate other agencies to provide. The location and information about the SARCs in the UK can be found through the Home Office website link www.homeoffice.gov.uk/crime-victims/reducing-crime/sexual-offences/sexual-assault-referral-centres/?view=Standard. Other specialised services include rape crisis centres and survivor groups which tend to offer support for adults dealing with rapes that occurred some time ago. However, these organisations as well as Victim Support and specialist police and health personnel may also provide support immediately after a rape if there are no SARCs in a particular geographical area.

Source: Lovett et al. (2004)

In concluding this section on social work practice we need to point out that we have only touched the surface in relation to sexual violence and practice issues. As you will probably have gathered, situations concerning sexual violence can be complex, involving many interrelated issues such as prostitution, drug use and trafficking. Very often these issues involve women who are asylum seekers or refugees who are already in a powerless and vulnerable position and feel that they cannot access support services. (See websites in

'Further reading'*)*. The recognised link also between sexual and domestic violence raises the complex and disturbing issue of women, in particular, being subjected to living in situations of ongoing sexual violence and coercion (Home Office, 2005). Government has recognised that it needs to prioritise the fight against sexual violence and social work practice will in the future be influenced by the multi-agency action plan on sexual violence and abuse (HM Government, 2007). Its key objectives are:

> *to maximise prevention of sexual violence and abuse, to increase access to support and health services for victims of sexual violence and abuse, to improve the criminal justice response to sexual violence and abuse.*

> (HM Government, 2007 p.ii)

C H A P T E R   S U M M A R Y

This chapter has introduced you to the concept of sexual violence in terms of definition, legislation and theories of explanation. We have encouraged you to use learning from other chapters in order to reflect on the links between sexual violence and discourses regarding masculinity and femininity. A key learning point is recognising that sexual violence is a complex area often related to other issues and dominated by myths and misinformation. With regard to social work practice a key learning point is the need of service users who experience sexual violence for substantial practical and emotional support, which can be accessed on a long-term basis and provided by a range of agencies working in partnership. Finally, this chapter has given you a basis on which to undertake further independent research in more depth regarding the wide spectrum of issues in relation to sexual violence.

FURTHER READING

Erooga, M and Masson, H (eds) (2006) *Children and young people who sexually abuse others: Current developments and practice responses*. 2nd edition. London and New York: Routledge.

Comprehensive book detailing the issues around children and young people who sexually abuse others.

Foreign and Commonwealth Office, Association of Directors of Social Services, Home Office, Department for Education and Skills, Department of Health (2004) *Young people and vulnerable adults facing forced marriage: Practice guidance for social workers*. Available at **www.adss.org.uk/publications/ guidance/marriage.pdf**

Guidelines for social workers give more information about forced marriages and the way forward in terms of best practice.

HM Government (2006) *Working together to safeguard children: A guide to interagency working to safeguard and promote the welfare of children*. London: Department for Education and Skills. Available **www.everychildmatters.gov.uk/workingtogether/**

Kelly, L (1988) *Surviving sexual violence*. Cambridge: Polity Press.

This book gives a feminist analysis of sexual violence and a critical exploration of the myths.

Kelly, L (1996b) When does the speaking profit us?: Reflections on the challenges of developing feminist perspectives on abuse and violence by women. In Hester, M, Kelly, L and Radford, J (eds) *Women, violence and male power: Feminist research, activism and practice*. Buckingham: Open University Press.

This chapter gives a feminist analysis of sexual violence perpetrated by women.

Kemshall, H and McIvor, G (eds) (2004) *Managing sex offender risk*. London and Philadelphia: Jessica Kingsley.

Accessible book discussing issues in relation to the offender of sexual violence.

Myers, S and Milner, J (2007) *Sexual issues in social work*. Bristol: BASW/Policy Press.

This book has useful sections discussing social work practice with 'victims' and offenders of sexual violence.

Vaughan, G (2000) Violence, sexuality and gay male domestic violence. In Buckley, K and Head P (eds) *Myths, risks and sexuality: The role of sexuality in working with people*. Lyme Regis: Russell House Publishing.

A chapter that discusses theory that may be helpful for gay men who experience domestic violence.

www.homeoffice.gov.uk/crime-victims/reducing-crime/sexual-offences/?version=4 The Home Office which provides links to information on initiatives and policies around sexual offences building on the legal provisions within the Sexual Offences Act 2003. Guides to the Act can be downloaded from the links provided by this website.

www.opsi.gov.uk/ACTS/acts2003/20030042.htm The Office of Public Sector Information which allows you to download a copy of the Sexual Offences Act 2003.

www.forwarduk.co.uk FORWARD is an international non-governmental organisation dedicated to improving the health and well-being of African women and girls and promoting action to stop harmful traditional practices such as female genital mutilation.

www.eaves4women.co.uk/POPPY_Project/POPPY_Project.php POPPY provides support and housing to women who have been trafficked into prostitution. POPPY combines direct services, support and advocacy with research, development and lobbying.

www.harpweb.org.uk HARPWEB, which consists of three websites providing information, practical tools and articles relating to the health issues of asylum seekers and refugees. There is a link to the issue of trafficking.

Chapter 8

Sexuality, best practice and social work

ACHIEVING A SOCIAL WORK DEGREE

This chapter will help you to meet the following National Occupational Standards.
Key Role 6: Demonstrate professional competence in social work practice.
- Research, analyse, evaluate, and use current knowledge of best social work practice.
- Contribute to the promotion of best social work practice.

It will also introduce you to the following academic standards as set out in the social work subject benchmark statement.
3.1.3 Values and ethics.
- The moral concepts of rights, responsibility, freedom, authority and power inherent in the practice of social workers as moral and statutory agents.

Introduction

This book has introduced you to a range of issues relating to sexuality and in particular we have encouraged you to engage with a broadly social constructionist approach. This has enabled you to analyse important issues such as the way that heterosexuality is constructed as 'normal' and 'acceptable' and as a result how 'dissident' (Bell and Binnie, 2000, p.10) sexualities, such as lesbian, gay and bisexuality, are constructed as 'abnormal' and 'unacceptable'. This approach has also been used to enable you to gain an understanding of issues of sexuality in relation to different groups of people, such as young people, older people and disabled people, as well as specific issues such as HIV and sexual violence. Throughout the book you have engaged with activities and case studies in order to develop and reflect on the knowledge, skills and values required in social work practice. In this concluding chapter we will be focusing on the issue of what makes for 'best' social work practice in relation to sexuality.

Sexuality and social work

An important starting point is the recognition that social work and social workers contribute through their theories and actions to the construction of sexuality. It is widely acknowledged that there has been until recently a lack of attention to issues of sexuality in social work education, research and literature (Trotter and Hafford-Letchfield, 2006). This apparent 'silence' as we have seen in previous chapters still contributes significantly to a construction of sexuality. Hicks (2005b) provides a comprehensive account of social work's view of sexuality over four decades using lesbian and gay parenting as his exemplar (see Hicks, 2005b in 'Further reading'). We give you a flavour of his analysis by providing some of the main points in the following research summary.

RESEARCH SUMMARY

Social work and sexuality through the decades

In the 1970s social work theory was silent on the subject of sexuality and within social work practice 'homosexuality' was viewed as a form of disability, illness or criminality. Some local authorities expressed concern about lesbian and gay staff working within residential settings with children and vulnerable young people. Many lesbian mothers lost custody of their children as they were deemed unfit to parent because of their sexual orientation. There was the emergence of radical social work theory influenced by feminism and gay liberationist ideas which started to challenge these oppressive views.

In the 1980s liberal views towards sexuality emerged in social work which regarded lesbians and gay men as having fixed identities and a particular set of needs. These views helped to raise awareness about discriminatory attitudes towards lesbian and gay sexuality through the recognition of homophobia and heterosexism. Despite this, lesbians and gay men were still viewed as 'unnatural' parents and a 'danger' to the 'normal' development of children. Based on these ideas the majority of applications from lesbians and gay men to foster/adopt children were rejected as unsuitable.

In the 1990s issues of sexuality within social work found a 'voice' through anti-discriminatory theory. However, debate regarding heterosexism tended to be marginalised in relation to other oppressions. Lesbians and gay men were starting to be accepted to foster/adopt children but in many instances were asked to be discreet about their sexuality and were used for 'hard-to-place' children.

Today social work theory and practice express a mixture of views carried over from the previous decades, although liberal views on sexuality tend to dominate. The challenge for social work is whether it can progress by having the ability to confront itself and the role it has played in promoting heterosexuality as the 'natural' way to be. Succeeding in this task would be a way forward for social work to be able to support and contribute to other ways of viewing sexuality.

Source: Hicks (2005b)

From reading the research summary you will have concluded that it is essential that as you practise social work you recognise the role you can play in constructing certain views of sexuality. This awareness allows you to recognise and challenge oppressive practice. It is one of the main guidelines for best practice as it enables you to start to become a professional who can support service users in an empowering way.

Sexual rights

Another important guideline that makes up the basis for best practice is the upholding of sexual rights. We referred to this issue in Chapter 2 when we highlighted the fact that some people could not achieve sexual well-being due to the denial of their sexual rights. So what are sexual rights? We have summarised the main points of the global statement on sexual rights adopted by the World Association for Sexual Health (2006) in the following research summary (see **www.worldsexology.org/about_sexualrights.asp** for the full statement).

RESEARCH SUMMARY

Declaration of sexual rights
The Declaration of Sexual Rights gives people the right to:

- *sexual freedom to express their full sexual potential excluding all forms of sexual coercion, exploitation, and abuse;*

- *sexual autonomy, sexual integrity and safety of the sexual body, which involves the ability to make autonomous decisions about their sexual life within a context of their own personal and social ethics;*

- *sexual privacy, which involves the right for individual decisions and behaviours about intimacy as long as they do not intrude on the sexual rights of others;*

- *sexual equality, which refers to freedom from all forms of discrimination regardless of sex, gender, sexual orientation, age, race, social class, religion or physical and emotional disability;*

- *sexual pleasure as this is a source of physical, psychological, intellectual and spiritual well-being;*

- *emotional sexual expression;*

- *sexually associate freely, which includes the possibility to marry or not, to divorce, and to establish other types of responsible sexual associations;*

- *make free and responsible reproductive choices, which encompasses the right to decide whether or not to have children and the right to full access to the means of fertility regulation;*

- *comprehensive sexuality education at any time of life;*

- *sexual health care for the prevention and treatment of all sexual concerns, problems, and disorders.*

Source: World Association for Sexual Health (2006)

Reflecting back on our discussion in Chapter 1 on diversity and power, we would argue that the access to and denial of sexual rights are linked to acceptability and power within our society. When we analyse the situation further we realise that sexual rights are not an independent 'stand-alone' list of rights but are in fact enshrined in the political, social, cultural and economic fabric of society. These structures of society construct through discourses what is acceptable in relation to sexuality and therefore who has access to and who is denied sexual rights. For example, in the UK a white heterosexual man has automatic access to his sexual rights whereas a black lesbian has had to fight for her sexual rights.

ACTIVITY 8.1

Reflecting on the above research summary, can you think of any situation in social work where it is justified to deny someone their sexual rights?

Comment

The World Association for Sexual Health regards sexual rights as fundamental and universal human rights which should be afforded to everyone. As we have seen throughout this book, people's sexual rights are often denied because of the way powerful discourses construct their sexuality as unacceptable or nonexistent. Examples we have come across include the denial of sexual rights for lesbian, gay or bisexual people through the assumption of heterosexuality, or the denial of sexual rights for disabled people and older people through the assumption of asexuality. As it is very clear that sexual rights do not include, nor have anything to do with, any type of sexual coercion, exploitation or abuse, we cannot think of a situation in social work where it is justified to deny someone their sexual rights. We would argue that the sexual rights listed in the research summary should form the value base for working with all service users around the issues of sexuality.

CRITICAL THINKING

Sexual citizenship – the example of lesbian, gay and bisexual people

Sexual politics is firmly in the public domain due to the attention given to sexual rights and sexual justice by both the political and legal systems (Bell and Binnie, 2000). For example, in the UK over the last decade lesbian, gay, and bisexual people have fought for and won a range of rights that have been denied them based on their sexual orientation. In the main they include equality with heterosexual people in the areas of age of consent, serving in the armed forces, adoption, employment protection and benefits, receiving goods and services, and forming legal sexual partnerships. It can be argued that acquiring access to specific sexual rights has opened the door to citizenship. Within the area of sexuality and citizenship, also referred to as 'sexual citizenship', there is much critical debate about the meaning and consequences of being or becoming a citizen. To be a citizen is to claim belonging to and inclusion in a particular society. However, citizenship is a socially constructed concept embodying ideas about what behaviour society considers as fit and proper. It is therefore a dynamic concept which is constantly influenced by the different discourses within society. For example, in the UK prior to the Sexual Offences Act 1967 two gay men having a sexual relationship could be imprisoned for their sexuality whereas

CRITICAL THINKING *continued*

after the Civil Partnership Act 2004 the same two gay men can now form a legally recog-nised and sanctioned sexual partnership. A critical question for lesbians, gay men and bisexual people is whether citizenship means becoming assimilated into heteronormative values and ways of thinking (Fish, 2006, p.206) and therefore the loss of radical challenge.

(See Bell and Binnie, 2000, and Richardson, 2000, in 'Further reading' for the range of critical discussions on sexual citizenship).

Sexuality, best practice and social work

ACTIVITY *8.2*

Revisit the case studies presented throughout this book. As you reflect on your comments and the ones we have provided, write down any general guidelines of best social work practice that could be applied in all the situations.

Comment

Every service user's situation is different but by engaging in reflective practice, you should be able to identify some general guidelines of good practice that can be applied to all situations. We have come up with the following guidelines which we feel are important when working with service users around the issues of sexuality. It is not an exhaustive list and you may have identified others which you feel are important.

Best practice guidelines

- The Declaration of Sexual Rights is an important value base to adopt, particularly when working with issues of sexuality.

- It is essential to be aware that your practice can influence how sexuality is constructed. Recognising how you are actively engaging with discourses gives you the potential to challenge and transform them.

- It is vital to be aware of the nature of discrimination around sexuality, in particular heterosexism, and being able to challenge your own attitudes and beliefs as well as that of colleagues and other service users. Awareness of the organisational context of your practice and the existence of any institutional discrimination is helpful in supporting the service user.

- You need to be comfortable about your own sexuality in order to be open and sensitive to the sexual issues of other people.

- It is important not to make any assumptions about a person's sexuality and in particular sexual orientation, as someone's behaviour, feelings and identity may not correspond.

- You need to ascertain how open service users are about their sexual orientation. It is essential to respect the wishes of service users if they want to keep their sexual orientation confidential. Despite confidentiality presenting you with a dilemma in terms of possibly not being able to undertake a full assessment of need, it is important to recognise that for some people it is often a necessary coping strategy (Wilton, 2000).

- When discussing issues of sexuality with service users it is vital to establish clear boundaries. For example, it may have to be made explicit that discussing sexual issues is not about being sexual or flirting with each other. Social workers have the responsibility for establishing and maintaining sexual boundaries in a social work relationship and any sexual relationship with a service user is an abuse of power contravening the Codes of Practice (GSCC, 2002), and in certain situations a criminal offence (Home Office, 2004a, 2004b).

- Good communication skills are a key aspect of working effectively with issues of sexuality. Developing a language of sexual expression and being able to talk about sex comfortably and explicitly are essential skills that will enable service users to express their own doubts, anxieties and problems. Listening sensitively and being aware of the areas of potential difficulty can also encourage service users to discuss sexual issues openly.

- Check your sexual knowledge and keep up to date with regard to sexual issues in terms of theories, practices, resources and networks. In order to practise within an empowering framework it is important to keep yourself open to radical and challenging ideas regarding sexuality. People experience their sexuality in relation to many influences such as their gender, class, ethnicity and age. Discrimination and social exclusion have a detrimental effect on sexual well-being and your perspective on sexuality should recognise this if you are to work effectively with service users.

C H A P T E R   S U M M A R Y

This chapter has introduced you to the concept of sexual rights and sexual citizenship. You have had an opportunity to reflect on the way that social work theories and actions can contribute to the social construction of sexuality in an oppressive way. Through reflecting on the case studies throughout this book you should feel confident to be able to demonstrate your understanding of the guidelines that underpin best practice in social work involving issues of sexuality. A key learning point from this chapter is that through engaging with the guidelines you will be able to demonstrate how social work can be challenging and empowering for service users.

FURTHER READING

Bell, D and Binnie, J (2000) *The sexual citizen: Queer politics and beyond*. Cambridge: Polity Press.

Good comprehensive discussions about the different views on sexual citizenship.

Brown, HC (1998) *Social work and sexuality: Working with lesbians and gay men*. Basingstoke: Macmillan/BASW.

Highlights a range of good practice working with lesbians and gay men across all service user groups.

Hicks, S (2005b) Sexuality: social work theories and practice. In Adams, R, Dominelli, L and Payne, M (eds) *Social work futures: Crossing boundaries, transforming practice*. Basingstoke and New York: Palgrave Macmillan.

Richardson, D (2000) *Rethinking sexuality*. London: Sage publications.

Chapters 4, 5 and 6 give critical discussions on sexual citizenship and sexual rights.

Conclusion

ACTIVITY

We want you to take a few minutes to reflect back on your reading and write down three key points that you feel you have learnt about sexuality.

Comment

We would like to share with you the three main aims of our book, which may be reflected in the key learning points that you have identified for yourself.

Sexuality – social construction

Our first aim has been to encourage you throughout the book to approach a range of issues about sexuality in a critical manner by adopting a social constructionist approach. If the idea of a socially constructed sexuality has been new to you, we hope you have found the introduction and engagement with the concept both exciting and challenging. If you were already familiar with the approach, then we hope this book has strengthened your understanding of the ideas and given you an opportunity to think of some of its tensions and limitations.

> *Sexuality is perhaps the last human dimension that many of us refuse to grant is socially created, historically variable and therefore deeply political.*

(Seidman, 1996, p.2)

We feel that a particular strength of the social constructionist approach is the way it identifies oppression and discrimination around issues of sexuality and challenges the notions of 'normality' and 'acceptability'. We hope the book has given you an understanding of diverse sexualities that you will be able to use to inform your practice.

Sexuality – an important area for social work

Our second aim has been to encourage you to apply the theories and ideas about issues of sexuality to social work practice. We hope we have shown you that sexuality is an important area for social work practice which is often neglected. A key learning point we hope you will take from the book as a whole is that social work is not just about problem issues in relation to sexuality but about positively promoting sexual well-being:

...sex is a central part of people's lived experience and also a right, with sexual expression a matter to be included in assessment and intervention in people's lives.

(Myers and Milner, 2007, p.1)

Sexuality – a right and a pleasure

Our third aim has been to encourage you to view sexuality as an issue for everyone and we hope we have enabled you to understand some of the complexities that some people face when trying to express their sexuality.

...sexuality as a source of pleasure and as an expression of love is not readily recognised for populations that have been traditionally marginalised in society.

(Tepper, 2000, p.285)

We have aimed to give older people, younger people and disabled people a voice in terms of sharing their views and experiences of sexuality and hope you feel able to support people through your practice in achieving their sexual rights.

References

Abbot, P (2006) Gender. In Payne, G (ed.) *Social divisions*. 2nd edition. Basingstoke and New York: Palgrave Macmillan.

Abbott, D and Howarth, J (2005) *Secret loves, hidden lives? Exploring issues for people with learning difficulties who are gay, lesbian or bisexual*. Bristol: The Policy Press.

African HIV Policy Network (2006a) *Stigma and discrimination*. Issue 10, October 2006. **www.ahpn.org/downloads/newsletters/AHPNNewsletters1006.pdf** (accessed 4/3/07).

African HIV Policy Network (2006b) *Department of Health action plan: HIV related stigma and discrimination: The African HIV Policy Network's response* . **www.ahpn.org/downloads/policies/Stigma_and_Discrimination_Action_Plan_-_AHPN_Mar2006.pdf** (accessed 4/3/07).

Alcorn, K (1997a) HIV transmission. In Alcorn, K (ed.) *AIDS reference manual* . London: National AIDS Manual Publication.

Alcorn, K (1997b) Understanding the epidemic. In Alcorn, K (ed.) *AIDS reference manual* . London: National AIDS Manual Publication.

Allen, KR (2005) Gay and lesbian elders. In Johnson, ML (ed.) *The Cambridge handbook of age and ageing* . Cambridge: Cambridge University Press.

Amnesty International UK (2005) *Sexual assault research: Summary report* . Prepared by ICM Research. **http://amnesty.org.uk/uploads/documents/doc_16619.doc** (accessed 9/4/07).

Andrews, S (2006) Sexuality and sexual health throughout the childhood and teenage years. In Balen, R and Crawshaw, M (eds) *Sexuality and fertility issues in ill health and disability* . London and Philadelphia: Jessica Kingsley.

Anorexia Nervosa and Related Eating Disorders, Inc. (2005) *Statistics: How many people have eating disorders?* **www.anred.com/stats.html** (accessed 2/07/07).

Batchelor, S and Raymond, M (2004) 'I slept with 40 boys in three months.' Teenage sexuality in the media: Too much too young. In Burtney, E and Duffy, M (eds) *Young people and sexual health* . Basingstoke and New York: Palgrave Macmillan.

Batty, D (2003) *Q&A: Sexual Offences Act*. In *The Guardian* 24/11/03 Society.

Bayliss, K (2000) Social work values, anti-discriminatory practice and working with older lesbian service users. *Social Work Education* 19 (1): 45–53.

Beasley, C (2005) *Gender and sexuality: Critical theories, critical thinkers*. London: Sage.

Beckett, C (2002) *Human growth and development*. London: Sage.

Bell, D and Binnie, J (2000) *The sexual citizen: Queer politics and beyond*. Cambridge: Polity Press.

Best, S (2005) *Understanding social divisions* . London: Sage.

Bildtgard, T (2000) The sexuality of elderly people on film – Visual limitations. *Journal of Aging and Identity* 5 (3): 169–183.

Bindel, J (2007) *Why is rape so easy to get away with?: Special reports* . **www.E:\Book\Guardian Unlimited.mht** (accessed 2/5/07)

Black Pride Festival **www.ukblackpride.org** (accessed 1/6/07).

Blake, S (2004) Not aliens or rocket science: Young men and sex and relationships work. In Burtney, E and Duffy, M (eds) *Young people and sexual health: Individual, social and policy contexts*. Basingstoke and New York: Palgrave Macmillan.

Bonnie, S (2004) Disabled people, disability and sexuality. In Swaine, J, French, S, Barnes, C and Thomas, C *Disabling barriers – enabling environments.* 2nd edition. London: Sage.

Borell, K and Ghazanfareeon Karlson, S (2003) Reconceptualizing intimacy and ageing: Living apart together. In Arber, S, Davidson, K and Ginn, J (eds) *Gender and ageing: Changing roles and relationships* . Buckingham: Open University Press.

Bortz, WM, Wallace, DH and Wiley, D (1999) Sexual function in 1202 aging males: Differentiating aspects. *Journal of Gerontology,* 54 (5): 237–241.

Bowman, WP, Arcelus, J and Benbow, SM (2006) Nottingham study of sexuality and ageing (NoSSA I). Attitudes regarding sexuality and older people: a review of the literature. *Sexual and Relationship Therapy*, 21 (2) May.

Bradshaw, S (2003) *Vatican: condoms don't stop AIDS. The Guardian* 9 October. See **http://www.guardian.co.uk/aids/story/0,7369,1059068,00.html** (accessed 4/6/06).

Brammer, A (2007) *Social work law,* 2nd edition. Harlow: Pearson Education.

Bremner, J and Hillin, A (1994) *Sexuality, young people and care.* Lyme Regis: Russell House Publishing.

Brown, HC (1998) *Social work and sexuality: Working with lesbians and gay men*. Basingstoke: Macmillan.

Brown, J and Russell, S (2005) My home, your workplace: People with physical disability negotiate their sexual health without crossing professional boundaries. *Disability and Society*, 20(4): 375–388.

Buckley, K and Head, P (2000) Stereotypes can be dangerous: Working with sexuality, power and risk. In Buckley, K and Head, P (eds) *Myths, risks and sexuality* . Dorset: Russell House Publishing.

Burtney, E and Duffy, M (2004) (eds) *Young people and sexual health*. Basingstoke and New York: Palgrave Macmillan.

Buston, K and Wright, D (2006) The salience and utility of school sex education to young men. *Sex Education*. 6 (2), May: 135–150.

Butler, RN (1969) Age-ism: Another form of bigotry. *The Gerontologist*, 9: 243–246.

Butler, J (1990) *Gender trouble*. London: Routledge.

Butler, RN and Lewis, MI (1986) *Love and sex after 40*. New York: Harper and Row.

Bytheway, B (2005) Ageism. In Johnson, ML (eds) *The Cambridge handbook of age and ageing*. Cambridge: Cambridge University Press.

Calasanti, TM and Slevin, KF (2001) *Gender, social inequalities and aging*. Walnut Creek, CA: Altamirapress.

Carabine, J (ed.) (2004) *Sexualities: Personal lives and social policy*. Bristol and Milton Keynes: Polity Press in association with the Open University.

Carr, A (2002) *Avoiding risky sex in adolescence*. Oxford and Malden: Blackwell.

Channel 4 TV (2006) *Can you believe it – gay Muslims?* **http://www.chanel4.com/culture/microsites/C/can_you_believe_it/debates/gaymuslims** (accessed 29/5/06).

Chappell, AL (1998) Still out in the cold: People with learning difficulties and the social model of disability. In Shakespeare, T (eds) *The disability reader: Social science perspectives*. London, NewYork: Continuum.

Choppin, E (2005) Sex talk silenced. **www.disabilitynow.org.uk/timetotalksex/feat_sep_2005.htm** (accessed 10/6/07).

Cincotta, N, Childs, J and Eichenfield, A (2006) Sexuality and growing up HIV-positive. In Balen, R and Crawshaw, M (eds) *Sexuality and fertility issues in ill health and disability: from early adolescence to adulthood*. London and Philadelphia: Jessica Kingsley.

Clarke, A, Bright, L and Greenwood, C (2002) *Sex and relationships: A guide for care homes*. London: Counsel and Care.

Cochrane, K (2007) *For your entertainment*. In *The Guardian* 1/05/07 G2, p. 4–7.

Coleman, J C and Hendry, LB (1999) *The nature of adolescence*. 3rd edition. London: Routledge.

Community Care (2007) HIV and AIDS information. **www.communitycare.co.uk/Articles/Article.aspx?liArticleID=103542&PrinterFriendly=true** (accessed 2/3/07).

Connell, RW (2003) The big picture: Masculinities in recent world history. In Weeks, J, Holland J and Waites, M (eds) *Sexualities and society: A reader*. Cambridge and Malden: Polity Press.

Cook, JA (2000) Sexuality and people with psychiatric disabilities. *Sexuality and Disability*, 18 (3): 195–206.

Cook, K (2004) *Rape appeal study: Summary findings*. **www.truthaboutrape.co.uk** (accessed 15/4/07).

Cooper, N (2004) *Making babies the gay way* . **www.channel4.com/health/microsites/0-9/ 4health/sex/lgb_babies.html#3** (accessed 14/2/07).

Corlyon, J and McGuire, C (1999) *Pregnancy and parenthood: The views and experiences of young people in public care.* London: National Children's Bureau.

Coyle, A (1998) Developing lesbian and gay identity in adolescence. In Coleman, J and Roker, D (eds) *Teenage sexuality: Health, risk and education* . London: Harwood Academic Press.

Crawford, K and Walker, J (2003) *Social work and human development.* Exeter: Learning Matters.

Crawford, K and Walker, J (2004) *Social work with older people* . Exeter: Learning Matters.

D'Augelli, RAH, Grossman, SL, Hershberger, and O'Connell, TS (2001) Aspects of mental health among older lesbian, gay, and bisexual adults. 'Aging and Mental Health, 5(2): 149–158'.

Davenport, W (1965) Sexual patterns and their regulation in a society of the South West Pacific. In Beach, F (ed.) *Sex and behaviour.* New York: Wiley.

Davies, D (1996) Homophobia and heterosexism. In Davies, D and Neal, C (eds) *Pink therapy.* Buckingham: Open University Press.

Davies, D (2000) Sharing our stories, empowering our lives: Don't dis me! *Sexuality and Disability* 18 (3): 179–186.

Davies, D and Neal, C (1996) (eds) *Pink therapy* . Buckingham: Open University Press.

De Palma, R and Atkinson, E (2006) The sound of silence: Talking about sexual orientation and schooling. *Journal of Sex Education* , 6 (4): 333–349.

Department for Education and Employment (2000) *Guidance of sex and relationship education.* London: The Stationery Office.

Department for Education and Skills (2000) *Don't suffer in silence.* **www.dfes.gov.uk/bullying** (accessed 14/4/07).

Department for Education and Skills (2006) *Care matters: Transforming the lives of children and young people in care.* London: HMSO.

Department for Work and Pensions (2005) *Factsheet 1: The definitions of disability.* **www.dwp.gov.uk/aboutus/provisions-dda.pdf** (accessed on 8/6/07).

Department of Health (1991) *The Children Act 1989: Guidance and regulations. Volume 4 Residential Care.* London: HMSO.

Department of Health (2000) *No secrets: Guidance on developing and implementing multi-agency policies and procedures to protect vulnerable adults.* London: HMSO.

Department of Health (2001a) *Better prevention, better services, better sexual health: The national strategy for sexual health and HIV.* **www.dh.gov.uk/assetRoot/04/05/89/45/04058945.pdf** (accessed 2/3/07).

Department of Health (2001b) *The national service framework for older people.* London: HMSO.

Department of Health (2001c) *The national sexual health strategy.* London: HMSO.

Department of Health (2001d) *Carers and Disabled Children Act 2000: Carers and people with parental responsibility for disabled children: policy guidance*. London: HMSO.

Department of Health (2001e) *Valuing people: A new strategy for learning disability for the 21st century*. **www.archive.official-documents.co.uk/document/cm50/5086/5086.pdf** (accessed 13/06/07).

Department of Health (2002a) *Care homes for older people: National minimum standards; Care homes regulations*. London: The Stationery Office.

Department of Health (2002b) *Requirements for social work training*. London: HMSO.

Department of Health (2002c) *Adoption and Children Act*. **http://www.opsi.gov.uk/acts/acts 2002/20020038.htm** (accessed 6/2/07)

Department of Health (2004) *Choosing health: Making healthy choices easier*. **www.dh.gov.uk/ PublicationsAndStatistics/Publications/PublicationsPolicyAndGuidance/ PublicationsPolicyAndGuidanceArticle/fs/en?CONTENT_ID=4094550&chk=aN5Cor** (accessed 2/3/07).

Department of Health (2005) *Action plan: HIV related stigma and discrimination*. **www.dh.gov.uk/en/Consultations/Closedconsultations/DH_4132988** (accessed 2/3/07).

Disability Now (2005) *Professionals challenged for seeing sex as a 'problem'*. **www.disabilitynow.org.uk/timetotalksex/news.apr.htm** (accessed 10/6/07).

Dodds, C, Keogh, P, Chime, O, Haruperi, T, Nabulya, B, Sseruma, WS and Weatherburn, P (2004) *Outsider status: Stigma and discrimination experienced by gay men and African people with HIV*. London: Sigma Research. **www.sigmaresearch.org.uk/downloads/report04f.pdf** (accessed 2/3/07).

Dogra, N, Parkin, A, Gale, F and Frake, C (2002) *A multi-disciplinary handbook of child and adolescent mental health for front-line professionals*. London: Jessica Kingsley.

Donelson, R and Rogers, T (2004) Negotiating a research protocol for studying school-based gay and lesbian issues. *Journal of Theory into Practice*, 43 (2): 128–135.

Donnellan, C (2005) *Sexuality and discrimination*. Cambridge: Independence.

Douglas-Scott, S (2004) Sexuality and learning disability. In Burtney, E and Duffy, M (eds) *Young people and sexual health*. Basingstoke and New York: Palgrave Macmillan.

Dworkin, A (1981) *Pornography: Men possessing women*. London: The Women's Press.

Earle, S (1999) Facilitated sex and the concept of sexual need: disabled students and their personal assistants. *Disability and Society*, 4 (3): 309–323.

Erooga, M and Masson, H (eds) (2006) *Children and young people who sexually abuse others: Current developments and practice responses*. 2nd edition. London and New York: Routledge.

Fenge, L (2006) Promoting inclusiveness: Developing empowering practice with minority groups of older people – the example of older lesbian women and gay men. In Brown, K (ed.) *Vulnerable adults and community care*. Exeter: Learning Matters.

Fergusson, DM and Mullen, PE (1999) *Childhood sexual abuse: An evidence based perspective*. Thousand Oaks, CA: Sage Publications.

Finger, A (1992) Forbidden fruit. *New Internationalist*, no. 233, 8–10.

Fish, J (2006) *Heterosexism in health and social care*. Basingstoke and New York: Palgrave.

Foley, M (1996) Who is in control?: Changing responses to women who have been raped and sexually abused. In Hester, M, Kelly, L and Radford, J (eds) *Women, violence and male power: Feminist research, activism and practice*. Buckingham: Open University Press.

Fooken, I (1994) Sexuality in the later years – the impact of health and body image in a sample of older women. *Patient Education and Counselling*, 23 (3): 227–233.

Ford, CS and Beach, A (1951) Patterns of sexual behaviour. In Giddens, A (1997) *Sociology*. 3rd edition. Oxford: Blackwell.

Foreign and Commonwealth Office, Association of Directors of Social Services, Home Office, Department for Education and Skills, Department of Health (2004) *Young people and vulnerable adults facing forced marriage: Practice guidance for social workers*. **www.adss.org.uk/publications/guidance/marriage.pdf** (accessed 15/4/07).

Fortier, E (2004) *Migration and HIV: Improving lives*. London: All Party Parliamentary Group on AIDS. **www.appgaids.org.uk/Publications/Migration%20and%20HIV%20Improving%20Lives.pdf** (accessed 30/5/07).

Foucault, M (1973) *The birth of the clinic: An archaeology of medical perception*. London: Tavistock Publications.

Foucault, M (1978) *The history of sexuality. Volume 1: An introduction*. London: Allen Lane.

Foucault, M (1981) The order of discourse. In Young, R (ed) *Untying the text*. New York: Routledge & Kegan Paul.

Foucault, M (1988) *Politics, philosophy, culture: Interviews and other writing 1977–1984*. London, Routledge.

Foundation for Women's Health, Research and Development (FORWARD) (2007a) *Female genital mutilation (FGM)*. **www.forwarduk.org.uk/key-issues/fgm** (accessed 15/4/07).

Foundation for Women's Health, Research and Development (FORWARD) (2007b) *Child marriage*. **www.forwarduk.org.uk/key-issues/child-marriage** (accessed 15/4/07).

Fox, N (1993) Postmodernism, sociology and health. Buckingham: Open University Press. Cited in Wilton, T (2000) *Sexualities in health and social care: A textbook*. Buckingham: Open University Press.

Frosh, S, Phoenix, A and Pattman, R (2002) *Young masculinities*. Basingstoke and New York: Palgrave.

Furley, R (2000) HIV and AIDS: Current issues for the social work role. *Social Work Review*, 12 (3): 26–28.

GALOP (1998) *Telling it like it is*. **www.galop.org.uk**.

GALOP (2001) The low down. **www.galop.org.uk**.

General Social Care Council (GSCC) (2002) *Codes of practice for social care workers and employers.* London: General Social Care Council.   •

Giddens, A (2006) *Sociology.* 5th edition. Cambridge: Polity Press.

Gilbert, LA, Walker, SJ, McKinney, S and Snell, JL (1999) Challenging discourse themes reproducing gender in heterosexual dating: An analog study. In *Sex Roles,* 41 (9–10): 753–774.

Golightley, M (2006) *Social work and mental health.* 2nd edition. Exeter: Learning Matters.

Golombok, S (2002) Adoption by lesbian couples: is it in the best interests of the child? *British Medical Journal,* 234: 1407–1408.

Golombok, S, Spencer, A. et al. (1983) Children in lesbian and single-parent households: psychosexual and psychiatric appraisal. *Journal of Child Psychology and Psychiatry* 24(4): 551–572.

Golombok, S and Tasker, F (1996) Do Parents Influence the Sexual Orientation of Their Children? *Developmental Psychology,* 32, (1): 9.

Golombok, S, Tasker, F and Murray, C (1997) Children raised in fatherless families from infancy: family relationships and the socio-emotional development of children of lesbian and single heterosexual mothers. *Child Psychol. Psychiatry,* 38–7: 783–791.

Goodley, D (2001) Learning difficulties: The social model of disability and impairment: challenging epistemologies. *Disability and Society,* 16 (2): 207–232.

Gott, M (2005) *Sexuality, sexual health and ageing.* Maidenhead and New York: OUP/McGraw-Hill Education.

Gough, B and McFadden, M (2001) *Critical social psychology: An introduction.* Basingstoke and New York: Palgrave.

Gradwell, L (1997/8) A rose by any other name. In *Healthmatters,* 32: 8–9. **www. healthmatters.org.uk/issue32/arose** (accessed 17/6/07).

Gray, R, Brewin, E, Noak, J, Wyke-Joseph, J and Sonik, B (2002) A review of the literature on HIV infection and schizophrenia: Implications for research, policy and clinical practice. *Journal of Psychiatric and Mental Health Nursing,* 9 (4): 405–409.

Haraway, DJ (2007) 'Gender' for a Marxist dictionary: The sexual politics of a word. In Parker, R and Aggleton, P (eds) 2nd edition *Culture, society and sexuality: a reader.* London and New York: Routledge.

Hawkes, G (1996) A sociology of sex and sexuality. In Gott, M (2005) *Sexuality, sexual health and ageing.* Maidenhead and New York: Open University Press/McGraw-Hill Education.

Hawkes, G and Scott, J (2005) Sex and society. In Hawkes, G and Scott, J (eds) *Perspectives in human sexuality.* Australia, Oxford, New York: Oxford University Press.

Hendricks, J and Hendricks, CJ (1977) Sexuality in later life. In Hendricks J (ed.) *Aging in mass society: Myths and realities.* Cambridge MA: Winthrop.

Herdt, G and Beeler, J (1998) Older gay men and lesbians in families. In Patterson, CJ and R.D'Augelli, A (eds) *Lesbian, gay, and bisexual identities in families: Psychological perspectives.* New York: Oxford University Press.

Hicks, S (1996) The 'last' resort? Lesbian and gay experiences of the social work assessment process in fostering and adoption. *Practice* 8 (2): 15–24.

Hicks, S (1997) Taking the risk? Assessing lesbian and gay carers. In Kemshall, H and Pritchard, J (eds) *Good practice in risk assessment and risk management 2: Protection, rights and responsibilities*. London: Jessica Kingsley.

Hicks, S (2005a) Lesbian and gay foster care and adoption: A brief UK history. *Adoption and Fostering*, 29 (3): 42–56.

Hicks, S (2005b) Sexuality: Social work theories and practice. In Adams, R, Dominelli, L and Payne, M (eds) *Social work futures: Crossing boundaries, transforming practice*. Basingstoke and New York: Palgrave Macmillan.

Hicks, S (2006) Genealogy's desire: Practices of kinship amongst lesbian and gay foster-carers and adopters. *British Journal of Social Work*, 36: 761–776.

Hill Collins, P (2000) *Black feminist thought: Knowledge, consciousness and the politics of empowerment.* 2nd edition. New York and London: Routledge.

Hinchliffe, S and Gott, M (2004) Intimacy, commitment, and adaptation: Sexual relationships within long-term marriages. *Journal of Social and Personal Relationships* 21(5): 595–609.

Hirst, J (2004) Researching young people's sexuality and learning about sex – Experience, need and sex and relationship education. *Culture, Health and Sexuality*, 6 (2): 115–129.

HM Government (2006) *Working together to safeguard children: A guide to interagency working to safeguard and promote the welfare of children*. London: Department of Education and Skills. **www.everychildmatters.gov.uk/workingtogether/** (accessed 14/4/07).

HM Government (2007) *Cross-government action plan on sexual violence and abuse.* London: Home Office. **www.homeoffice.gov.uk/documents/Sexual-violence-action-plan** (accessed 15/4/07).

Hockey, J and James, A (2003) *Social identities across the life course*. Basingstoke and New York: Palgrave Macmillan.

Holland, J, Ramazanoglu, C, Sharpe, S and Thompson, R (1998) *The male in the head: Young people, heterosexuality and power*. London: Tufnell Press.

Holland, J, Ramazanoglu, C, Sharpe, S and Thompson, R (2003) When bodies come together: Power, control and desire. In Weeks, J, Holland, J and Waites, M (eds) *Sexualities and society: A reader*. Cambridge, Oxford, Malden: Polity Press.

Holloway, W (1984) Gender differences and the production of subjectivity. In Henriques, J, Holloway, W, Urwin, C, Venn, C and Walkerdine, V (eds) *Changing the subject*. London: Methuen.

Home Office (2000) *Setting the boundaries: Reforming the law on sex offences (Volume 1)*. London: Home Office Communication Directorate. **http://www.lawbore.net/articles/setting-the-boundaries.pdf** (accessed 10/4/07).

Home Office (2004a) *Adults: Safer from sexual crime: The Sexual Offences Act 2003*. **www.homeoffice.gov.uk/documents/adult-safer-fr-sex-harm-leaflet** (accessed 10/4/07).

Home Office (2004b) *Children and families: Safer from sexual crime. The Sexual Offences Act 2003.* **www.homeoffice.gov.uk/documents/children-safer-fr-sex-crime?view=Binary** (accessed 10/4/07).

Home office (2004c) *Working within the Sexual Offences Act 2003* **http://www.voiceuk.org.uk/docs/care-workers.pdf** (accessed 13/06/07).

Home Office (2005) *Tackling sexual violence: Guidance for local partnerships* . London: Home Office. **www.crimereduction.gov.uk/dv/dv13.pdf** (accessed 14/4/07).

hooks, bell (1992) *Black looks: race and representation.* Boston, MA: South End Press.

Hope, VD and Macarthur, C (1998) Safer sex and social class: Findings from a study of men using the 'gay scene' in the West Midlands region of the United Kingdom. *AIDS Care,* 10 (1): 81–88.

Hughes, B (2004) Disability and the body. In Swain, J, French, S, Barnes, C and Thomas, C (eds) 2nd edition *Disabling barriers – enabling environments* . London, Thousand Oaks, New Delhi: Sage.

Humphreys, L (1970) *The tearoom trade.* London: Duckworth.

Hunt, S (2005) *The life course: A sociological introduction* . Basingstoke and New York: Palgrave Macmillan.

Hyde, M (2006) Disability. In Payne, G (eds) 2nd edition. *Social divisions.* Basingstoke and New York: Palgrave Macmillan.

International Federation of Social Workers (1990) *International policy on HIV/AIDS* . **www.ifsw.org/en/p38000082.html** (accessed 9/3/07).

International Federation of Social Workers (2000) *Social work manifesto on HIV/AIDS.* **www.ifsw.org/en/p38000241.html** (accessed 9/3/07).

Jackson, S (1999) *Heterosexuality in question.* London: Sage.

Jackson, S (2006) Heterosexuality, sexuality and gender: Rethinking the intersections. In Richardson, D, McLaughlin, J and Casey, ME (eds) *Intersections between feminist and queer theory.* Basingstoke and New York: Palgrave Macmillan.

Jackson, S and Scott, S (2006) Sexuality. In Payne, G (eds) *Social divisions* . 2nd edition. Hampshire: Palgrave Macmillan.

Jeary, K (2004) Sexual abuse of elderly people: Would we rather not know the details? *Journal of Adult Protection,* 6 (2): 21–31.

Jeffries, S (1985) *The spinster and her enemy.* London: HarperCollins.

Johns, R (2005) *Using the law in social work.* 2nd edition. Exeter: Learning Matters.

Johnson, MH (2004) A biological perspective on human sexuality. In Brooks-Gordon, et al., *Sexuality repositioned: diversity and the law.* Oxford: Hart Publishing.

Jones, RL (2002) 'That's very rude, I shouldn't be telling you that': Older women talking about sex. *Narrative Inquiry* , 12 (1): 121–42.

Kallianes, V and Rubenfield, P (1997) Disabled women and reproductive rights. *Disability & Society*, 12 (2): 203–221.

Katz, S and Marshall, BL (2003) Is the functional 'normal'? Aging, sexuality and the bio-marking of successful living. *History of the Human Sciences*, 17 (1): 53–75.

Kedde, H and van Berlo, W (2006) Sexual satisfaction and sexual self images of people with physical disabilities in the Netherlands. *Sexuality and Disability*, 24, (1): 53–68.

Kelly, L (1988) *Surviving sexual violence*. Cambridge: Polity Press.

Kelly, L (1996a) Weasel words: Paedophiles and the cycle of abuse. *Trouble and Strife Issues,* 33: 44–49. **www.womenssupportproject.co.uk/files/pdf/WeaselWords.pdf** (accessed 16/4/07).

Kelly, L (1996b) When does the speaking profit us?: Reflections on the challenges of developing feminist perspectives on abuse and violence by women. In Hester, M, Kelly, L and Radford, J (eds) *Women, violence and male power: Feminist research, activism and practice*. Buckingham: Open University Press.

Kelly, L, Lovett, J and Regan, L (2005) *A gap or chasm? Attrition in reported rape cases.* London: Home Office. **www.homeoffice.gov.uk/rds/pdfs05/hors293.pdf** (accessed 17/4/07).

Kemshall, H and McIvor, G (eds) (2004) *Managing sex offender risk*. London and Philadelphia: Jessica Kingsley.

Kenny, C (2004) More abuse of older people in residential homes, finds charity helpline. **www.communitycare.co.uk/Articles/2004/11/29/47289/more-abuse-of-older-people-in-residential-homes-findscharity.html?key=ELDER%20AND%20ABUSE** (accessed 5/2/07).

King, M (2003) *Mental health and wellbeing of gay men, lesbians and bisexuals in England and Wales*. London: MIND.

Kinsey Institute (1999) Kinsey's heterosexual-homosexual rating scale. **www.kinseyinstitute.org/rresources/ak-hhscale.html** (accessed 4/5/07).

Kinsey, AC, Pomeroy, WP and Martin, C (1948) *Sexual behaviour in the human male*. Philadelphia, PA: Saunders.

Kitwood, T (1997) *Dementia reconsidered: The person comes first.* Buckingham, Philadelphia, PA: Open University Press.

Krug, EG, Dahlberg, LL, Mercy, JA, Zwi, AB and Lozano, R (2002) *World report on violence and health*. Geneva: World Health Organisation. **www.who.int/violence_injury_prevention/violence/world_report/en/full_en.pdf** (accessed on 2/5/07).

Lamb, E (ed.) (1999) *Parenting and child development in 'non-traditional' families*. London: L. Erlbaum Associates.

Langley, J (2001) Developing anti-oppressive empowering social work practice with older lesbian women and gay men. *British Journal of Social Work,* 31: 917–932.

Lavin, N (2004) *Long-time companions*. Community Care, 22 July **www.community.careco.uk** (accessed 2/2/07).

Levy, JA (1999) Sex and sexuality in later life stages. In Rossi, AS (ed.) *Sexuality across the life course*. Chicago, IL: University of Chicago Press.

Lewis, J (1984) *Women in England 1870–1950: sexual divisions and social change*. Brighton: Wheatsheaf.

Lindsay, J (2005) Don't panic!: Young people and the social organisation of sex. In Hawkes, G and Scott, J (eds) *Perspectives in human sexuality*. Victoria, Oxford, and New York: Oxford University Press.

Local Authority Social Services Letter (LASSL) (2004) Female Genital Mutilation Act 2003. London: Department for Education and Skills. Available at **http://www.dh.gov.uk/en/ Publicationsandstatistics/Lettersandcirculars/Localauthoritysocialservicesletters/ AllLASSLs/DH_4074779** (accessed on 14/4/07).

Loe, M (2004) *The rise of Viagra: How the little blue pill changed sex in America.* New York: New York University Press.

London Borough of Waltham Forest (2005) *Confidentiality and HIV/AIDS.* **www.walthamforest. gov.uk/com-doc-cs348pdf** (accessed 2/3/07).

Lorber, J (1994) *Paradoxes of gender.* New Haven, CT: Yale University Press.

Lovell, E (2002) *I think I may need some help with this problem: Responding to children and young people who display sexual harmful behaviour.* London: NSPCC.

Lovett, J, Regan, L, and Kelly, L (2004) *Sexual assault referral centres: Developing good practice and maximising potentials*. London: Home Office Research Development Study. **www.homeoffice.gov.uk/rds/pdfs04/hors285pdf** (accessed 4/6/07).

Low, LPL, Lui, MHL, Lee, DTF, Thompson, DR and Chau, JPC (2005) Promoting awareness of sexuality of older people in residential care. Electronic *Journal of Human Sexuality* 8, August 24 **www.ejhs.org** (accessed 19/1/07).

McCarthy, M (1999) *Sexuality and women with learning disabilities.* London: Jessica Kingsley.

McCarthy, M and Thompson, D (2007) *Sex and the 3R's: Rights, responsibilities and risks*. Brighton: Pavilion Publishing.

McDermott, E (2006) Surviving in dangerous places: Lesbian identity performances in the workplace, social class and psychological health. *Feminism and Psychology*, 16(2): 193–211.

McFarlane, L (1998) *Diagnosis: Homophobic: The experiences of lesbians, gay men and bisexuals in the mental health services.* London: PACE.

Miller, R and Murray, D (1998) *Social work and HIV/AIDS: Practitioner guide.* Birmingham: Venture Press.

Milligan, M and Neufeldt, A (2001) The myth of asexuality: A survey of social and empirical evidence. *Sexuality and Disability*, 19 (2): 91–109.

Molloy, D, Knight, T and Woodfield, K (2003) Diversity in disability: exploring the interactions between disability, ethnicity, age, gender and sexuality. In Department of Work and Pensions. *Research Report 188, October*. London. **http://www.dwp.gov.uk/asd/asd5/rports 2003- 2004/rrep188.asp** (accessed 2/7/07).

Mona, LR, Gardos, PS and Brown, RC (1994) Sexual self views of women with disabilities: The relationship among age-of-onset, nature of disability and sexual self-esteem. *Sexuality and Disability*, 12: 261–277.

Moore, S and Rosenthal, D (1998) Adolescent sexual behaviour. In Coleman, J and Roker, D (eds) *Teenage sexuality: Health, risk and education*. London: Harwood Academic Press.

Moore, TM, Strauss, JL, Herman, S and Donatucci, CF (2003) Erectile dysfunction in early, middle and late adulthood: Symptom patterns and psychosocial correlates. *Journal of Sex and Marital Therapy* 29 (5): 381–399.

Myers, S and Milner, J (2007) *Sexual issues in social work*. Bristol: Policy Press.

Nagel, J (2003) *Race, ethnicity and sexuality: Intimate intersections, forbidden frontiers*. Oxford and New York: Oxford University Press.

National Aids Trust (2004) *The needs of people living with HIV in the UK: A guide*. London: National Aids Trust. **www.nat.org.uk/download?rootDocumentId=99&eid= WVC6CAP DIQD4Y&WebDeck.ICO=true** (accessed 2/3/07).

National Aids Trust (2006) *HIV in the United Kingdom: A progress report – 2006*. London: National Aids Trust. **www.nat.org.uk/documents/148** (accessed 8/3/07).

National Aids Trust (2006a) *Criminal prosecution of HIV transmission: NAT policy update*. **www.nat.org.uk/document/68** (accessed 5/3/07).

National Aids Trust (2006b) *Crown prosecution service policy for prosecuting cases of disability hate crime*. **www.nat.org.uk/document/210** (accessed 5/3/07).

National Institute of Health (1992) *Impotence: NIH Consensus Development Conference Statement December* **www.consensus.nih.gov/1992/1992Impotence091html.htm** (accessed 23/1/07).

Northampton County Council (2006) *Facts and figures about disability in the UK*. **www.northamptonshire.gov.uk/ncc/Templates/PrintFriendly.aspx?guid={A4EDA04F-5911-4E43-8244-0548D69002D0}** (accessed 2 July 2007).

Office for Criminal Justice Reform (2006) *Convicting rapists and protecting victims – justice for victims of rape: a consultation paper*. **www.cjsonline.giv.uk/the_cjs/whats_news/news-3299.html** (accessed on 19/2/07).

Ofsted (2007) *Time for change? Personal, social and health education*. **www.ofsted.gov.uk/ publications/070049** (accessed 12/4/07).

Oppenheimer, C (2002) Sexuality in old age. In Jacoby, R and Oppenheimer, C (eds) *Psychiatry in the elderly*. Oxford: Oxford University Press.

O'Toole, CJ (2000) The view from below: Developing a knowledge base about an unknown population. *Sexuality and Disability*, 18 (3): 207–224.

Parker, J and Bradley, G (2003) *Social work practice: Assessment, planning, intervention and review*. Exeter: Learning Matters.

Patel-Kanwal, H (2004) Service provision for meeting the sexual health needs of young people from Indian, Pakistani and Bangladeshi communities. In Burtney, E and Duffy, M (eds) *Young people and sexual health*. Basingstoke and New York: Palgrave Macmillan.

Payne, G (ed.) (2006) *Social divisions.* Basingstoke: Palgrave Macmillan.

Petrelis, M (2005) *Muslim scholar wants UAE gay arrestees executed* . Petrelis Files: **www.mpetrelis. blogspot.com/2005/12/gulf-news-muslim-scholar-wants-uae-gay.htlm** (accessed 4/6/06).

Phillips, LM (2000) *Flirting with danger: Young women's reflections on sexuality and domination.* London: New York University Press.

Pierson, J (2002) *Tackling social exclusion.* London and New York: Routledge.

Plante, RF (2004) Sexuality and subversion: University peer sexuality educators and the possibilities for change. In Kimmel, MS and Plante, RF (eds) *Sexualities: Identities, behaviours and society* . Oxford: Oxford University Press.

Plummer, K (1975) *Sexual stigma: an interactive account.* London: Routledge & Kegan Paul.

Plummer, K (1995) *Telling sexual stories: Power, change and social worlds.* London: Routledge.

Priestley, M (2003) *Disability, a life course approach.* Cambridge: Polity Press.

Pugh, S (2005) Assessing the cultural needs of older lesbians and gay men: Implications for practice. *Practice* 17 (3): 207–218.

Pulerwitz, J, Amaro, H, DeJong, W, Gortmaker, SL and Rudd, R (2002) Relationship power, condom use and HIV risk among women in the USA. *AIDS Care,* 14 (6): 789–800.

Puri, BK, Brown, RA, McKee, HJ and Treasden, IH (2005) *Mental health law: A practical guide* . London: Hodder Arnold.

Rainbow Ripples and Butler, R (2006) *The Rainbow Ripples report: Lesbian, gay and bisexual disabled people's experiences of service provision in Leeds* . **www.rainbowripples.org.uk/ the_rainbow_ripples_report.doc** (accessed 7/6/06).

Rape Crisis, England and Wales (2006) *Myths* . **www.rapecrisis.org.uk/myths.html** (accessed 15/4/07).

Reed, J, Stanley, D and Clarke, C (2004) *Health, well-being and older people.* Bristol: Policy Press.

Reiss, IL and Reiss, HM (2003) The role of religion in our sexual lives. In Heasley, R and Crane, B (eds) *Sexual lives: A reader on the theories and realities of human sexualities.* London: McGraw-Hill.

Renold, E (2007) Primary school 'studs': (de)constructing young boys' heterosexual masculinities. *Men and Masculinities,* 9: 275–297.

Rich, A (1980) Compulsory heterosexuality and lesbian existence. *Signs,* 5 (4): 630–60.

Richardson, D (2000) *Re-thinking sexuality.* London: Sage.

Risman, B and Schwartz, P (2004) After the sexual revolution: Gender politics in teen dating. In Stombler, M, Baunach, DM, Burgess, EO, Donnelly, D and Simonds, W (eds) *Sex matters: The sexuality and society reader.* Boston: Pearson Education.

Rubin, G (1993) Thinking sex: Notes for a radical theory of the politics of sexuality. In Kauffman, LS (eds) *American feminist thought at century's end: A reader* . Cambridge: Blackwell.

Ryan, A (2005) From dangerous sexualities to risky sex: Regulation sexuality in the name of public health. In Hawkes, G and Scott, J (eds) *Perspectives in human sexuality* . Australia, Oxford, New York: Oxford University Press.

Sale, AU (2002) *Back in the closet* . Community Care 30 May **www.communitycare.co.uk**. (accessed 13/2/07).

Saul, JM (2003) *Feminism: Issues and arguments*. Oxford: Oxford University Press.

Scott, S and Jackson, S (2006) Sexuality. In Payne, G 2nd edition. *Social divisions* . Basingstoke and New York: Palgrave Macmillan.

Scott-Sheldon, LAJ, Marsh, KL, Johnson, BT, and Glasford, DE (2006) Condoms + pleasure=safer sex? A missing addend in the safer sex message. *AIDS Care,* 18 (7): 750–754.

Seidman, S (1996) Introduction. In Seidman, S (ed.) *Queer theory/sociology*. Massachusetts and Oxford: Blackwell.

Shakespeare, T (1999) Coming out and coming home . *Journal of Gay, Lesbian and Bisexual Identity,* 4 (1): 39–51.

Shakespeare, T (2000) Disabled sexuality: Toward rights and recognition. *Sexuality and Disability*, 18 (3): 159–166.

Shakespeare, T (2003) 'I haven't seen that in the Karma Sutra': The sexual stories of disabled people. In Weeks, J, Holland, J and Waites, M (eds) *Sexualities and society: A reader.* Cambridge, Oxford, Malden: Polity Press.

Shakespeare, T, Gillespie-Sells, K and Davies, D (1996) *The sexual politics of disability: Untold desires*. London: Cassell.

Sheffield, CJ (2004) Sexual terrorism. In Kimmel, MS and Plante, RF (eds) *Sexualities: Identities, behaviours and society* . New York, Oxford: Oxford University Press.

Shepard, G (1987) Rank, gender and homosexuality: Mombassa as a key to understanding sexual options. In Caplan, P (ed.) *The social construction of sexuality*. London: Tavistock.

Sherman, B (1999) *Sex, intimacy and aged care* . London and Philadelphia, PA: Jessica Kingsley.

Shildrick, M (2004) Silencing sexuality: The regulation of the disabled body. In Carabine, J (ed.) *Sexualities: personal lives and social policy*. Bristol: Policy Press in conjunction with Open University.

Shucksmith, J (2004) A risk worth the taking: Sex and selfhood in adolescence. In Burtney, E and Duffy, M (eds) *Young people and sexual health*. Basingstoke and New York: Palgrave Macmillan.

Skeates, J and Jabri, D (eds) (1988) *Fostering and adoption by lesbians and gay men*. London: London Strategic Policy Unit.

Smith, PP (1992) Encounters with older lesbians in psychiatric practice. *Sexual and Marital Therapy,* 7 (1): 79–86.

Smith, AMA, Rosenthal, DA and Reichler, H (2004) High schoolers' masturbatory practices: Their relationship to sexual intercourse and personal characteristics. In Kimmel, MS and Plante, RF (eds) *Sexualities: Identities, behaviours and society*. New York and Oxford: Oxford University Press.

Speak, S (1997) *Young single fathers: Participation in fatherhood*. **www.jrf.org.uk/knowledge/ findings/socialpolicy/sp137.asp** (accessed 14/4/07).

Steiner, S (2002) *Sharia law*: **www.guardian.co.uk/theissues/article/0,6512,777972,00.html** (accessed 4/6/06).

Stephen, K (2002) Sexualised bodies. In Evans, M and Lee, E (eds) *Real bodies: A sociological introduction*. Basingstoke: Palgrave.

Stoltenberg, J (2004) Toward gender justice. In Murphy, F (ed.) *Feminism and masculinities*. Oxford: Oxford University Press.

Stonewall (2007) *Homophobic bullying*. **www.stonewall.org.uk/information_bank/education/ homophobic_bullying/default.asp** (accessed 14/4/07).

Surrey County Council (2007) *The Fraser Guidelines*. **www.surreycc.gov.uk/sccwebsite/ sccwspages. nsf/LookupWebPageByTITLE_RTF/The+Fraser+Guidelines?opendocument** (accessed 19/4/07).

Tasker, FL and Golombok, S (1997) *Growing up in a lesbian family: Effects on child development*. New York: Guilford.

Temkin, J (1987) *Rape and the legal process*. London: Routledge & Kegan Paul.

Tepper, MS (2000) Sexuality and disability: The missing discourse of pleasure. *Sexuality and Disability*, 18 (4): 283–290.

Terrence Higgins Trust (2001a) *Prejudice, discrimination and HIV: A report*. London: Terrence Higgins Trust. **www.tht.org.uk/informationresources/publications/policyreports/ prejudice report581.pdf** (accessed 8/3/07).

Terrence Higgins Trust (2001b) *Social exclusion and HIV: A report*. London: Terrence Higgins Trust. **www.tht.org.uk/informationresources/publications/policyreports/socialexclusionandhiv 582.pdf** (accessed 8/3/07).

Terrence Higgins Trust (2007) *Disturbing symptoms 5: How primary care trusts managed sexual health and HIV in 2006 and how specialist clinicians viewed their progress: a research report February 2007*. **www.tht.org.uk/informationresources/publications/policyreports/disturbingsymptoms 5.pdf** (accessed 2/3/07).

Thomson, R (2004) Sexuality and young people. In Carabine, J (ed.) *Sexualities: Personal lives and social policy*. Bristol and Milton Keynes: Polity Press in association with the Open University.

Thomson, R and Holland, J (1998) Sexual relationships, negotiation and decision making. In Coleman, J and Roker, D (eds) *Teenage sexuality: Health, risk and education*. Reading: Harwood Academic.

Thompson, A and Siddiqui, H (1999) *Clash of cultures*. Community Care Archive article, 7 August 1999.

Thompson, N (2006) *Anti-discriminatory practice*. 4th edition. Basingstoke: Palgrave Macmillan.

Took, M (2004) *Rethink policy statement 56: Sexual issues relating to people with severe mental illness, including harassment, sexual dysfunction, psychosexual education and sexuality.* **www.rethink.org/ document.rm?id=526** (accessed 10/7/06).

Trotter, J and Hafford-Letchfield, T (2006) *Let's talk about sexuality.* In *Community Care* 9–15 November, pp.36–37.

Trumbach, R (2003) Sex and the gender revolution. In Weeks, J et al., (eds) *Sexuality and societies: A reader .* Cambridge: Polity Press.

Turner, C (1992) *HIV and AIDS in the Diploma in Social Work .* London: Central Council for Education and Training in Social Work.

Ussher, JM (2005) The meaning of sexual desire: Experiences of heterosexual and lesbian girls . *Feminism and Psychology*, 15 (1): 27–32.

Valios, N. (2001) *Desire denied .* **www.communitycare.co.uk/Articles/Article.aspx?liArticle ID=3319** (accessed 5/5/07).

Vaughan, G (2000) Violence, sexuality and gay male domestic violence. In Buckley, K and Head, P (eds) *Myths, risks and sexuality: The role of sexuality in working with people .* Lyme Regis: Russell House.

Victim Support (2006) *Crime and prejudice: The support needs of victims of hate crime: a research report.* Victim Support, June 2006. **www.victimsupport.org.uk/vs_england_wales/ about_us/publications/hate_crime/crime_prejudice.pdf** (accessed 2/3/07).

Ward, CA (1995) *Attitudes towards rape: Feminist and social psychological perspectives .* London, Thousand Oaks, New Dehli: Sage.

Waites, M (2005) *The age of consent.* Basingstoke: Palgrave Macmillan.

Waldby, C (1996) *AIDS and the body politic: Biomedicine and sexual difference.* London: Routledge.

Walz, T (2002) Crones, dirty old men, sexy seniors: Representations of the sexuality of older persons. *Journal of Aging and Identity*, 7 (2): 99–112.

Warwick, I and Douglas, N (2001) *Safe for all: A best practice guide to prevent homophobic bullying in secondary schools .* **www.stonewall.org.uk/documents/mfbn_Safe_For_All_PDF_ Format.pdf** (accessed 14/4/07).

Warner, J, McKeown, E, Griffin, M, Johnson, K, Ramsay, A, Cort, C and King, M (2004) Rates and predictors of mental illness in gay men, lesbians and bisexual men and women: Results from a survey based in England and Wales. *Journal of British Psychiatry ,* Dec., 185: 479–485.

Weatherburn, P, Ssanyu-Sseruma, W, Hickson, F, McLean, S and Reid, D (2003) *Project Nasah: an investigation into the HIV treatment information and other needs of African people with HIV resident in England.* London: Sigma Research. **www.sigmaresearch.org.uk/downloads/report03a.pdf** (accessed 4/6/06).

WebMD (2005) *Is there a gay gene?* **www.webMD.com/content/article/100/105486.htm** (accessed 4/6/06).

Weeks, J (1986) *Sexuality.* London: Routledge.

Weeks, J (2000) *Making sexual history*. Cambridge and Malden: Polity Press.

Weeks, J (2003) *Sexuality. second edition*. London: Routledge.

Wellings, K, Field, J, Johnson, A M, and Wadsworth, J (1994) *Sexual behaviour in Britain: The national survey of sexual attitudes and lifestyles*. London: Penguin.

Wellings, K, Nanchahal, K, Macdowall, W, McManus, S, Erens, B, Mercer, CH, Johnson, AM, Copas, AJ, Korovessis, C, Fenton, KA and Field, J (2001) Sexual behaviour in Britain: Early heterosexual experience. *The Lancet*, 358: 1843–50.

Wheeler, R (2006) Gillick or Fraser? A plea for consistency over competence in children. *British Medical Journal*, 332: 807. **www.bmj.com/cgi/content/full/332/7545/807** (accessed 19/4/07).

Whitney, C (2006) Intersections in identity–identity development among queer women with disabilities. *Sexuality and Disability*, 24 (1).

Wight, D and Henderson, M (2004) The diversity of young people's heterosexual behaviour. In Burtney, E and Duffy, M (eds) *Young people and sexual health*. Basingstoke and New York: Palgrave Macmillan.

Williams, P (2006) *Social work with people with learning difficulties*. Exeter: Learning Matters.

Wilson, G (2000) *Understanding old age: Critical and global perspectives* . London, Thousand Oaks, New Delhi: Sage.

Wilton, T (2000) *Sexualities in health and social care: A textbook*. Basingstoke: Open University Press.

Wilton, T (2004) *Sexual (dis)orientation: gender, sex, desire and self-fashioning*. Basingstoke and New York: Palgrave Macmillan.

Wintour, P, Woodward, W and Bates, S (2007) *Catholic agencies given deadline to comply on same sex adoptions* . **www.guardian.co.uk/frontpage/story/0,,2001834,00.html** (accessed on 20/02/2007).

Women's National Commission (2005) *The Women's National Commission Sexual Violence Subgroup response to the consultation on the possession of extreme pornography. 1 December 2005* . **www.thewnc.org.uk/pubs/extremepornographyconsultation2005.doc** (accessed 1/5/07)

World Association for Sexual Health (WAS) (2006) *Declaration of Sexual Rights*. **www.worldsexology.org/about_sexualrights.asp** (accessed 17/2/07).

World Health Organisation (2002) *Defining sexual health: Report of a technical consultation 28–31 January 2002, Geneva*. **www.who.int/reproductivehealth/publications/sexualhealth/defining_sh.pdf** (accessed 24/1/07).

Glossary

Bisexual describes the sexual orientation of a person who is sexually and/or emotionally attracted to both men and women. Bisexuality is perceived as being the most fluid of sexual orientations.

Cross-dresser refers to a person who wears the clothing styled for the opposite sex, for example a woman wearing 'male' clothing or a man wearing 'female' clothing. Many cross-dressers are heterosexual and identify with their biological sex.

Drag King and **Drag Queen** refer to people who cross-dress and perform 'drag acts' in order to challenge gender stereotypes. They usually want to be identified as a 'drag queen' (a man dressed as a woman) or a 'drag king' (a woman dressed as a man) and differ from cross-dressers or transvestites who often want to be regarded or 'pass' as a person of the opposite sex.

GAY means 'Good As You' and can be used for women whose primary sexual attraction is to other women, but is a term more often used for a man whose primary sexual attraction is to other men. The definition describes the identity of the person, not the relationship, as not all men who have sex with men identify as gay and not all gay men are exclusively attracted to other men.

Gender is the psychological, social and cultural differences between males and females which give rise to the concepts of 'masculine' and 'feminine'. However, there is debate about whether gender includes all differences, which we discuss in Chapter 1. The term 'gender identity' is used to refer to how individuals view themselves, which may be different to their biological sex.

Heteronormativity refers to the historical, social and culture beliefs, ideas and norms that construct heterosexuality as the normal 'way to be'. These heterosexual norms construct people who are not heterosexual or who are not heterosexual in the 'normal' way as 'deviant' or 'abnormal'.

Heterosexual refers to a sexual orientation where people are exclusively or almost exclusively sexually and/or romantically attracted to people of the opposite sex or with opposite gender identity.

Heterosexism refers to a set of assumptions and practices which promote heterosexuality as the only normal, acceptable and viable way to live our lives. It is built on the belief that heterosexuality is superior and thereby assumes an inferiority status for all same-sex relationships.

Homosexual is a medicalised term suggesting an illness that can be cured. It is used to describe sexual behaviour between people of the same sex/gender, but tends to be used particularly to describe men. The word has negative connotations and is very rarely used by lesbians and gay men themselves as it is often felt to be oppressive and offensive.

Homophobia refers to the intolerance, fear and hatred that people have of lesbians, gay men and bisexuals. It is however an inadequate term as the word 'phobia' tends to imply possible mental health issues, a degree of irrational and unconscious behaviour, and implies the phobia is only located within the individual concerned.

Intersexuality is where a person is born with characteristics of both male and female reproductive organs and often babies with 'ambiguous genitalia' have undergone surgical operations to 'become male' or 'become female'. This type of intervention is now heavily criticised and good practice is to wait for the individual person to decide their sex/gender for themselves when they are older.

Lesbian refers to a woman whose primary sexual attraction is to other women. The definition relates to the woman herself, not to the relationship, as not all women who have sex with other women identify as lesbian, and not all lesbians are exclusively attracted to women.

Men who have sex with men is a term used to classify men who have sex with men, regardless of whether they identify as gay, bisexual or heterosexual.

Sex can be used to describe the biological differences between males and females and also to describe sexual activity or sexual behaviour such as 'having sex'.

Sexuality is complex, fluid and includes our beliefs, acts, behaviours, desires, relationships and identities. It is influenced by the historical, social, cultural and political aspects of society and involves relationships with ourselves, those around us and the society in which we live, whether we identify as gay, heterosexual, lesbian, bisexual or celibate.

Sexual orientation is a term used to describe the focus of a person's sexual attractions and desires. Heterosexual, bisexual, homosexual, lesbian and gay are all common terms to describe a person's sexual orientation. Sexual identity and sexual preference are also terms which are used to mean sexual orientation.

Sexism refers to prejudice and discrimination on the basis of gender and in particular refers to the oppression of women by men. In its extreme form, sexism is also known as misogyny, a word derived from the Greek for 'hatred of females'.

Transgender is a term used to include anyone who does not consider themselves to fit into the traditional female/male, sex/gender constructs within society.

Transsexual is a person who has undergone gender reassignment, that is changed from a woman to a man or vice versa, using a range of medical interventions.

Transvestite is a person who cross-dresses with a desire to adopt the appearance, clothing and behaviour of the opposite sex.

Index

abortion 22, 24, 50, 51, 96, 104
adolescence 37
adoption 29, 30, 128
Adoption and Children Act 2002 29
African communities 97, 99
African HIV Policy Network 99, 100
Age Concern 57, 64
age of consent 22–3, 38, 50–2, 113–14, 130
ageing 36, 56, 57–8, 61, 62, 65, 70
ageism 20, 57, 60, 65, 66
AIDS *see* HIV/AIDS
Alexander the Great 6
Alzheimer's Society 66
Amnesty International 118–19
Anorexia Nervosa 40, 52
anti-discriminatory theory 128
apartheid 25, 26
Aquinas, St. Thomas 7
Aristotle 6
arranged marriages 46, 115
asexuality
  disabled people 78–9, 84, 85, 106
  older people 58, 59, 60, 62, 63, 68, 69, 70, 106, 130
  silence and 11
  young disabled women 40
assault, sexual 23, 71, 113, 116–19, 120, 121, 124
assessment
  for adoption 30–1
  disabled people 84–6
  older people 66–7
  people with HIV 102–3
asylum seekers 99, 100, 124

beauty 40, 58, 69
beliefs 3, 6, 9, 20, 28, 29, 46, 63, 83, 115, 131
best practice 31, 52, 115, 127–32
birth control 96
bisexuality 28, 127
British Association of Social Workers 93
British Council of Disabled People 75
British Crime Survey 116

bullying, homophobic 43, 45, 49, 88, 106
Butler, Robert N. 57

cancer 75, 93
care homes 59, 67, 70–1
carers 30, 68, 85–6
  and disabled 85–6
  lesbian and gay 29–32
  and privacy 68
celibacy 3, 5
child beauty pageants 38
childhood innocence 38
children
  class and 26–7
  contraceptive advice 52
  disabled treated as 78–9
  forced marriage 115
  and HIV 103
  lesbian and gay parenting 29–32, 128
  sexual abuse of 117
  sexual activity 113–14
  sexualised images 38
Children Act 1989 48, 49, 114
Children Act 2004 114
Christianity 7, 96
church, Christian 7, 8, 100
citizenship, sexual 130–1
Civil Partnership Act 2004 18, 65, 131
class 26–7, 28–9, 45
Clinton, Bill 23
cognitive impairment 78, 79–80, 83, 84, 86–8
colonisation 25
coming out 44, 66–7, 80, 88
compounded/multiple disadvantage 76
condoms 8, 40, 41, 51, 54, 104, 105, 106–7
confidentiality 101–2, 107, 108
  dilemma 132
  GUM clinics 109
contraception 19, 24, 45, 50, 51, 52, 80, 86, 104

dementia 62, 66, 70–1, 72, 122
depression 36, 65, 89

deviant heterosexuality 98
diabetes 40, 69
direct payments scheme 68, 85, 102
disability 74–91
  definition 75
  medical model of 76, 80, 83
  rights 81, 88
  social construction of 76
  social model of 76, 83, 84, 87
disabled people
  condom use 106
  diversity of 75
Disability Discrimination Acts 1995 & 2005
    75, 102–3
discourse(s) 5–6, 14
  dominant 17, 18
  male-in-the-head 42
  male sexual drive 118
  medical 39, 52, 61, 76
  oversexed 79–80
  patriarchy versus 21–2
  predatory 41
  romantic 40, 41
discrimination
  age 59
  barrier to accessing services 101
  HIV 98–100
diversity 5–6, 16–34
  disabled people 75, 83
  older people 57, 63, 64
  and religion 8–9
  young people 38
divorce 63, 96, 129
drug companies 61
dysfunctions 61

education
  sex and relationship 49–50
Ellis, Havelock 10
Equality Act 2006 29, 65
Erikson, Erik 42, 59
ethnic minorities 26, 28, 29, 46–7, 57, 98,
    99–100, 101
ethnicity 6, 17, 20, 21, 25–6, 29, 36, 39,
    46–7, 53, 57, 64, 65, 75, 76, 78, 98,
    99, 101, 105, 132
eugenics 80
exclusion 53, 59, 61, 66, 76, 77, 79, 81,
    98, 106, 132
exposure 113

facilitated sex 85–6
Family Planning Association 87
female genital mutilation 114–15

Female Genital Mutilation Act 2003 115
femininity 2, 22, 39–40, 41, 42, 54, 58,
    82, 121
feminism 27, 120, 121, 128
feminist theory 2–3, 21, 120, 121
feminists 106
  postmodern 22
films 120
forced marriages 115
fostering 29, 30, 128
Foucault, Michael 5–6, 8, 13, 14, 17, 59,
    96
Fraser guidelines 52
Freud, Sigmund 10, 42, 59

gang membership 36
gay liberation 29, 128
gay men 42
gender 2–3, 6, 39–42, 57
  divisions challenged 32–3
  heterosexuality and 21–5
  inequality 118, 120
  social divisions 20–1
  traits 13
Gender Recognition Act 2003 33
general population 75, 97–8
genitourinary medicine clinic 70, 108
Gillick competence 52
globalisation 25, 26
Greeks, ancient 6–7
grievous bodily harm 109
Grindhouse 120

Hamer, Dean 4
harassment, sexual 22, 25, 41, 44, 71, 88,
    90, 112
hate crime 18
hetero-patriarchy 10
heterosexism 18–20, 24, 27, 28, 30, 43,
    88, 98, 99, 101, 128, 131
  impact on older people 65–6
heterosexuality 17–18, 119
  and class 26–7
  considered natural 10
  disabled people 80
  and ethnicity 25–6
  and gender 21–2
  institution and identity 17
  norm 17, 19, 42, 49, 58, 98, 127
  privilege 19–20
  and social divisions 20–7
  in young people 39–42, 44
highly active antiretroviral treatment
    (HAART) 102
Hindus 8

HIV/AIDS 8, 33, 40, 70, 92–110
  definition 93
  prevention 103–7
  risk 95–7
  social context 96–100
  testing for 107–9
  transmission 94
homelessness 36, 53, 106
homophobia 18–20, 27, 128

immigration 99, 100
inferior-stigmatised status 76
International Federation of Social Workers
  93

jokes, sexist 120

knowledge 6, 141

learning difficulties 75, 77, 79–80, 86–8,
  90
legislation, role of 116
Lesbian and Gay Carer's Network 66
lesbians 23, 27–8, 42, 64–8
  as mothers 65
  older 64–8
  parenting 29–32
  in workplace 29
Lewinsky, Monica 23
living apart together (LAT) 63
Local Government Act 1988 30, 49
looked after children 48–9

marginalisation 50, 53, 59, 89, 134
marriage 8, 10, 17, 18, 25, 26, 27, 49, 64,
  96
  arranged 46
  forced 114, 115
  rape within 23, 112
masculinity 2, 24–5, 27, 39, 41, 42, 82,
  118, 119, 120, 121
masturbation 5, 8, 38–9, 79, 85, 114
medication 69, 89, 90
men
  sexual drive 10
  young 41–2
mental health 52, 65, 78, 79–80, 83, 84,
  89–90
  masturbation and 39
  phobia as problem 18–19
Mental Health Act 1983 90
mental illness 75
  as disability 75
  homosexuality as 89

mosques 100
mothers
  disabled 80
  lesbian 30, 31, 65, 128
  unmarried 7
  young 45
multiple sclerosis 75
Muslims 8–9
Mustanski, Brian 4–5

National Aids Trust 98, 99, 100, 101, 106,
  109
National Health Service (Venereal Diseases)
  Regulations 1974 101
National Minimum Standards 70
National Service Framework for Older
  People 57, 59
National Sexual Health Strategy 59
National Survey of Sexual Attitudes and
  Lifestyles 23, 59
nature versus nurture 2, 4, 9, 38, 119
NAZ project 29
'need to know', HIV and 101–2
NHS Community Care Act 1990 85, 122
'No Secrets' guidelines 71, 90, 114

Offences Against the Person Act 1861 109
older people 56–73
  asexuality 58
  condom use 106
  definition 57
  voice of 63
Opening Doors Conference 64
othering 17, 76, 118
oversexed 26, 78, 79–80, 84

PACE 89
paedophilia 121
parenting
  corporate 48–9
  lesbian and gay men 29–30, 32, 128
  older 58
  young 45
partners, availability of 69
passivity 10, 22–3, 78
patriarchy 21–2, 120
physical impairment 78, 82, 84–6
Plato 6
pleasure, disabled people and 82
Poor Law 7, 26–7
pornography 23–4, 26, 112, 114, 117,
  120–1
poverty 7, 26, 53, 57, 99, 105, 106
power 5–6, 7, 20–2

Greeks and 7
safer sex 105
unequal 105
and violence 120–1
pregnancy
advice on 51
preventing 83
teenage 49
unplanned 45
premarital sex 96
prisoners 106
privacy 39, 68, 70, 84, 87, 89, 129
Prohibition of Female Circumcision Act
1985 115
prosecution
HIV 109
young people 51, 113
prostitution 26, 112, 113, 114, 117, 124
puberty 36, 37, 41

queer theory 33
Qur'an 8

race 25–6, 121
racism 47, 99
rape 8, 23, 26, 71, 112, 113, 116, 119,
120, 124
medical examination 123
myths 118, 122–3
statistics 116–17
underreported 117
reflective practice 131
religion 7–9, 10, 17, 38, 96
religious fundamentalism 9, 10, 29
representation 11, 12, 13, 19
disabled people 80
older people 61
reproduction 7–8, 17, 24, 58, 96
reputation 54
residential homes 59, 66, 67–8, 70–1, 87
risk 53–4
HIV transmission 94–6, 97–8, 104, 109

safe sex 54, 87, 89, 99, 103–8
barriers to adopting 105
Safra project 29, 47
same-sex marriages/relationships 8, 9, 18,
28, 31, 44, 49, 88, 96
Sappho 6
self-esteem 43, 45, 49, 53, 65, 69, 89, 106
sex education 38, 86, 87
ethnic minorities 46–7
looked after children 48–50
marginalisation of young men 50
sexism 20, 21, 24

sexual abuse 61
disabled people 78, 79, 86, 87
older people 61, 71–3
Sexual Assault Referral Centres (SARCs)
124
sexual grooming 112, 114, 116
sexual health needs 40, 49, 52, 53
disabled people 89
holistic approach 51–2
older people 69
sexual identity 22, 28, 29, 31, 33, 36, 37,
39, 42, 43–4, 64, 69, 103
Sexual Offences Act 1967 130
Sexual Offences Act 1993 22
Sexual Offences Act 2003 50–1, 54, 90,
112–14
sexual orientation 4–5
choice 13–14
confidentiality 132
older people 57
young people 42–4
sexual rights 33–4, 129–131
sexual violence 48, 54, 89, 90, 112–25
continuum of 120
myths 118, 122–3
gay victims 121
gendered 120
perpetrated by women 121
social construction of 117–19
underreported 116
victims vulnerable 117
sexual well-being 53, 82, 90
social work role and 48, 114, 133–4
sexually transmitted infections (STIs) 38,
51, 52, 70, 83, 92, 103, 123
Sharia Law 8–9
Sikhs 8, 9
silence 11–12, 19, 41, 49, 56, 60, 61–2,
79, 121, 128
Single Equality Bill 103
slavery 25–6, 28
slaves 7
social divisions 20–1, 26, 35, 39, 57, 75,
76, 98
social exclusion 106, 132
social isolation 66–7
social workers 83–4, 127–8
anti-discriminatory 30–1, 60
communication skills 132
enabling role 87
fight against HIV 93, 100, 102, 103
sexual relationships 132
use of legislation 114
and young people 36, 48

sodomy 8
stereotypes 19, 25, 27, 30, 32, 36, 40, 46,
        57, 62, 66, 70
sterilisation 24, 80
Stonewall Riots 29
substance use 36, 53
suicide 44, 45

teachers 38
Terence Higgins Trust 92, 98, 99, 106
transgender people 18, 29, 32–3, 42
truancy 45

UK Black Pride 29
USA 26

Vagrancy Act 1898 10
Valuing People 86
Viagra 61, 62
Victim Support 124
Victorian Britain 7
voyeurism 113

Weeks, Jeffrey 13
women
  non-monogamous 104
  passivity 10, 22–3
  physical appearance 5, 40
  sexual violence and 117, 118, 119
  young 39–40
Working together to safeguard children
        114
World Association for Sexual Health   33,
        129, 130

young people 35–55
  definition problematic 36
  emotional well being 54
  gender 39–42
  HIV and 103
  perpetrators of sexual offences 117
  safe sex and 105, 106–7
  sexual violence 113–4
  voice of 47–8
youth offending 36